From Parchment
to Power

From Parchment to Power

How James Madison Used the Bill of Rights to Save the Constitution

Robert A. Goldwin

The AEI Press

Publisher for the American Enterprise Institute
WASHINGTON, D.C.
1997

Distributed to the Trade by National Book Network, 15200 NBN Way, Blue Ridge Summit, PA 17214. To order call toll free 1-800-462-6420 or 1-717-794-3800. For all other inquiries please contact the AEI Press, 1150 Seventeenth Street, N.W., Washington, D.C. 20036 or call 1-800-862-5801.

Library of Congress Cataloging-in-Publication Data

Goldwin, Robert A., 1922-.
    From parchment to power: how James Madison used the Bill of Rights to save the Constitution / Robert Goldwin.
       p. cm.
    Includes bibliographical references and index.
    ISBN 0-8447-4012-8 (cloth). — ISBN 0-8447-4013-6 (pbk.)
    1. Constitutional history—United States. 2. Madison, James, 1751-1836.
I. Title.
KF4541.G65 1997
342.43'029—dc21   96-51947
                                                   CIP

3 5 7 9 10 8 6 4

ISBN 978-0-8447-4013-3

THE AEI PRESS
Publisher for the American Enterprise Institute
1150 17th Street, N.W., Washington, D.C. 20036

To Nancy, Jane, Liz, and Seth

Contents

Foreword

Amazingly enough, considering the years that have elapsed since the founding and the number of historians and political scientists at work in this country, Robert Goldwin's is the first book to provide a full narrative account of how, and to what end, the Bill of Rights was added to the Constitution.

Parts of that story are, of course, known by even the most casual students of the period, and well known to scholars: how, in a unanimous vote of the states, the Constitutional Convention refused to add a Bill of Rights to the Constitution; how the authors of *The Federalist* (Alexander Hamilton, James Madison, and John Jay) opposed amendments, insisting that they were unnecessary because the Constitution was, itself, a bill of rights; how men like Patrick Henry and Thomas Jefferson insisted that the Constitution not be ratified without amendments; how, beginning with Massachusetts, various states ratified the Constitution with the understanding that it would be amended; how the reluctant Madison, after promising to do so during the ratification debates in Virginia, succeeded in getting the very reluctant First Congress to propose amendments; and how the ten we know as the Bill of Rights were subsequently ratified by the requisite number of states. What is little known, and less understood or appreciated, is that, while taking the form of amendments, they did not in fact amend—by which I mean change or even modify—the Constitution. This was Madison's doing, and Goldwin's masterful account of how he singlehandedly maneuvered his amendments through a reluctant Congress makes fascinating reading.

But if Madison's amendments did not amend, what did they do, or what purpose did they serve? According to Madison, the objective of the amendments was to "give satisfaction to the doubting part of [his] fellow citizens." But the amendments did not satisfy the hard core Anti-Federalists, who wanted to change the Constitution in fundamental respects. They likened Madison's amendments to "whip-syllabub, frothy and full of wind, formed only to please the palate," or to "a pinch of snuff [securing] rights never in danger." But Madison never expected to win them over to his cause; as he told Jefferson, his strategy was to isolate the Anti-Federalist leaders from their followers, the body of the people who needed reassurance that their individual liberties were not threatened by the new Constitution. His conciliatory amendments, carefully crafted to change not one word of the original Constitution, succeeded in doing this.

Goldwin says his original intention was to write a straightforward account of the adoption of the Bill of Rights, but this book is much more than that. It is a study of the role of public opinion in a democracy, of the qualities of political leadership needed to establish and maintain political freedom, of the theoretical understanding and practical political skills involved in successful constitution making—in a word, a study of Madison's statecraft. Long described as the Father of the Constitution, Madison, as Goldwin persuasively demonstrates, also deserves to be called the Father of the Bill of Rights.

WALTER BERNS
University Professor of Government, Emeritus
Georgetown University

Preface

On the day I joined the American Enterprise Institute, near the end of 1976, the institute's president, the late William Baroody, Sr., said to my wife, "You know, my dear, there's no tenure here at AEI." He paused, and then added, "But some people do stay a helluva long time."

Two decades later I am happy to acknowledge my unbounded gratitude to the American Enterprise Institute for the opportunity it has provided me to spend so long a time at one position, almost all of it directing programs and editing books that enabled me to learn about constitutions and constitution making.

Nothing in my previous career led me to expect I would spend twenty years in one place. In 1961 I was a lecturer in political science at the University of Chicago; in 1964 I took a leave of absence from the university to serve as issues campaign manager and speech writer for the (unsuccessful) Republican candidate for governor of Illinois; in 1966 I spent a year in London, as a Guggenheim Foundation Fellow, studying the writings of John Locke; that was followed by two years in Ohio, as associate professor of political science at Kenyon College, three years in Annapolis, as dean of St. John's College, two years in Brussels, as special adviser to the United States ambassador to NATO, and, finally, two years in the White House, as special consultant to the president and, concurrently, adviser to the secretary of defense—and all of that in just fifteen years. I'm quite sure I did not realize it then, but in retrospect it seems clear that it was time for me to settle down and find a steady job.

AEI is usually described as a "conservative think tank," but that label fails to do it justice as the unusual educational institution it is. What I have found most valuable and admirable is its openness to honest and reasoned differences of political positions, its commitment to civil discourse with those who disagree, so long as the disagreements are instructive.

My duties at AEI have primarily been organizing and leading a series of conferences on the Constitution of the United States with judges, law professors, political scientists, historians, journalists, and federal and state elected officials. I was encouraged to invite participants to our conferences who spoke for the full range of political persuasions. And the AEI books I have edited have been books of controversy, essays by authors of opposing views, chosen as the most authoritative, persuasive, and instructive spokesmen for their viewpoints. And when we held international conferences on constitutions of other countries, the range of views was even greater, reflecting those of constitutional experts and constitution writers from countries with very different political systems from all corners of the world.

I have benefited over the decades, commencing long before I came to AEI, from excellent colleagues from whom I learned the most important things about politics and constitutions, and who also have been cherished friends: Edward Banfield, Walter Berns, Joseph Cropsey, Robert Licht, Philip Merrill, Charles Nelson, and, while they lived, Martin Diamond and Herbert Storing. William Schambra and Art Kaufman were indispensable colleagues for many productive years at AEI. Christopher DeMuth, the president of AEI, in addition to being the best boss one could hope for, provided the title for this book, and sustained my efforts with patience and praise over many years.

I have benefited from the suggestions and criticisms from all these friends and colleagues, and I have taken seriously their advice, but they will understand that I have not always been able to follow it, since they often disagreed with each other in their recommendations.

AEI recruits fine young undergraduate and graduate student interns, and I have been blessed with the help of some of the best of them: Adam Zurofsky, Stanford University; Hannah Allen, Rutgers University; Zubin Khambatta, University of Pennsylvania; Daniel Feinberg, Harvard University; and Michael Eagles, Georgetown University.

Finally, I acknowledge with heartfelt gratitude the support I have received from the trustees of the Earhart Foundation. I owe a special debt of thanks to the leaders of that excellent foundation, Richard Ware, David Kennedy, and Antony Sullivan, for their steadfast encouragement for so many years.

Constitution Making, Now and Then: An Introduction

Though few Americans seem to realize it, for many decades now the world has been in the midst of a constitution-writing era. During the two decades from 1971 to 1990, 110 of the world's 162 national constitutions—more than two-thirds of all the national constitutions in effect in 1990—either were newly written and adopted or were so extensively rewritten that they could be considered to be new. And the pace of constitution writing continues: on average, more than five new national constitutions are adopted somewhere in the world every year.

Some of them, of course, are written for newly formed or newly independent nations; but a surprising number are wholly new constitutions or major revisions of the constitutions of long-existing, well-established nations, among them Egypt (1971), Morocco (1972), Pakistan (1973), Turkey (1974), Greece (1975), Sweden (1975), the former U.S.S.R. (1977), Spain (1978), Canada (1982), Turkey again (1982), the People's Republic of China (1982), the Netherlands (1983), the Philippines (1987), Brazil (1988), and Portugal (1989).[1] The dissolution of the Soviet Union into fifteen separate nations and the overthrow of the governments throughout the former Soviet bloc brought many more new constitutions into existence. Add to these the scores of major revisions or new constitutions during the same twenty-year period for nations such as Bangladesh, the Bahamas, Zambia, Grenada, Myanmar, Gabon, São Tome and Principe, Trinidad and Tobago, Kirabati, the Seychelles, and Yemen, to mention only a few, and it becomes clear that constitution writing continues at a steady pace in nations of every variety and size, all over the world.

1

Why is there so much constitution writing? After all, the decision to attempt to replace a constitution is not one to be taken lightly. Writing a new constitution can be the cause of great turmoil and disruption of national life. The populations of modern nations, almost without exception, are diverse—including within them differences of race, religion, nationality, and language, not to mention economic and regional diversities. The effort to heal the divisions and achieve harmony among these diverse elements, which is one aim of the project to make a new constitution, always arouses great fears and often stirs up fierce animosities and, consequently, severe internal struggles. For these reasons, nations usually undertake constitutional revision only when it seems unavoidable, when there is a severe national crisis. And even then they often wait too long and suffer overthrow of the government before a more peaceful resolution can be effected. But whenever they begin, constitutional assemblies spend months and even years struggling to resolve internal disputes.

The Compelling Reasons for Constitution Writing

Despite all these powerful reasons for avoiding the writing of a new constitution, there are always constitution writers at work somewhere in the world. Two obvious reasons for this phenomenon come to mind. Overriding the reasons for not embarking on constitutional revision is one dominant fact: that great hopes are attached to new constitutions, hopes that they will provide some or all of what is lacking in the national life, be it order, stability, tranquillity, personal freedom, political equality, legal justice, economic prosperity, or all of these. High hopes—that is the main reason why nations decide to seek a new constitution, despite the dangers and the difficulties that constitution making always begets.

Add to this a second reason. A new constitution is sought because the old constitution has failed. If the consequences of that failure are sufficiently widespread and harsh, they bring a nation to the point of trying to reconstitute itself. The frequency of major revisions of constitutions is a measure of the frequency of the collapse of failed constitutions. It is evidence that it is extremely difficult to make a good constitution, one that secures the fundamental rights of individuals; that enables ordinary citizens to go about their everyday business in peace and safety; that provides balance among the diverse elements of the society; that achieves sufficient national unity; that lasts long enough to give stability and continuity to the national life; and that provides the citizenry with a reason to feel proud of themselves and their nation. Because so few constitutions succeed in achieving the hopes invested in them initially, nations find it necessary to return to the task and try again. In the chapters that follow, we shall see that all these elements were involved in the American decision to attempt to write a new constitution in 1787.

Why do so few constitutions succeed in building a durable and just regime? Not every national population is suited to the kind of thought and conduct required to sustain a constitutionally limited government. Most do not have experience in the institutions, principles, and procedures of self-government. The problems of diversity and unity, pulling in opposite directions, are difficult to resolve or tolerate without resort to violence. The temptation is strong to assert group interests and rights, despite the worldwide record of chaotic divisions that result within society. For these reasons, among others, the future of constitutionalism is always in jeopardy, not only in nations newly striving to establish a democratic regime, but also in long-established constitutional democracies, including ours, that seem to be losing their way. In an age when the public impatiently expects quick responses to its every demand, is there sufficient tolerance for time-consuming procedures of deliberation? In an age when almost every aspect of life is offered in the form of exciting entertainment, is there a capacity for mundane, even boring, politics?

1789 and Its Consequences

For most of the world, the mention of "1789" evokes images of the storming of the Bastille and the French Revolution, not the peaceful ratification of the American Constitution. The lengthy legislative procedural wrangling in numerous state conventions and in the Congress, as described in the chapters that follow, leading to the ratification of the Constitution and to the remarkably undramatic adoption of the Bill of Rights, pales in comparison with the stirring scenes of the bloody revolution occurring in France during the same three-year period. Nothing on the American political scene rivaled the compelling drama of the overthrow of the French monarchy, and the clarion call of the Declaration of the Rights of Man and the Citizen, still to this day the preamble to the French constitution, with its resounding pronouncement that "ignorance, forgetfulness or contempt of the rights of man are the only causes for public misfortunes and the corruption of governments."[2]

3

The American constitution writers, I think, would consider that assertion in the French declaration to be a foolish exaggeration and oversimplification. They would not deny the primacy of rights, nor would they shrink from declaring that governments are established to secure the rights of man. But they would insist that neglect, or ignorance, or even abuses of rights cannot be "the only causes" of misgovernment. That would neglect or ignore the importance of other critical factors, such as the separation of powers; a sound representative system; a bicameral legislature; free, fair, and frequent elections by secret ballot; an independent judiciary; an energetic executive; a federal structure; an extended territory; a multiplicity of interests among the citizenry; and all the many other elements that help to provide the checks and balances characteristic of a stable, limited, constitutional government. Would it be an exaggeration to ascribe to this difference in political acumen, at least in part, the results that emerged in the years immediately after 1789: in America, a constitution that has endured for more than two hundred years; in France, a constitution that lasted for less than three years and then descended into the Terror, the guillotine, and, eventually, the dictatorship of Napoleon?

Constitution writing is not much on the minds of most Americans, chiefly because we have not had the experience of writing and adopting a new national constitution for ourselves for more than two hundred years. Contrast that with the experience of our fellow democrats—the French, for example, who have had fifteen constitutions since 1789, the most recent one adopted in 1958;[3] or our neighbors the Canadians, who have suffered almost uninterrupted constitutional revision, and even uncertainty that the nation will survive intact, since adopting a new constitution in 1982.[4]

The Americans adopted a new constitution but once, and, fortunately, they did it well. Familiarity with that long-ago experience of the making of the longest-lasting written national constitution in the world might be instructive and useful to all who still have hopes that the cause of constitutional democracy might flourish throughout the world. When I speak of useful instruction I have in mind the advice that Alexis de Tocqueville proffered to his countrymen after the overthrow of the French monarchy in 1848, when the French faced the task of reconstituting themselves as a republic. "The institutions of America, which were a subject only of curiosity to monarchical France," he wrote,

ought to be a subject of study for republican France. Though it is no longer a question whether we shall have a monarchy or a republic in France, we are yet to learn . . . whether it shall be . . . pacific or warlike, liberal or oppressive, a republic that menaces the sacred rights of property and family, or one that honors and protects them both . . . . Let us look to America . . . less to find examples than instruction; let us borrow from her the principles, rather than the details, of her laws. The laws of the French republic may be, and ought to be in many cases, different from those which govern the United States; but the principles on which the American constitutions rest, those principles of order, of the balance of powers, of true liberty, of deep and sincere respect for right, are indispensable to all republics.[5]

The American Experience

In that spirit of instruction in the principles, rather than in the details, of free government, I offer the example of the American experience of constitution making and its exceptionally successful constitution makers, for the benefit of citizens of the United States as well as of other countries. I have tried to tell the story, in straightforward narrative form, of the disputes, difficulties, confusions, conflicts, intimidations, stratagems, theories, deceptions, setbacks, compromises, miscalculations, accidents, and pure good luck that went into the making of the Constitution of the United States of America and its Bill of Rights. It is primarily a political story, full of lessons on what it takes to establish a durable, democratic constitutional republic, lessons that are both theoretical and practical.

I did not set out initially to write a book about the making of the Constitution. My original intention was more limited, to explain how and why the First Congress added the Bill of Rights to the Constitution. I trust that the reader will agree, in the end, that I have succeeded in explaining that, and much more. Very simply, the story expanded of its own accord, because it was not possible to explain why the First Congress took up the Bill of Rights without first describing the great constitutional controversies that raged during the ratification process, before there was a First Congress. It became clear that the amendments were brought forward as an attempt to solve problems lingering from the ratification struggle and that the amendments were added as an essential step in completing the making of the Constitution. One of my main arguments is that the task of making the Constitution of the United States was not complete until the

Bill of Rights was adopted. Readers may be surprised, however, by the sense in which the project of establishing the Constitution was considered incomplete, and by the way the amendments were regarded by the men who wrote and deliberated and passed those amendments. As another author has cautioned his readers, "You may find it a different story from the one you learned in school."[6]

This book differs in important respects from most others that deal with the making of the Constitution. It begins close to where many of the others end, that is, in the closing weeks of the Constitutional Convention in Philadelphia, at the end of August and the beginning of September 1787—not at the beginning of the convention, in early May of that year. It does not end at the end of the convention, or even with the ratification of the Constitution, as many other books do, but continues to follow the story through to the remarkably strange conclusion, the official adoption of the Bill of Rights.

The Plan of the Book

The book is divided into three parts. Part one begins with the closing days of the Convention in Philadelphia, when the delegates' thoughts were turning from the task of writing the document to the political task of getting it ratified; from the small, indoor world they had made for themselves and lived in for four months, to the great, out-of-doors world where the nation awaited their momentous report. As we shall see, these highly principled, honorable, and public-spirited lawgivers were also clever, resourceful, skillful, experienced, and practical politicians, who were not above using questionable means to accomplish noble ends. In short, the constitution-making process began with morally and constitutionally dubious decisions. The delegates left Philadelphia determined to do whatever was necessary to achieve ratification.

From Philadelphia the action moved to the Continental Congress in New York, where the Constitution's lack of certain amendments aroused a dispute that persisted and spread throughout the country, and where the first serious opposition was overcome in a very short time and, as we shall see, in a manner surpassingly strange. From there the process moved on to the states, not to the legislatures but to conventions "chosen by the people," with the opposition growing stronger as it progressed from state to state, and with the margins of victory in successive state ratifying conventions growing smaller and smaller. But victories they were, and in due course eleven states approved it and the Constitution was ratified. All of that part of the story is told in part one.

Part two deals primarily with the "why" of this story—why James Madison decided to push the amendments through a Congress that resisted him at every step of the way. The Constitution had been ratified, elections for Congress and the presidency had been held, the First Congress had convened, George Washington had been inaugurated, and the new government had begun to function. At this point in the story of the making of the Bill of Rights, James Madison took center stage. Madison had played a leading role in the Constitutional Convention, in the Virginia ratifying convention, and in influencing public opinion as one of the authors of *The Federalist*. Now, as a congressman from Virginia, he proved to be, in the eyes of his congressional colleagues, the most annoying and disruptive member of the House of Representatives by insisting on proposing amendments to the Constitution in the first few weeks of the first session of the First Congress. This was met with a chorus of complaints that Madison had his priorities all wrong and that it made no sense to consider amendments before there was any experience with the Constitution that might reveal what needed to be amended. In addition, there were urgent matters such as raising revenue and organizing the government that ought not be delayed. Why Madison acted as he did, and how he succeeded in his project of amendments against almost unanimous opposition, is a central element of the story of the making of the Constitution, and one of the great feats in the history of constitution making.

Madison was a towering figure in the American founding, but it has been his fate to be less appreciated than he deserves. As the historian Jack Rakove has pointed out, Madison had almost no commanding personal characteristics except "the power of his intellect":

> Madison lacked the stern but charismatic dignity of Washington, the obstreperous and restless temper of John Adams, and the warmth and charm of his good friend, Thomas Jefferson . . . . He was less bold than Alexander Hamilton, less cosmopolitan than Benjamin Franklin, less ambitious than Robert Morris or James Wilson. Thomas Paine was a far more effective writer, and Patrick Henry and Richard Henry Lee, his Virginia rivals, far more stirring orators.[7]

But Rakove goes on to agree with his fellow historian Michael Kammen that Madison was "the most profound, original, and far-seeing among all his peers." To which I add my own amen!

Throughout the ratification process, the most strident demand of the opposition had been to add a bill of rights to the Constitution. That the original Constitution did not have a bill of rights was the result of a conscious decision, not an oversight, on the part of the framers in the Constitutional Convention. When a delegate moved that a bill of rights be added, the motion was voted down, ten states to none. For a variety of reasons, most of the chief authors of the Constitution thought a bill of rights was unnecessary in a constitution such as theirs, and perhaps even dangerous to the security of rights. There is no doubt that all of them were devoted to the cause of the rights of individuals and adhered to the principle of the Declaration of Independence that governments are established to secure the great rights of mankind. But they did not think such a declaration had a place in the Constitution, and they had serious doubts about the effectiveness of a bill of rights in securing the rights they held precious.

Part two traces the development of Madison's thought from skeptic to advocate of a bill of rights. Madison was devoted to the cause of securing private rights, but he had long expressed doubts that a bill of rights was the best way to secure them. For him the fundamental question was, What truly secures rights? He thought that rights were best protected by a properly constructed constitution and that by itself a bill of rights was but a "parchment barrier," especially ineffective in protecting the minority against an oppressive majority. How a man of such convictions became the chief proponent of the Bill of Rights is the central part of this story.

In the course of a marvelous dialogue, by correspondence, with his illustrious friend Thomas Jefferson, then serving as the American minister in Paris, Madison overcame his doubts and persuaded himself that a bill of rights could serve an essential function in the American constitutional scheme. In a letter to Jefferson, he posed this question, more to himself than to his correspondent: "What use . . . can a bill of rights serve in popular governments?" Only after Madison had satisfied himself that he could answer that question did he begin the amending process in the First Congress that ended in his becoming the "Father of the Bill of Rights." Madison was of the opinion that the task of establishing the Constitution could not be considered complete as long as a sizable minority of Americans continued to be uneasy about the extensive powers it granted to the new federal government. In his view, it was not enough for the new Constitution to have the support of the majority. He thought the Constitution had to be an extraordinary force in American political life, powerful enough to overwhelm and restrain an oppressive majority whenever one might arise, and the Constitution could not be that powerful unless it had the universal allegiance of "the great mass of the people." Madison saw his amendments as the perfect instrument for winning that support. As we shall see, the task he imposed on himself was a daunting one—to push through an uncomprehending Congress the solution to a problem that only he seemed to perceive.

Part three picks up the story of "how" it was done, a detailed account of the debates in the First Congress, where Madison's amendments were proposed, debated, revised, and finally passed by the required two-thirds majorities of both houses and then passed on to the state legislatures for eventual ratification of the Bill of Rights. After Madison won the struggle to introduce the amendments, he commenced the long and grueling task of persuading reluctant congressmen and state legislators to adopt his amendments and to reject others proposed by opponents of the Constitution—a task he performed with remarkable skill and dogged persistence. Madison was blessed with an unusual combination of statesmanlike powers. He had a penetrating intellect, as exhibited by the theoretical discourse in his correspondence with Jefferson, as well as by his authorship of the most profound of *The Federalist* papers, and this was combined with a talent for political tactics and the legislative temperament suited to dealing with practical politicians. Edmund Burke's description of the "combining mind" of the exemplary lawgiver capable of founding a free government fits Madison perfectly:

> To make a government requires no great prudence. Settle the seat of power, teach obedience, and the work is done. To give freedom is still more easy. It is not necessary to guide; it only requires to let go the rein. But to form a *free government*—that is, to temper together these opposite elements of liberty and restraint in one consistent work—requires much thought, deep reflection, a sagacious, powerful, and combining mind.[8]

If Burke ever enlarged on this theme, I am not aware of it, but Madison so completely exemplified the concept of the "combining mind" required "to form a free government" that a treatise on the subject is not needed. We need only contemplate Madison's words and deeds during this period of constitution making from 1787 to 1792.

The reader will find this book full of historical facts, but it is not the work of a historian. It is the work of a student of politics, especially the politics of constitution making. I have not attempted any original factual "research"; instead, I have relied for the factual material on the best authorities, eminent historians of the founding era: Lance Banning, Michael Allen Gillespie, Leonard W. Levy, Michael Lienesch, Dennis J. Mahoney, Forrest McDonald, Jackson Turner Main, Jack N. Rakove, Clinton Rossiter, and Robert Rutland, among others. For original documentary materials I have used the indispensable collections of Henry Steele Commager; Max Farrand; Bernard Schwartz; Helen E. Veit, Kenneth R. Bowling, and Charles Bangs Bickford; Philip B. Kurland and Ralph Lerner; and Charles G. Tansill. Writing a book of this sort would be immeasurably more difficult without access to the invaluable works of these authors and editors.

This book of facts also has many reflections suggested by them. I borrow the phrase "facts, and reflections suggested by them" directly from Madison. In one of his letters to Jefferson, Madison emphasized the importance of the right facts as the basis of reflections in the search for the truth. Jefferson was then residing in Paris, observing the turmoil of tottering monarchical rule about to be overthrown while actively engaged in advising Lafayette in developing the French Declaration of the Rights of Man and the Citizen; at the same time, Madison was observing the distress of American majority rule while actively engaged in guiding it through a period of transition. Madison asserted that Jefferson might not be able to see for himself "a truth of great importance" about rule by the majority simply because he did not have before him the observable facts available to Madison:

> In our Governments the real power lies in the majority of the Community, and the invasion of private rights is chiefly to be apprehended, not from acts of Government contrary to the sense of its constituents, but from acts in which the Government is the mere instrument of the major number of the Constituents. This is *a truth of great importance*, but not yet sufficiently attended to; and is probably more strongly impressed on my mind by *facts, and reflections suggested by them*, than on yours which has contemplated abuses of power issuing from a very different quarter.[9]

In any historical account, it is necessary to make a selection of facts from the superabundance of them available, and there is always room for dispute about which were selected and which neglected. My facts were drawn from original documents and from the works of others, but the selection of which to include and which to pass by was necessarily my own. It is the reflections, however, which are also my own, that form the basis of my claim that this book contains some "truths of great importance."

Many of the facts presented here are both well known and little known: well known to historians of the founding era, but little known to many others. Included among the list of these "well-known, little-known facts" are these: that the Constitution was ratified by a very narrow margin and probably would have been defeated had it been submitted to a nationwide popular referendum; that the procedure adopted for ratification of the Constitution was a conscious violation of the requirements of the Articles of Confederation; that the word *unanimous* preceding the signatures in the text of the Constitution was deliberately misleading, concealing the fact that many of the delegates to the convention were not among the signatories; that although there was a widespread demand for amendments, most of the states expressed no concern for adding provisions protecting freedoms of religion, press, and speech; that the resounding phrase *We the People,* with which the Preamble of the Constitution begins, was something of an accident; that everyone in the First Congress, Federalists and Anti-Federalists alike, was opposed to consideration of amendments, and that even Madison had almost no words of praise for the amendments he himself proposed; that the Anti-Federalist leaders, who agitated for a bill of rights throughout the ratification struggle, subsequently voted consistently against the Bill of Rights in the First Congress, from start to finish; that ratification of the Bill of Rights was not a victory for the Anti-Federalists, but a crushing defeat for them, from which they never did recover; that the final adoption of the Bill of Rights was hardly noticed by the public, was hardly mentioned in the press of the day, and was certainly not celebrated. These "well-known, little-known facts" add spice to a story that would be, even without them, a fascinating one.

Although Madison was the central figure in the making of the Constitution and of the Bill of Rights, he was unlike the great solitary lawgivers of ancient times, Lycurgus of Sparta and Solon of Athens.[10] His achievement was not in acting alone, but rather the opposite. Scores of others were involved—and, ultimately, as I argue at the end of the book, millions of others were drawn in—in establishing the Constitution. It was, in fact, inherent in the nature of Madison's effort that a multitude of others had to become involved. Even those who persisted in trying to emasculate the Constitution after ratification found that they had to become participants in the constitution making: they had to take an oath to support the Constitution as a prerequisite to serving in Congress, where they continued their amending efforts.

With all of the foregoing as introduction, let us turn now to the Constitutional Convention in Philadelphia, where the story begins. Why did the Americans decide first to try to repair the Articles of Confederation, and why did they instead end up with a wholly new constitution? The nation was beset in 1787 with a variety of severe difficulties. The Articles of Confederation were more like a treaty of alliance among the states than a true constitution. Under the provisions of the articles, the Continental Congress had little ability to raise revenue, was too weak to deal effectively with encroaching great powers like Britain and Spain, could not make foreign loans because its credit was so bad, and was incapable of rectifying these defects because the articles could be amended only by unanimous consent of the states, and there were too many conflicting interests among them to achieve unanimity on almost any question. Spain was blocking shipping on the Mississippi River; Britain was restricting American exports; and the Congress was powerless to deal with them. Regional differences were such that there were well-grounded fears that the Union could break up into two or three confederacies.

In the face of this crisis threatening the survival of the United States, in the twelfth year of independence, the Continental Congress, after prolonged hesitation and many delays, finally agreed to authorize a Constitutional Convention to recommend alterations of the Articles of Confederation.[11] And so it was that delegates from the several states began to gather in Philadelphia in May 1787.

PART ONE

How to Ratify a Constitution

1

Philadelphia: The Last Days of Summer, 1787

In the final weeks of the Constitutional Convention in Philadelphia, in late August and early September of 1787, all the great substantive issues had been voted on and the final text of the proposed new Constitution for the United States of America was practically ready to be engrossed on four pages of parchment. All that remained to be decided was how to finish the job.

The Constitution that the convention delegates had written would be transmitted to the Continental Congress as a "report," at which point the convention would cease to exist and other persons and other assemblies would begin to participate in controlling its fate. Every state had its own constitutional government, but the United States as a whole had almost no government; the little bit of government it had was provided by the instrument called the Articles of Confederation, and the chief institution under the Articles of Confederation was the Continental Congress. The Constitutional Convention had been established by the Continental Congress and derived all of its authority, such as it was, from the Congress.[1]

The question that convention delegates had to address in those last weeks in Philadelphia was how to transform their proposed Constitution, at that point nothing more than the recommendation of a temporary assembly,[2] into the new, official, operating instrument of government; that is, how to make the transition from parchment to power.

Obstacles to Ratification

The delegates identified and concentrated their attention on five major obstacles in the way of ratification:

- the amending provision in the Articles of Confederation
- the instructions from the Continental Congress establishing the convention
- the Continental Congress itself
- the state legislatures
- three prestigious dissenting delegates

If the delegates could not find the way to overcome or circumvent these five obstacles, the Constitution would be a dead letter,[3] and all their hard work over the long, hot summer would be lost—not to speak of the damage to the Union and to the future safety, prosperity, and even existence of the United States. What were these five obstacles?

First, the amending provision in the Articles of Confederation read as follows:

> nor shall any alteration at any time hereafter be made . . . unless such alteration be agreed to in a congress of the united states, and be afterwards confirmed by the legislatures of every state.[4]

Many of the delegates predicted that getting approval from Congress would be very difficult; but even if they should succeed there, all of them knew that having it confirmed by every one of the state legislatures was impossible. Several states had already demonstrated their opposition to the Constitution. Rhode Island had refused to send delegates to the Constitutional Convention;[5] delegates from New York and Maryland had walked out of the convention in protest; and a majority of Virginia's legislature, dominated by Patrick Henry, the fiery orator and leading Anti-Federalist, was known to be hostile to the new plan.

Second, the Congress had instructed the convention that it was being established "for the sole and express purpose of revising the Articles of Confederation." But the convention delegates had gone far beyond mere revisions; instead they were about to propose an entirely new form of government. The Continental Congress had sought to be precise in the wording of the instrument establishing the Constitutional Convention, limiting its functions and specifying the procedural sequence for approving any recommendations they might propose. Hence the convention, at its inception, was instructed by the Continental Congress that it was being established

> for the sole and express purpose of revising the Articles of Confederation and reporting to Congress and the several legislatures such alterations and provisions therein as shall when agreed to in Congress and confirmed by the states render the federal constitution adequate to the exigencies of Government & the preservation of the Union.[6]

The language of the instructions, in the judgment of the delegates, contained a massive contradiction. The stated end, to "render the federal Constitution adequate to the exigencies of government and the preservation of the union," and the means to be used, mere "alterations" of the Articles, were incommensurate. What was required to achieve the goal, they had decided, was a fundamentally different scheme of governance. In so deciding, the convention had exceeded the limitations placed on its delegated powers, perhaps unavoidably, but certainly unmistakably.[7] It is not surprising, therefore, that most of the delegates thought it would be foolhardy to ask the Continental Congress to approve what they had done.

A third obstacle to ratification was the character of the Continental Congress itself. The quality of most of the members of Congress was not high. As the leading chronicler of the Continental Congress has observed, "Little men a-plenty strode up and down the Congress hall in those days . . . men so small that their souls would rattle in a mustard seed."[8] They were a disheartened and disgruntled bunch, powerless to raise revenue or to enact and carry out decisive policies, going weeks on end without being able to muster a quorum, but with enough resolve left in those so disposed to take a stab at obstructing ratification. The Articles of Confederation bound the thirteen states together in something less than a government; as the document expressed it, they were sovereign states joined in "a firm league of friendship with each other." The Continental Congress, "the united states in congress assembled," provided its members with the only opportunity for public service beyond the state level. The question for the delegates to the Constitutional Convention was whether these petty men could be big enough to approve a new plan that would put the Continental Congress out of business and probably also put an end to their political careers.

The state legislatures presented a similar problem. Human nature being what it is, delegates thought that state legislators would be reluctant to agree to surrender so much of their own power and to transfer it to the new Congress. Would it be prudent to rely on these legislators to vote for a plan designed to diminish themselves so severely?

Finally, there was the unsettling circumstance that three prestigious delegates—Elbridge Gerry of Massachusetts, Governor Edmund Randolph of Virginia, and Colonel George Mason, also of Virginia—had announced that they would not sign the Constitution. They had proposed the addition of a number of provisions, including a bill of rights, that the delegates had debated and voted down. The concern was that if the public saw there were opponents of the Constitution among leading members of the convention, it would have a severe, adverse impact on the reception of the document once it emerged from the convention. This was the fifth obstacle in the way of ratification—dissension within the convention itself at the final moment when they wanted to come forth with the clearest possible appearance of unity.

Imagine, then, the mood of the delegates at this time, the last day of August, just two-and-a-half weeks before they would dispatch their report to the Continental Congress in New York. On the one hand, they had been remarkably successful in resolving very dangerous controversies—differences between big and small states, between proslavery and antislavery delegates, between commercial and agricultural interests, between those who sought to perpetuate the sovereignty of the individual states and those who sought to subordinate them within a union under one general government. Significant compromises had been achieved, for the most part without compromising the principles of liberty and justice (except, most glaringly and, to many delegates, most distressingly, with regard to slavery). They had produced a historically unprecedented framework of representative government, with strong but limited powers, a result worthy of pride and praise, surely one of the greatest achievements in the entire political history of the world.

On the other hand, after four months of arduous and highly successful constitution writing, any sense of elation or self-congratulation that the delegates might have felt must have been greatly diminished if not eradicated by feelings of apprehension and even dismay at what now clearly lay ahead. In the concluding moments of their deliberations, it must have been ominously obvious that the obstacles to transforming this manuscript into the working Constitution would be formidable.

18

Evasions and Solutions

The delegates examined these obstacles in detail; they debated them with considerable fervor, often bitterly divided in their opinions of what to do, admonishing each other sometimes with harsh criticisms and even denunciations. In the end they voted to evade every obstacle they could. Those they could not evade they attacked with stunning audacity.

The solutions they came up with can be found, but not easily, in the texts of the pieces of their "report" to the Congress, tucked away and barely visible in the Constitution itself and in the accompanying resolution of the convention. For example, the original version of the accompanying resolution began as follows: "Resolved, That the preceding Constitution be laid before the United States in Congress assembled for their approbation." But after impassioned debate, the delegates voted to delete the words "for their approbation."[9] Further, they decided, again after heated exchanges, not to take a chance with the state legislatures but to bypass them and instead seek state approval from popularly elected conventions in each state. These evasions, of the Continental Congress and of the state legislatures, we see, very inconspicuously, by omission, in the final text of the resolution:

> Resolved,
> That the preceding Constitution be laid before the United States in Congress assembled, and that it is the opinion of this Convention, that it should afterwards be submitted to a Convention of Delegates, chosen in each state by the people thereof.[10]

They did not say that the procedures they recommended would not authorize the Congress or the state legislatures to judge this Constitution, but that was the effect. The Congress could transmit or refuse to transmit the Constitution to the states, but that was the only choice it was offered—take it or leave it. And the state legislatures were called on to order elections to elect delegates to the ratifying conventions, but they were offered no other role. The delegates went even further and called on those assemblies to cooperate fully in facilitating ratification, arranging for presidential and congressional elections, and organizing the many steps required of the old institutions to get the new government established and running.

The impossibility of winning the approval of all thirteen state legislatures was dealt with in similar fashion, this time in the Constitution itself, in Article VII, the last and the least of the articles in the Constitution of the United States. Unlike the major articles of the Constitution, Article VII has no sections or clauses or paragraphs; it is just one simple declarative sentence, twenty-four words in all.[11] It reads as follows:

> The Ratification of the Conventions of nine States, shall be sufficient for the Establishment of this Constitution between the States so ratifying the Same.

Just as there was no indication in the convention's resolution that the words "for their approbation" had been deleted, or that the state legislatures had been eliminated from the ratification process in favor of ratifying conventions more likely to be favorably disposed, so in Article VII there is no mention that this nine-state provision violates the Articles of Confederation's requirement for approval by all thirteen state legislatures.

Among the delegates opposed to bypassing the Congress or authorizing anything less than unanimous approval by the states were two strange bedfellows: Alexander Hamilton, who had returned to the convention in these last days of the meetings in order to sign the document for New York, preliminary to his strenuous efforts in support of ratification as coauthor of *The Federalist* and as the powerful leader of the Federalist delegation in the New York state ratifying convention; and Elbridge Gerry, the able, argumentative, and conscientious delegate from Massachusetts who was nevertheless about to refuse to sign and then, on leaving the convention, to go home and take an outspoken stand in opposition to unconditional ratification. Despite their profound disagreements, Gerry and Hamilton were fully agreed on the procedures they thought the convention was obliged to follow.

Gerry expressed himself as scandalized by the proposal that as few as nine states could establish the new Constitution and put an end to the confederation; he scolded the convention for what he described as

> the indecency and pernicious tendency of dissolving in so slight a manner, the solemn obligations of the articles of confederation. If nine out of thirteen can dissolve the compact, Six out of nine will be just as able to dissolve the new one hereafter.[12]

Hamilton supported Gerry's position that it was wrong "to allow nine States . . . to institute a new Government on the ruins of the existing one," but he objected more strenuously to "the indecorum of not requiring the approbation of Congress." He ended by offering a motion, immediately seconded by Gerry,[13] that the new Constitution be submitted to the Continental Congress for their approval, and then be sent to the state legislatures, leaving it to them to decide whether ratification by nine states would suffice to establish the new government.

Hamilton's motion did not receive a warm welcome. James Wilson opposed it, saying "it is necessary now to speak freely" against any plan that made the fate of the Constitution depend on "the approbation of Congress." It would be "worse than folly," he said,

> to rely on the concurrence of the Rhode Island members of Congs. in the plan. Maryland had voted on this floor for requiring the unanimous assent of the 13 States to the proposed change in the federal System. N— York has not been represented for a long time past in the convention. Many individual deputies from other States have spoken much against the plan. Under these circumstances Can it be safe to make the assent of Congress necessary. After spending four or five months in the laborious & arduous task of forming a Government for our Country, we are ourselves at the close throwing insuperable obstacles in the way of its success.[14]

Delegates saw the risk in asking for the approval of Congress, but they also saw the risk in trying to bypass the Congress. It seemed equally insulting either to ask them to give their assent to their dissolution on a take-it-or-leave-it basis or not to ask for their assent at all.

The new Constitution would dissolve the old Congress and replace it with a bicameral legislature with greatly increased powers, based on different and novel principles of representation, and most likely with different members. Would the Continental Congress accede to its own political demise, and very probably the end of many of the members' own political careers? Could they be expected to approve this new document without the opportunity to make changes?

And even if the delegates could find the way to get the new Constitution past Congress, they would still be faced with the next problem—how to get the approval of the state legislators, whose status and powers would be greatly reduced by establishment of a more powerful general government. What would be the best way to approach them for acceptance of the new scheme?

Gouverneur Morris argued that they were more likely to get

the cooperation of the state legislatures if the states were left free "to pursue their own modes of ratification,"[15] each state to choose its own method; he urged therefore that they not make ratifying conventions mandatory in every state. Rufus King immediately responded that "striking out 'Conventions' as the requisite mode was equivalent to giving up the business altogether."[16] Madison agreed, reminding his colleagues of the obvious facts of human nature, especially the power of self-interest and its effect on political behavior. State legislators, he argued, had strong interests in opposing this new Constitution, because it would deprive them of so much of their present power. Bypassing them by going directly to "the people," by the device of conventions whose members were popularly elected, was not only rhetorically effective but was also consistent with republican principles. Above all, it was the only prudent course for getting the Constitution ratified. It was best, Madison said, to require conventions,

> Among other reasons, for this, that the powers given to the Genl. Govt. being taken from the State Govts[,] the Legislatures would be more disinclined than conventions composed in part at least of other men; and if disinclined, they [that is, state legislators] could devise modes apparently promoting, but really thwarting the ratification . . . . The people were, in fact, the fountain of all power, and by resorting to them, all difficulties were got over. They [i.e., the people] could alter constitutions as they pleased.[17]

Finally the vote was called for on Hamilton's motion to require the approval of Congress and to leave it to the states to determine the number of states needed to ratify. Hamilton, the only delegate then representing New York, cast his state's vote, as one would expect, in favor of his own motion, but he gathered no support; it was defeated, ten states to one.

And so instead of attacking the obstacles posed by the Continental Congress and the state legislatures, the delegates chose to evade them, consciously violating their instructions from the Congress and the procedural requirements of the Articles of Confederation. But of course those assemblies were, we might say, only representative of the fundamental difficulty. The massive underlying problems looming ahead for the prospect of ratification were the widespread confusion, uneasiness, suspicion, and hostility to the new plan of government in many places throughout the country, all of which would surely be manifested in every representative body—

the Congress, the state legislatures, or ratifying conventions chosen by the people.

Public opinion had to be their chief concern. The delegates knew that the Constitution needed as much authoritative prestige as could be mustered coming out of the convention in order to succeed in the campaign to win over the public. That is why the matter of delegates who were reluctant to sign was considered to be such an important problem.

Another Constitutional Convention?

Just about every major delegate had reservations about one part or another of the Constitution. For example, James Wilson, in his famous State House Yard Speech during the campaign for ratification in Pennsylvania, said, "I will confess that I am not a blind admirer of this plan of government and that there are some parts of it which, if my wish had prevailed, would certainly have been altered."[18] Charles Pinckney of South Carolina said he had as many objections to the plan as had others; among other things, "he objected to the contemptible weakness & dependence of the Executive [and] he objected to the power of the majority only of Congs over Commerce."[19] And Hamilton said that "No man's ideas were more remote from the plan than his own were known to be."[20] And these were the statements of some of the staunchest supporters of the Constitution, delegates who were firmly committed to signing it.

Troubling announcements began to come on August 31, from delegates who said they would not sign the Constitution or support ratification unless radical changes were made. Gerry denounced "the system as full of vices," and Mason chose to express his distaste in dramatic form, saying that

> he would sooner chop off his right hand than put it to the Constitution as it now stands. He wished to see some points not yet decided brought to a decision . . . . Should these points be improperly settled, his wish would then be to bring the whole subject before another general Convention.[21]

Randolph then picked up on Mason's suggestion to call another constitutional convention, and began to develop it in more detail; in the ensuing two weeks, as it became clear that his numerous disagreements were not going to be dispelled, Randolph returned to it repeatedly. He realized, he said, that his colleagues would not agree to the proposal to call for a second convention, "but the discharge of his duty in making the attempt, would give quiet to his own mind." Randolph unburdened himself of the long list of his reasons for not signing, which had to be mightily discouraging to the other delegates because of the obvious impossibility, at this late date, of making many of the changes he called for. His objections

> turned on the Senate's being made the Court of Impeachment for trying the Executive—on the necessity of 3/4 instead of 2/3 of each house to overrule the negative of the President—on the smallness of the number of the Representative branch—on the want of limitation to a standing army—on the general clause concerning necessary and proper laws—on the want of some particular restraint on Navigation acts—

and so on, for six more specific provisions.[22]

It should be emphasized that none of these objections was unreasonable. In fact, some last-minute changes were made in response to the objections of Randolph and others, reducing to two-thirds the number required to override a presidential veto, and increasing the size of the House of Representatives. But the number of his objections in support of provisions that had been extensively discussed and voted down by the delegates made it clear to all that Randolph could not be satisfied. His objections were not unreasonable, but they were unacceptable; so, too, was his proposal for a second constitutional convention.

Mason was the other prestigious Virginia delegate who had a long list of reasons for not signing. In the course of a discussion of whether to add to the Constitution a provision for juries in all civil cases, Mason brought up a subject that, surprisingly, had not been mentioned before. He said

> he wished the plan had been prefaced with a Bill of Rights .... It would give great quiet to the people; and with the aid of the State declarations, a bill might be prepared in a few hours.[23]

Gerry thereupon moved for a committee to prepare a bill of rights, and Mason seconded the motion. But after the briefest possible discussion, questioning the necessity of a bill of rights, the motion was defeated decisively: "Ayes—0; noes—10; absent—1."[24]

Mason had many other complaints, but the chief one, because of its effects on the commerce of Virginia and other Southern states, concerned the power given to Congress by a bare majority to pass navigation acts, which he said . . . would enable a few rich merchants in Philada N. York & Boston, to monopolize the Staples of the Southern States & reduce their value perhaps 50 Per Ct.

To protect Southern interests he made a motion that passage of all navigation acts require "the consent of 2/3 of each branch of the Legislature";[25] the *Records* do not report any discussion of this proposal by Mason. Apparently the time was past for lengthy deliberations or reconsideration of what had already been decided. Delegates voted at once, and Mason's motion was defeated, seven states to three, with every Northern state voting against him.[26]

Now, for the third time in two weeks, Randolph made one last attempt to persuade the delegates to agree to his plan for another constitutional convention:

Mr Randolph . . . expressing the pain he felt at differing from the body of the Convention, on the close of the great & awful subject of their labours, and anxiously wishing for some accommodating expedient which would relieve him from his embarrassments, made a motion importing "that amendments to the plan might be offered by the State Conventions, which should be submitted to and finally decided on by another general Convention." Should this proposition be disregarded, it would he said be impossible for him to put his name to the instrument. Whether he should oppose it afterwards he would not then decide but he would not deprive himself of the freedom to do so in his own State, if that course should be prescribed by his final judgment.

Mason seconded Randolph's motion and added his own reasons for calling a second convention:

This Constitution had been formed without the knowledge or idea of the people. A second Convention will know more of the sense of the people, and be able to provide a system more consonant to it. It was improper to say to the people, take this or nothing. As the Constitution now stands, he could neither give it his support or vote in Virginia; and he could not sign here what he could not support there. With the expedient of another Convention as proposed, he could sign.[27]

Gerry added his voice to the dissenting group, by presenting his list of eleven "objections which determined him to withhold his name from the Constitution." Given all the flaws of the Constitution, "the best that could be done he conceived was to provide for a second general Convention."

Achieving "Unanimous Consent"

It was by now close to six o'clock in the afternoon on Saturday, September 15—not the best time to invite fatigued and impatient delegates to deliberate a major change of procedure that, if adopted, would have sweeping and unforeseeable consequences. The three nonsigners had had their say and all could see they were not to be swayed except by major concessions that the rest of the delegates were unwilling to make. The final moment had obviously come, and the convention now moved swiftly. As soon as Gerry concluded his remarks in support of Randolph's motion, the account of the proceedings reads as follows:

> On the question on the proposition of Mr. Randolph.
> All the States answered—no.
> On the question to agree to the Constitution. . . . All the States ay.
> The Constitution was then ordered to be engrossed.
> And the House adjourned.[28]

It testifies to the importance the delegates attached to getting every possible signature that, when the convention reconvened on the following Monday, September 17, for the reading of the engrossed Constitution, on what turned out to be the final day of the convention, they made still one more effort to persuade the reluctant delegates. Because so many delegates, not only the three announced nonsigners, had expressed so many different reservations, Gouverneur Morris had undertaken to devise a formula that he hoped would enable all delegates to sign. Morris persuaded Benjamin Franklin to present this signing formula as his own in hopes that Franklin's prestige would make it more acceptable. As Morris explained it to the delegates, "signing in the form proposed related only to the fact that the States" were giving their "consent" to the Constitution, not that the delegate signing his name was approving any or all of the text.[29] A signer would therefore be free, once he had left the convention, to express criticisms or even opposition to ratification.

Some delegates said that this formula was helpful. William Blount of North Carolina, for one, said he could not sign if it meant he was pledging himself to support the plan, but he could sign "to attest the fact that the plan was the unanimous act of the states in Convention." But Gerry said "the proposed form made no difference with him." Mason, who had said "he would sooner chop off his right hand than put it to the Constitution," kept his word—and his right hand. Randolph said "he could not but regard the signing in the proposed form, as the same with signing the Constitution."[30]

Charles Pinckney pleaded that such negative "declarations from members so respectable at the close of this important scene, give a peculiar solemnity to the present moment,"[31] and Hamilton added that "A few characters of consequence, by opposing or even refusing to sign the Constitution, might do infinite mischief."[32] But these entreaties had no effect. The three did not sign.

The convention had started out with fifty-five delegates appointed. Some never showed up, some left during the proceedings. There were forty-two present at the end, with thirty-nine signing, representing twelve states. Thus sixteen signatures out of fifty-five were missing, almost 30 percent; and yet the enacting clause, composed by Gouverneur Morris and proposed by Benjamin Franklin, includes the word "unanimous." In the Constitution it follows directly after Article VII and reads as follows:

> Done in Convention by the Unanimous Consent of the States present . . . IN WITNESS whereof We have hereunto subscribed our Names.

This was followed by the signatures, grouped by states. Pennsylvania had eight signatures, but five states had no more than two. Alexander Hamilton, the only delegate from his state still in attendance on the last day of the convention, signed alone for New York; there was no mention of the two other delegates from New York who had left early in protest at the convention's exceeding its powers. Elbridge Gerry did not sign, but Nathaniel Gorham and Rufus King did, and so Massachusetts was also included among the twelve states giving their "unanimous consent." Edmund Randolph and George Mason did not sign, but George Washington (who signed in his dual capacities as president of the convention and deputy from Virginia), James Madison, and John Blair did, and so Virginia also was part of the "unanimous consent."

One has to acknowledge, and even admire, the political skill that produced this double result, easing the way for delegates to sign who had reservations and, at the same time, making it possible, truth-

27

fully, albeit misleadingly, to use the word—*unanimous*—that they all considered to be so powerful and necessary. As we shall see, this was not the last maneuver in the name of unanimity in the effort to influence public opinion and complete the business of making the Constitution.

2
New York: The Continental Congress and the Quest for Unanimity

The signing of the Constitution took place in Philadelphia on September 17, 1787. The "report," consisting of three items—the Constitution, the resolution setting out the recommended ratification procedure, and a covering letter of transmittal to the Continental Congress from George Washington as president of the convention—was dispatched the next day and received by Congress in New York City on September 20. Once the report was in their hands it was clear that several members of the Continental Congress viewed it unfavorably, just as had been predicted: some because of the procedural violations, others because of the substance of the new plan of government.

Why then did the Congress do exactly as asked by the convention and vote, unanimously, within just a week, to send the Constitution on to the state legislatures to be submitted to conventions chosen by the people? The congressional resolution, adopted on September 28, reads as follows:

> Congress having received the report of the Convention lately assembled in Philadelphia, *Resolved* Unanimously that the said Report with the resolutions and letter accompanying the same be transmitted to the several legislatures in Order to be submitted to a convention of Delegates chosen in each state by the people thereof in conformity to the resolves of the Convention made and provided in that case.[1]

Why did the Congress cooperate in the stratagem to bypass themselves, an arrangement so contrary to the political interests of the members of Congress? Why did they accede to ratification by only nine states? Why did they accept a take-it-or-leave-it process? Why was the vote unanimous?

More Feeble than Fearful

The task of finding the answers to these questions is complicated by the fact that there is no official account of the proceedings; the record of all deliberations during that momentous week was erased from the Congress's Journal by a strange agreement of both sides. But the answers can be found, despite the absence of the official record, in the letters written by those members of Congress who were there to political colleagues who were not, telling what happened and explaining the reasoning behind the decisions.

Several factors combined to help move the Constitution through the Congress. Undoubtedly the most important was the incurable weakness of the confederation and its Congress. A "great majority" in Congress was predisposed to support almost any plan the Convention might propose,[2] so long as it provided for government stronger than the confederation. That predisposition was a direct consequence of the weakness, bordering on impotence, of the Continental Congress. For this we have the testimony of many members of Congress. One, for example, gave this despairing description of the state of American affairs, blaming it on congressional powerlessness:

> The public treasury without money, the people discontented and the States either refusing or not complying with the requisitions of Congress. . . .Congress annually vote requisitions for the foreign and domestic interest, which are totally disregarded.[3]

In similar vein, the North Carolina delegates reported to their legislature that because Congress was powerless to collect requisitions from the states, "Congress have been reduced to the dreadful alternative of borrowing principal to pay interest." The Union was therefore "at the eave of a bankruptcy and of a total dissolution of Government."[4]

Congress had rarely had as many as seven states in attendance, the prescribed quorum, throughout the previous year,[5] and in the six weeks leading up to September 20 there had not been a single day when they had had a quorum. The president of Congress, Arthur St.

Clair, had been trying to rally the states to send enough delegates to receive and act on the report of the Constitutional Convention whenever it should arrive. On August 13 he issued a plaintive appeal for the states to send members to attend:

> What must the nations of the world think of us when they shall be informed that we have appointed an Assembly and invested it with the sole and exclusive power of Peace and War, and the management of all National concerns, and during the course of almost a whole year, it has not been capable, except for a few days, for want of a sufficient number of members, to attend to these matters . . . . Besides, the National Convention, which the people look up to for so much good, will soon rise, and it appears of great consequence that, when their report comes under consideration of Congress, it should be a full Congress, and the important business which will be laid before them meet with no unnecessary delay.[6]

The response was not immediate, but on September 20, the day the convention's report was delivered in Congress, they finally achieved a quorum, with nine states in attendance. A few days later eleven states were on the floor, with only Rhode Island and Maryland missing. But apparently only the business of the new Constitution offered sufficient incentive to bring the Congress, however briefly, to life. Once they had voted, on September 28, to transmit the Constitution to the states, attendance again dwindled. Two weeks later, the Congress was once again unable to muster a quorum.

It was, of course, not a negligible advantage to the cause of ratification, in addition to the weakness of the Congress, that many of the delegates to the Convention were also members of Congress. These delegates hurried from Philadelphia to New York and promptly took their seats in Congress to vote on their own handiwork. For example, Madison provided the decisive vote in Virginia's congressional delegation, which had been split, two for the Constitution and two against, until he arrived. Richard Henry Lee, a leading opponent of the Constitution from Virginia, was offended by this dual role of convention delegate and Congress member. He himself had refused to serve as a delegate to the convention on the principled ground that

> being a member of Congress where the plan of the Convention must be approved, there appeared an inconsistency for members of the former to have session with the

latter, and so pass judgment at New York upon their opinion at Philadelphia.[7]

By Lee's count, "so many members" of the Convention came to Congress "that the votes of three states being of them, two states divided
by them, and many others mixed with them, it is easy to see that
Congress could have little opinion upon the subject."[8]

But surely the chief factor in the surprising compliance of the
Congress was its profound weakness relative to the vigor of the Constitutional Convention. The convention had captured national attention; hopes and expectations were high, as President St. Clair had
said: "the people look up to [the convention] for so much good"; all
this was too powerful for a debilitated Congress to resist. The Congress had neither the stature nor the capacity to stand up to the convention. In sum, the opposition the Philadelphia delegates had feared
they would encounter in Congress turned out to be more feeble than
fearful. The momentum in these earliest days was all in the direction
of forward progress for the new plan of government.

The opposition to ratification in Congress was no match for
Madison's overwhelming rhetorical skills in debate. For example,
when the anticipated complaint was voiced on the floor of Congress
that the convention had gone far beyond mere revisions of the Articles of Confederation, Madison was ready with a head-on attack. On
this point there was no evasion. It was true, he said, that part of their
instructions had been to do no more than revise the Articles of Confederation, but the instructions went on to describe the kind of "alterations
and provisions" that were wanted: they were to be such as would
"render the federal Constitution adequate to the exigencies of Government and the preservation of the Union." The opinion of the convention was that they could not achieve that exalted end by mere
tinkering with the Articles of Confederation, which was fundamentally flawed. In such a case, Madison argued, when the means and
ends are incompatible, a choice must be made of one or the other.
The rule is that the less important, in this case the means, must give
way to the more important, in this case the end of achieving a "federal Constitution adequate to the exigencies of Government and the
preservation of the Union."

The question also came to the floor why Congress should be
precluded from considering amendments to this proposed Constitution. Richard Henry Lee quickly drafted a lengthy set of them, but
Madison attacked once again, unloading what must have seemed a
bewildering barrage of political, legal, and constitutional arguments

against the very idea of amendments by this Congress. He argued

> that it was clearly the intention of the States that the plan to be proposed should be the act of the Convention with the assent of Congress, which would not be the case, if alterations were made, the Convention no longer being in existence to adopt them; that as the Act of the Convention when altered would instantly become the mere act of Congress, and must be proposed by them as such, and of course be addressed to the legislatures, not conventions of the states, and require the ratification of thirteen instead of nine states, and as the unaltered act would go forth to the States directly from the Convention under the auspices of that Body, some States might ratify the one and some the other of the plans, and confusion and disappointment be the least evils that could ensue.[9]

Lee, even so, tried to move ahead with his amendments and called for a vote on them that would be recorded in the Journal of the Congress. He knew that he could not prevail in a vote, but he wanted his amendments and the vote on them to be printed in the Journal. On the other side, the Federalists, though assured of a majority on any vote, wanted to avoid putting Lee's amendments and any votes for them on the record. They had resolved in Philadelphia not to seek approval of the Constitution in Congress but rather to ask only that it be transmitted to the states. But once in New York they allowed enthusiastic supporters of the Constitution, who had not been in the convention, to talk about winning congressional approval. And this gave them something to trade away, thus making compromise possible.

The Appearance of Unanimity

The pro-Constitution forces offered to give up a vote of congressional approval, which they did not want anyway, and accept instead unanimous agreement simply to transmit the Constitution, on condition that Lee's amendments not be entered in the Journal and, in fact, that none of that week's proceedings be entered in the Journal. In exchange, the anti-Constitution forces were able to claim a victory in preventing a vote of approval of the Constitution, in exchange for agreeing to give up their push for amendments, which they knew had no chance of adoption anyway. In short, both sides gave up something they did not want or could not have gotten and received instead something they tried to turn to advantage. Lee was able to assume a position of leadership among the Anti-Federalists by circulating his amendments, now certified by the Federalist leaders to be dangerous and therefore potent. In his letters he could boast of his victory in the congressional maneuvering:

> I moved the amendments . . . and demanded the yeas and nays, that they might appear on the Journal. This seemed to alarm; and to prevent such appearance on the Journal, it was agreed to transmit the Constitution without a syllable of approbation or disapprobation; so that the term "unanimously" only applied to the transmission. . . .[10]

Supporters of the Constitution reported the same facts, but gave them a different emphasis, explaining their cleverness in trading approval for unanimity. Another Virginia congressman, an enthusiastic Federalist, wrote to Jefferson, then in Paris:

> When the report was before Congress, it was not without its direct opponents, but a great majority were for giving it a warm approbation. It was thought best, however, by its friends, barely to recommend to the several legislatures, the holding of conventions for its consideration, rather than send it forth with even a single negative to an approbatory act. The people do not scrutinize terms; the unanimity of Congress in recommending a measure to their consideration, naturally implies approbation; but any negative to a direct approbation, would have disavowed a dissension, which would have been used to favor divisions in the states.[11]

Madison, in a letter to Jefferson, confirmed that unanimity was the prize they sought. Given the "very serious effort" by Richard Henry Lee to "embarrass" the plan, "to obtain unanimity it was necessary to couch the resolution in very moderate terms."[12]

Washington let Madison know that he fully supported the bargain made for the sake of "the appearance of unanimity," and gave his reasons in terms that provide a rare peep behind the curtain of Washington's private thoughts:

> I am better pleased that the proceedings of the Convention is handed from Congress by a unanimous vote (feeble as it is) than if it had appeared under stronger marks of approbation without it.—This apparent unanimity will have its effect.—Not every one has opportunities to peep behind the curtain; and as the multitude often judge from externals, the appearance of unanimity in that body, on this occasn., will be of great importance.[13]

It might seem, if one were to judge from externals, that the Continental Congress demonstrated a spurt of energy and efficiency in dispatching the business of the proposed Constitution in just one week. They received the "report" of the Convention on September 20; scheduled the vote for the 26th; deliberated briefly and then voted, unanimously, on the 28th to send the Constitution on to the states. But a closer examination of what transpired in those few days makes it clear that the Congress was not exhibiting institutional strength but was rather collapsing under pressure from a superior force. They could criticize, they could complain, they could object, they could even offer a brief resistance; but the members of Congress could not stop, or even slow, the forward progress of the Constitution. It had been moved past or over or through one obstacle after another until now it was on its way to the state legislatures.

3
The States: The Politics of Ratification

Even though they would not be the ones to vote on ratification, each state legislature had to set the date and the rules for electing delegates to its ratifying convention. At first it was as if a race had been declared, with supporters of the Constitution organizing more quickly and effectively than their opponents. The Congress had barely voted to transmit the Constitution when several state legislatures voted to call elections for delegates. In fact, one state did not wait for the word from New York. The convention in Philadelphia had done its work "literally downstairs from the sitting session of the Pennsylvania legislature,"[1] and they had a copy of the Constitution as soon as the convention adjourned—well before the official copy reached the Congress in New York.

Supporters of the Constitution, a majority in the Pennsylvania legislature, sought to move as quickly as possible, to hold elections for delegates throughout the state and to have their ratifying convention seated, all within six weeks. The opponents of ratification, facing certain defeat if elections for the convention were held before there was a chance for extended public discussion, stayed away from the legislative session in sufficient numbers to prevent a quorum. A mob was organized to drag two of the minority members from their rooming house back to the assembly chambers. The sergeants-at-arms locked the doors to prevent their escape. And the legislature, now with a quorum, voted to hold the ratifying convention on November

20. But this turned out to be a costly victory for the Constitution. News of the strong-arm tactics spread, and resentment mounted. Opposition to the Constitution continued to grow in Pennsylvania even after the state had officially ratified, and this resentment helped to fuel opposition in other states yet to ratify.

Early, Easy Victories

But the haste in calling elections for convention delegates in Pennsylvania and other states produced the desired effect, winning majorities for ratification. Support for the Constitution was concentrated in cities and towns along the coast in almost every state; opponents of the Constitution were scattered in the rural areas away from the coast. Slowness of travel and communications made it more difficult, on short notice, to organize and rally the opponents than the supporters. The less time allowed before the elections, the better for the cause of ratification. The Pennsylvania election results gave the Federalists a two-to-one majority, forty-six to twenty-three, in the convention. When the convention voted in favor of ratification on December 12, not one vote had changed.

Delaware, starting later than Pennsylvania, moved faster; it ratified unanimously on December 7. New Jersey ratified ten days later, also unanimously; Georgia two weeks later, also unanimously; and a week later, Connecticut. And so, in less than four months, five of the nine states needed had held statewide elections and chosen delegates overwhelmingly committed to ratification. In these five conventions, more than 80 percent of the delegates, popularly elected, cast their votes for ratification. In all of them, the outcome was predetermined by the popular elections. The delegate candidates announced their position, were elected on that basis, and did not change. In none of them was one vote changed by the deliberations.

The Federalists were prevailing because they were better organized, they had better speakers and writers to influence the elections of delegates, they controlled the press and made good use of it, and they moved too fast for the opposition to be able to organize. But the trend was not to continue. In Massachusetts, the sixth state, the opponents were able to make a stand for the first time.

The easiest states had ratified; the hardest ones lay ahead. Everyone knew that the Constitution would not be truly established, even if nine should ratify, without Massachusetts, New York, and Virginia, three big and rich states. The outcome in Massachusetts

37

would have a powerful influence on the conventions in the remaining states, especially New York and Virginia. If the Constitution lost in Massachusetts, it would almost certainly not be ratified.

Massachusetts—Prospect of Defeat

Massachusetts, the scene of Shays's Rebellion just a year earlier, was politically polarized in January 1788, when the convention began. The state was sharply divided, rich against poor, western farmers against eastern merchants, cities and towns against rural areas, creditors against debtors, and so on. The dominant statewide issues were enormous public debt, oppressive tax collection, widespread mortgage foreclosures, issuance of paper money—the kind of issues that tend to divide violently the few and the many.[2] That division was the context of the elections for delegates to the ratifying convention. The coastal cities and towns elected only supporters of the Constitution; the rural areas, away from the coast, elected only opponents of the Constitution, and the opponents won a majority of the seats in the convention.

The Massachusetts convention was an odd assembly. All the Anti-Federalist leaders, like Elbridge Gerry, who lived in Cambridge, were defeated in the elections, because they lived in eastern towns that favored ratification.[3] As a result, all the best speakers in the convention, all the learned political and legal minds, favored ratification. There seemed to be no deliberative talent on the other side, but they were a decisive majority in the convention and made up in resentment, mistrust, and numbers what they lacked in rhetorical skills.

The disparity in talent was not advantageous to the Federalist cause. The delegates had deep reservations that they were unable to express, and so the pro-Constitution speakers found themselves in the curious position of having to deliver both sides of the debate, first formulating the objections their opponents might hold in order then to dispel or refute them.

Logical arguments did not have much effect; opposition was based more on suspicions and prejudices than on reasoned convictions, and was thus resistant to logic. Their comments were often baffling; for example, one delegate said that these well-educated speakers were able to make the worse appear the better, and "if we had men of this description on our side" we would be able to refute them. Another, responding to a Federalist argument lauding the Constitution, said, "A good thing does not need praise. . . . If these great men would speak half as much against it, we could complete our business and go home in forty-eight hours."[4]

If the convention had voted on ratification of the Constitution as a whole, up or down, in the first day or two, the nays would have prevailed; but the Federalists won agreement to consider the Constitution paragraph by paragraph, which gave them time to seek for a way out. The obstacle was not an objection to this or that part of the text of the Constitution, but rather suspicion on the part of the poor, the debtors, the less well educated that the campaign to impose this new plan of government was part of a plot against them. As Rufus King said, "their real objection was not to the Constitution, but to the men who made it."[5] They did not trust a system produced by the educated, the rich, the successful, the powerful.

When it became clear that arguments were not being effective, other methods were explored, some of them of the sort that justified the delegates' suspicions. Debtors among the delegates were pressured by their creditors to vote for ratification. And the word was spread that the pay many of the delegates needed to get back home after the convention adjourned would be forthcoming if the convention ratified, but not otherwise.[6]

The decisive turning point was the winning over of the state's two most influential leaders: John Hancock, the governor of Massachusetts and also the president of the convention, and Samuel Adams, the president of the state senate. They both had serious reservations about the Constitution, but they had been elected to the convention as declared "neutrals" on the question of ratification.

There are stories, undoubtedly true, about some of the tactics used in the attempt to bring these two prominent patriots to support ratification. In a mass meeting of 400 tradesmen organized in Adams's own home district, a petition demanding that he support ratification was drawn up and delivered to him, in person, by none other than Paul Revere.[7]

Hancock was visited by a delegation of Federalists who offered him glittering prospects if he would lead Massachusetts to ratify the Constitution. His opponents promised to support him in his next campaign for governor; further, they would support him for vice president under the new Constitution if George Washington were a candidate for president. Perhaps most enticing, if Virginia did not ratify, and Washington were therefore not eligible for the presidency, they would support Hancock for president of the United States.[8]

The testimony of many participants leaves no doubt that these events really did occur, but one can doubt, nevertheless, that they were decisive influences. The convention had been going on for nearly a month, and a kind of stalemate had developed. The opponents did not have enough votes for outright rejection of the Constitution; the proponents did not have the votes to win ratification without amendments; and no one knew how to get valid amendments before ratification. In the face of this stalemate, Hancock, who had absented himself from the convention, pleading ill health, made an appearance and came up with the solution.[9]

The Turning Point

Historians disagree about who worked out the formula Hancock presented to the convention, though they do agree it was not Hancock; nevertheless, Hancock presented the package to the convention delegates as all his own. It was a novel solution, a major breakthrough that almost certainly saved the Constitution from ultimate defeat. Hancock stepped down from the chair and from the floor proposed that the convention "assent to and ratify the said Constitution" without conditions, and that it simultaneously recommend a set of amendments to the First Congress, to be enacted according to the amending provisions in Article V of the Constitution. Also, the convention should "enjoin" their future congressmen "to exert all their influence, and use all reasonable and legal methods to obtain ratification" of the proposed amendments. His set of proposed amendments dealt with such things as protecting states' powers, restricting congressional powers over elections and taxation, prohibiting monopolies, requiring grand jury indictments, limiting the powers of federal courts, and some lesser matters. None of them touched on subjects we might have expected, such as religion, press, speech, assembly, or petition.

The distinctive feature of Hancock's move was that these amendments were being offered not as conditions for ratification, but only as recommendations. In putting the question to a vote, Hancock uttered decisive words: "I give my assent to the Constitution *in full confidence that* the amendments proposed will soon become a part of the Constitution." Those words, *in full confidence that,* instead of, say, *on condition that,* made the difference between a disguised rejection of the Constitution and a real, if begrudging, acceptance of it.

With Hancock back in the chair and Adams supporting his move from the floor, enough votes were changed to win ratification by the slim margin of 19 votes out of 355 cast, 187 to 168. On February 6, Massachusetts became the sixth state to ratify, using a formula—unconditional ratification accompanied by recommended amendments—that was subsequently used by six of the remaining seven state ratifying conventions.

We may never be able to ascertain with certainty what persuaded Adams and Hancock. But in my opinion Adams was enough of a politician to know that the mass meeting in his district was a staged event, and Hancock was much too popular (he was reelected governor in the next election by a margin of four-to-one) to be swayed by promises of support from his opposition. As for the presidency, he could have foreseen that by leading Massachusetts to ratification he would increase the likelihood that Virginia would then also ratify, thus making George Washington eligible for the presidency and ending Hancock's own chance to be elected president.

It seems reasonable to conclude that Hancock and Adams decided in favor of unconditional ratification not out of concern for their personal and political advantage, although they certainly were not neglectful of such considerations, but rather primarily for patriotic reasons, because they thought the Constitution, with all its faults, and with some amendments, was necessary for the well-being of Massachusetts and the nation.[10]

Why did enough delegates follow Hancock and Adams to change the minority in favor of ratification into a majority? In my opinion, they followed because they trusted Hancock and Adams. If they were opposed to the Constitution because they distrusted the men who produced it, they now switched because they trusted the men who asked them to support it. The delegates who originally opposed the Constitution could not be persuaded, but since Hancock and Adams could be, ratification was achieved. But even with such trustworthy leadership, the margin of victory was very narrow. Opposition continued to be widespread and stubborn in the remaining states. The Constitution was still in peril.

Virginia—Sharply and Evenly Divided

In April and May, Maryland and South Carolina ratified, both by comfortable margins, and now, with eight ratifications, the stage was set for the decisive conventions in Virginia and New York. The Virginia legislature, led by Patrick Henry, had in fact timed its convention for the beginning of June, in the expectation that eight states

41

would have ratified by then. Thus Virginia's decision, up or down, would decide the fate of the Constitution. The Virginia convention was unlike the Massachusetts convention in one important respect: both sides were represented by the most able men in the state. In other ways the two conventions were similar. Just as Shays's Rebellion in Massachusetts marked the division within the state and convention, so an issue peculiar to Virginia, how best to keep navigation open on the Mississippi River, divided these delegates. Virginians feared that the Jay-Gardoqui Treaty would be agreed to with Spain, to close the Mississippi River to American shipping, with devastating consequences for Western territories. Many Virginians had close ties of many sorts with settlers in the Western territories, especially in the Southwest. The future of Virginia, and of the South as a whole, was seen as dependent on keeping the Mississippi open to American shipping.[11]

This issue, navigation on the Mississippi, may have been the main reason why Patrick Henry declined to participate as a delegate in the Constitutional Convention.[12] It was also the main reason why George Mason, in the Constitutional Convention, was insistent on including a constitutional provision that navigation laws, in order to protect the interests of the Southern states, must have a two-thirds congressional majority for passage. The convention's refusal to agree to this proposal may well have been Mason's main reason for withholding his signature.[13]

Mason and Patrick Henry used this local issue to argue for amendments that would restore powers to the states, in this case to enable Virginia to keep the shipping open on the Mississippi, and would diminish what they considered to be excessive powers vested in the federal government to control navigation. Madison, however, used the very same local issue to make the opposite argument. He contended that navigation on the Mississippi was endangered not by too much unchecked federal power to enact navigation laws, but by national weakness, too little power in the hands of an impotent Congress under the Articles of Confederation. The better way to defend Virginia's interests was to strengthen the national institutions, to give them the power to deal effectively with a great nation like Spain. Virginia's interests and the national interests coincided, and both would be served by ratifying the Constitution.[14]

The division of delegates was so close that neither side could be sure it had a majority. Almost every prominent personage in Virginia was elected as a delegate, and these leaders, "as homogeneous a group as any in the country—were divided very evenly and sharply over questions of the state's essential interests."[15] Patrick Henry's objective in the convention was not to reject the Constitution but rather to obtain amendments to it, *prior* to ratification, by means of a second constitutional convention empowered to consider all the amendments recommended by the several state ratifying conventions. This proposal, first made by Governor Edmund Randolph back in Philadelphia, was not only still alive, it was growing as a movement among the opponents to ratification in Virginia and New York. There was, however, one decisive exception: Randolph himself had ceased to support his own proposal.

When the Virginia legislature, dominated by an Anti-Federalist majority, voted to hold elections for delegates to the state ratifying convention, they adopted a resolution at the same time in favor of a second constitutional convention. They directed Governor Randolph to transmit this act to the other governors, to be laid before their legislatures, asking for their cooperation. Randolph's letter was mailed to Governor George Clinton of New York on December 27, 1787, but for some mysterious reason it took more than two months to reach him, too late for the New York legislature to act on it. Had it been received sooner, New York would certainly have agreed to cooperate and, with the combined support of the governors and legislatures of the states of New York and Virginia, a second constitutional convention prior to ratification would then have been inevitable.[16]

Madison and Washington were concentrating their attention on persuading Randolph to reconsider his demand for a second convention. The circumstances were now greatly changed, with eight states having ratified. Randolph became convinced, he said, that there was now only one issue, Union or no Union. On that issue he became a determined spokesman for unconditional ratification. On the floor of the ratifying convention, with his arm upraised (the record does not reveal whether it was his left or right arm), he said, "I will assent to the lopping off of this limb before I assent to the dissolution of the Union," thus surpassing George Mason in the extent of his self-amputatory zeal.[17]

For some reason, Governor Clinton, after receiving Governor Randolph's delayed letter of December 27, waited two more months, until May, to respond to it, perhaps intending to have his letter arrive just when the Virginia convention was nearing a decision. When Randolph received it, he held it for several days, waiting for the next scheduled meeting of his Executive Council, to ask their opinion whether Clinton's letter was a private letter or an official communication. The council, not surprisingly, decided it was indeed an official communication and that it should be presented to the Virginia legislature, which in turn would deliver it to the ratifying convention. The message of the letter was that the New York legislature agreed to cooperate with the Virginia legislature in calling for a second constitutional convention to consider the numerous amendments proposed by the several states, prior to ratification.

Randolph accordingly had Clinton's letter delivered to the legislature, where the envelope sat on a table, unopened. It just so happened that Patrick Henry was scheduled that day to make his climactic speech to the ratifying convention, urging them not to ratify before amendments were obtained in a second constitutional convention. So many of the state legislators went over to the convention to join the audience to hear the great orator's speech that there was not a quorum in the legislature to act on, or even look at, Clinton's letter, which many authorities think would have been more effective in the cause of a second convention than Henry's speech was. Clinton's letter was eventually opened, read by the legislature, and forwarded to the convention, but not until the day after they had ratified, unconditionally, using the Massachusetts formula, by the narrow margin of eighty-nine to seventy-nine.[18]

The decisive switch was made by Governor Randolph. He contended that with eight states having ratified, refusing to ratify would be tantamount to splitting away from them. The decisive argument, for him, was that a ninth state was needed to prevent the dissolution of the Union. Unbeknownst to Randolph and the rest of the Virginia delegates, New Hampshire had ratified four days earlier, also by a ten-vote margin, fifty-seven to forty-seven, making them the decisive ninth state and Virginia the tenth.

Patrick Henry's final remark in the Virginia ratifying convention was a brief masterpiece of multiple meanings. He said, "My head, my hand, and my heart shall be at liberty to remove the defects of the system in a constitutional way," thus acknowledging defeat, promising to persevere in seeking amendments, and accepting the rule of the Constitution and the institutional procedures it established, all in one compact sentence.[19]

New York—Sharply and Unevenly Divided

The Virginia convention was still in session, with the outcome uncertain, when the New York convention opened. The New York Anti-Federalists were led by Governor Clinton, who was very popular in most of upstate New York; the Federalists were led by Alexander Hamilton, who was equally popular in New York City and its environs. Despite carrying more than 90 percent of the vote in New York City, the Federalists were swamped in the voting in the rest of the state. The Federalists came into the convention in Poughkeepsie at a two-to-one disadvantage, but before two weeks had passed the Anti-Federalists were the ones who found themselves in a perilous situation.

Hamilton made several masterful moves as the Federalist leader. First, the Federalists joined the Anti-Federalists in electing Governor Clinton, unanimously, as president of the convention, thus establishing a disarmingly harmonious atmosphere while minimizing the popular governor's participation in debate. Second, they proposed, and the Anti-Federalists agreed, that there would be no vote until the Constitution had been discussed clause by clause. What Hamilton had in mind was to delay as long as possible a decision by the overwhelming majority against him, in hopes that word would come that Virginia, or New Hampshire, or both had ratified, which is of course what did happen within two weeks.

The Anti-Federalist majority was not monolithic, varying in views and especially in the intensity of their opposition to ratification. They had the votes to defeat unconditional ratification, but they did not have a majority in favor of outright rejection of the Constitution. What they sought, unsuccessfully, was some way to ratify on condition that their long list of amendments would be a part of the Constitution, a proposal that the Federalists called "a gilded rejection." When that failed, their next motion was to ratify while reserving the right of New York to withdraw from the Union if Congress did not call a convention to consider amendments within four years.

Hamilton sought Madison's opinion whether this latest Anti-Federalist proposal would be acceptable. The next day he read to the convention Madison's reply, that it would not be accepted by Congress as a valid ratification:

> Such conditional ratification would not make New York a member of the Union. The Constitution requires an adoption *in toto* and forever. The idea of reserving a right to

withdraw was started in Richmond, and was considered a conditional ratification, which was itself abandoned as worse than a rejection.[20]

The motion was voted down, with even Melancton Smith, the Anti-Federalist floor leader, who was now beginning to waver, voting against the motion he had originally made.

The news that New Hampshire and Virginia had ratified unconditionally had a profound effect on several of the Anti-Federalists, especially Melancton Smith. He changed his position and announced himself in favor of ratification in the Massachusetts form. "My great object," he explained, "is to procure . . . good amendments," and with the Constitution already ratified by ten states, the only way he and other New York Anti-Federalists could participate in getting the amendments they sought was by becoming part of the Union. The new circumstances, he argued, now required New York to ratify. Hamilton, too, explained the surprising switch of a small but decisive number of Anti-Federalist leaders in the same way. "Our arguments confound, but do not convince—Some of the leaders however appear to me to be convinced by circumstances."

On July 26, more than a month after convening, the New York delegates ratified by a margin of just three votes, using the Massachusetts language, "in full confidence" that their amendments would be considered. But though the Anti-Federalist majority lost, they were not beaten. They were able to exact a heavy price for their votes. The convention resolved the next day, "by unanimous order of the New York Convention," to send a circular letter, signed by Governor Clinton, to the governors of all the states, urging them to submit applications to the new Congress to call a constitutional convention, as provided for in Article V of the Constitution. We can easily imagine the terms of the trade involved in obtaining enough Anti-Federalist votes for unconditional ratification, in exchange for every one of the Federalist votes, including even Hamilton's, in favor of Clinton's call for a second constitutional convention.

Madison was appalled by Governor Clinton's circular letter and the effect it seemed to be having, and said so in a letter to Washington, written from New York:

> The circular letter from this state is certainly a matter of as much regret as the unanimity with which it passed is a surprise. I find it everywhere, and particularly in Virginia, laid hold of as a signal for the united exertions in pursuit of early amendments.[21]

46

Most observers assumed that Hamilton was faced with a choice between agreeing to the circular letter or rejection of the Constitution, and that he chose to pay the price of the circular letter in order to gain ratification. Madison went so far as to contend that it would have been wiser to let the convention reject the Constitution than to agree to the circular letter:

> I begin now to accede to the opinion which has been avowed for some time by many, that the circumstances involved in the ratification of the state of New York will prove more injurious than a rejection would have done. The latter would rather have alarmed the well-meaning Federalists elsewhere, would have had no ill effect on the other party, would have excited the indignation of the neighbor states, and would necessarily have been followed by a speedy reconsideration of the subject.[22]

Washington expressed a more charitable judgment of Hamilton's decision, in a letter to John Jay:

> Considering the great majority that appeared to cling together in the Convention, and the decided temper of the leaders, I did not, I confess, see how it could be avoided.[23]

And in a letter to Hamilton himself, Washington's tone, though stern and critical, was also understanding of the hard choice Hamilton had faced, as well as cautiously optimistic for the new government's prospects:

> The Circular Letter from your Convention, I presume, was the equivalent by wch. you obtained an acquiescence in the proposed Constitution: Notwithstanding I am not very well satisfied with the tendency of it; yet the Foederal affairs have proceeded, with few exceptions, in so good a train, that I hope the political Machine may be put in motion, without much effort or hazard of miscarrying.[24]

Washington had summed up quite well the way matters stood. There were still many reasons to worry, but there were also reasons to be hopeful that "the political machine" was close to being "put in motion." Eleven states had ratified; the Constitution was established, at least formally; the initial battles were over. But they had been close. The margin in Massachusetts was 19 votes out of 355, in Virginia 10 votes out of 168, in New York 3 votes out of 57. Put another way, a change of just eighteen delegate votes in those three states would have defeated the Constitution. The Constitution was now safely ratified, but its supporters had to face the fact that if there had been a direct popular referendum throughout the United States, ratification without prior amendments would probably have been defeated.

Reflections on Part One

What lessons can be drawn from this story of the making of the democratic republic, displaying so dramatically both the accord and the discord of its major components, its profoundly democratic foundation and its complex republican structure? This old story, of how the Constitution was ratified, is rich in political lessons, although most of the events themselves were not especially remarkable. After all, these politicians engaged in rather commonplace tactics, of a sort familiar to Americans. We should not be much surprised that there were instances of deliberate deceptions and half-truths; parliamentary maneuvers to thwart the majority or intimidate the minority; fiddling with election rules, dates, and districting; intentional misleading of the voting public; pressure on rank-and-file politicians; appeals to the vanity or the personal advantage of prominent political figures; skillful use, abuse, and misuse of the press; and much more. And it is also not remarkable that the elections were, by and large, free and fair, and that both sides accepted without protest the outcomes of elections and conventions. All of this is pretty much what we would expect and unremarkable to anyone with any sense of the character of American politics.

What makes the unremarkable remarkable, the commonplace extraordinary in this case, is that it all occurred *before* the Constitution was ratified. What that means is that these familiar American political habits were not originally developed and ingrained in the

American character by the Constitution. They existed in full force before the Constitution existed. The genius of the Framers was in writing a constitution that captured American democratic politicking as it was practiced, designing institutions and a structure of society that would perpetuate, not redesign, the way Americans were already constituted.

The next thing to note is that, despite their often sharp differences, all the leaders, on both sides, were committed to the principles of political liberty. There were no monarchists, no oligarchists, no proponents of any kind of nonrepublican, nonconstitutional regime. All were devoted to establishing a constitutional republic founded on the principles of the primacy of the rights of individuals and government by the consent of the governed. They agreed about the end they sought; they differed about the best ways to achieve it. They agreed about fundamental principles; they differed about the best ways to implement them.

Even the most critical opponents of ratification, like Patrick Henry, Elbridge Gerry, and George Clinton, were not against a new constitution "adequate to the exigencies of Government and the preservation of the Union," to use the wording of the instructions of the Continental Congress to the Constitutional Convention. They were opposed to ratifying this Constitution without prior amendments. The Anti-Federalist objective was to amend first, then ratify. The amendments they sought were primarily structural amendments, designed to reduce the powers of the Congress to control elections, to levy taxes, to regulate commerce, and to command the military. But the amendments they sought were in no way inconsistent with republican principles. The Anti-Federalists wanted to amend the Constitution before ratifying it because they were skeptical, with good reason, that Congress would lead the way in reducing its own legislative powers once the Constitution was established.

Some, but not most, of the states called for amendments similar to the Bill of Rights amendments later passed by the First Congress. In many states there was no opposition at all to ratification; in states where there was some, it always came down to this one issue, prior amendment or subsequent amendment. The Anti-Federalists did not seek, and could not have achieved, outright rejection of the Constitution; but they came very close to preventing ratification prior to amending.

Further, Americans were the most experienced and accomplished self-governing citizens in the world at the time. Before and after independence, Americans had been governing themselves through representative assemblies for more than 150 years, under colonial charters they had modified and constitutions they had made for themselves. American politicians were the world's leading practitioners of the processes of constitutional democracy. They knew how to campaign, supervise elections, hold conventions, and run popularly elected legislatures. During the Revolutionary War they welcomed assistance from foreign military commanders and advisers, but no one would have thought of asking for foreign advisers to help them constitute a democratic republic for themselves. If any people could resolve the kind of difficulties they faced, it was these politically skilled Americans.

Many of the most important features of the proposed Constitution, explained to the public as innovations in *The Federalist*, were prominently in evidence and already in practice in the ratification process—that is, before the Constitution was established. For example, we see the workings of the multiplicity of interests, the theme of Madison's great theoretical contribution to *The Federalist*. The multiplicity of interests represented in the state conventions provided excellent protection from the evil consequences of an overbearing majority, just as Madison said it would. In state after state there were represented in the convention a variety of interests, all with their spokesmen and their votes. Even when a constitution was the issue, all politics was local. The interests varied within each state and from state to state, but in no state, and certainly not in the nation as a whole, was any interest or group able to impose its will on others without taking into account the concerns of the others. Some interests prevailed, but everything had to go through a deliberative process that required attention to, and concessions to, the interests of others. Opposed interests could not be, and were not, ignored. Some won and some lost, but none was crushed. Even in defeat the losers were left able to carry on their fight for amendments.

Where there is a multiplicity of interests, there is necessarily a strong incentive to compromise interests as beneficially as possible. Throughout the ratification process, the disposition to compromise and the special skills necessary to effect compromise were evident everywhere. The grand example of compromise was, of course, the Massachusetts formula, which enabled every closely divided state to take the decisive step to ratify unconditionally and yet allow the large minority to continue to act on their conviction that amendments were necessary.

The system of representation by small districts, as opposed to direct democracy, had many beneficial related consequences. Local and regional interests were able to make their concerns known and heard. Because their votes were sought in the conventions, all possible concessions were made. The complexity of the representative system, again as opposed to direct democracy, also had the advantage of taking much time. Quick decisions were avoided, which made deliberation and conciliation possible and likely. The exceptions, as in the case of the Pennsylvania ratifying convention, were regrettable and regretted, useful examples to illustrate that there were better ways to proceed. Pure majority rule, a direct democratic referendum on a take-it-or-leave-it basis, would probably have rejected the Constitution, especially if it had occurred early in the process. As time went on, after extended public discussion and explanation, public opinion became more reconciled to the Constitution. By the time it was established, voters in state after state were evidently pleased with it and with those who supported it. They elected an overwhelming Federalist majority to the First Congress. All of this suggests that there are benefits in the complexity of constitutional procedures and the time they allow for citizens to understand the issues, compose the differences among competing interests, and make their decisions.

New Hampshire presented an example of how a representative assembly can sometimes do a better job than direct democracy in giving the people what they want and what is best for them. The New Hampshire convention was originally elected with a decisive Anti-Federalist majority. The delegates came together bound by instructions from their constituents to vote No; but a few days of deliberation persuaded many of them that they ought to ratify the Constitution, not reject it. The delegates voted to adjourn, went home to speak to their constituents, received new instructions, came back four months later, and ratified in a three-day convention.

Federalism as described in *The Federalist* was also a factor in the ratification process. There was constant communication and cooperation among the states, and concerns peculiar to one state were taken into consideration in the deliberations of other states. The extended territory made possible by a federal system had another obvious beneficial consequence anticipated in *The Federalist*: the enlarged pool of leadership in all the states was more than any one of them could have provided. James Wilson in Pennsylvania, John Hancock and Samuel Adams in Massachusetts, James Madison in Virginia,

Alexander Hamilton in New York, and George Washington off-stage but exerting his influence everywhere, were all indispensable. The Constitution would not have been ratified without them. But the process welcomed them; it could not have been better designed to give full effect to the extraordinarily high levels of constructive leadership they displayed.

The statesmanship of Anti-Federalists like Patrick Henry, Melancton Smith, and George Clinton must also be considered, because in defeat they all eschewed any form of unconstitutional resistance. Many Anti-Federalists, for example, ran for seats in the First Congress, and several were elected, but that meant that they accepted the establishment of the Constitution. The requirement in Article VI that all legislators "and all executive and judicial Officers, both of the United States and of the several States, shall be bound by Oath or Affirmation, to support this Constitution," combined with the desire of Anti-Federalists to persist in seeking amendments as provided for in Article V, transformed those opponents into adherents sworn to uphold the Constitution. Many years later, when Madison was elected president of the United States, his first vice president was George Clinton; after Clinton died in office, Madison's next vice president was Elbridge Gerry.

Because it was a constitution they were trying to establish, the wisest of the majority, especially James Madison, saw the necessity, with increasing clarity as ratification progressed from state to state, to bring along those who opposed. After victory it would be necessary to have the allegiance of everyone, not just those who voted for ratification. By not alienating the defeated minority, by leading in a fashion appropriate to constitution making, the Federalist leaders solidified the unity of the Union. They were statesmen who did not scorn the skills of ordinary politicians. They were willing to scrounge for votes where they could find them, without losing sight of the fact that they were engaged in the extraordinary task of making the world's first written national constitution.[1]

This took a special kind of politicking and made for a complicated and difficult sort of conduct, at once confrontational and conciliatory. It had been a very close call, and the struggle did not end with ratification. Even after the government was functioning, opposition continued to be widespread and stubborn. Although the ratification battle was over, all the combatants were still on their feet, and the movement to call a second convention to consider amendments was very much alive.

What now remains to be told is how James Madison took the scores of amendments proposed by opponents of the Constitution in the several state ratifying conventions, refashioned them with his own purpose in mind, and then used them to put an end to just about all opposition to the Constitution—and especially to put an end to the movement for a second constitutional convention.

PART TWO

How Madison Became the
Father of the Bill of Rights

4
"What Use Can a Bill of Rights Serve?" A Madison-Jefferson Dialogue

That there is a bill of rights in the Constitution we owe in considerable part to the Anti-Federalists and their energetic agitation for amendments; but that we have the Bill of Rights we have, rather than a number of quite different amendments, we owe in larger part, in fact almost exclusively, to James Madison.

As we have seen, the demand for amendments that began in the final weeks of the Constitutional Convention, and continued during the proceedings of the Continental Congress, became more intense as the deliberations moved on to the later state ratifying conventions and the subsequent elections. Calls for amendments were heard everywhere, and the longer the ratification process went on, the longer and more specific and more radical the list of amendments became.

When Madison became a congressional candidate in Virginia, the pressure was especially strong on him to assure the voters in his district that he was amenable to amendments to guard private rights, because it was so well known that he had repeatedly expressed opposition to such amendments. Patrick Henry, who dominated the Virginia legislature, had "gerrymandered" (before there was such a term) the district where Madison would run for Congress so that it included Anti-Federalist strongholds. When Madison made the journey from New York to Virginia in late December 1787, he was immediately persuaded by his supporters that he would have to publicize his support for amendments if he were to have any chance of winning the election. In a letter intended to be made public, he wrote to a prominent Baptist preacher that although he had "opposed all previous alterations" to the Constitution while ratification was the issue and the outcome was still in doubt,

> Circumstances are now changed: The Constitution is established on the ratifications of eleven States and a very great majority of the American people; and amendments, if pursued with a proper moderation and in a proper mode, will be not only safe, but may serve the double purpose of satisfying the minds of well meaning opponents, and of providing additional guards in favour of liberty. Under this change of circumstances, it is my sincere opinion that the Constitution ought to be revised, and that the first Congress meeting under it ought to prepare and recommend to the States for ratification, the most satisfactory provisions for all essential rights, particularly the rights of conscience in the fullest latitude, the freedom of the press, trials by jury, security against general warrants &c.[1]

And so we confront the problem of trying to understand and explain how Madison, one of the most penetrating critics of bills of rights, came to the First Congress pledged to support a bill of rights and, in the process, against the determined opposition of both the Anti-Federalist minority and the Federalist majority in both houses of Congress, became the historically renowned Father of the Bill of Rights.

Madison's Report to Jefferson

A few weeks after the Constitutional Convention completed its work, Madison wrote a memorable letter from New York to his good friend, Thomas Jefferson, then serving as the minister representing the United States in Paris.[2] He enclosed a copy of the new Constitution, giving Jefferson a remarkable first-hand report of the work of the convention and explaining key features of the Constitution. In that long letter—it runs seventeen handwritten pages—Madison referred just once to the absence of a bill of rights in the Constitution, apparently not yet alert to the importance of the issue that would become central to ratification, as well as the major topic of his ensuing exchange of letters with Jefferson.

In this initial letter the subject was mentioned only in passing, as Madison reported that George Mason was one of the delegates who had refused to sign the Constitution.

> Col. Mason left Philada. in an exceeding ill humour indeed. A number of little circumstances arising in part from the impatience which prevailed towards the close of the business, conspired to whet his acrimony. He returned to Virginia with a fixed disposition to prevent the adoption of the plan if possible. He considers the want of a Bill of Rights as a fatal objection.[3]

But Madison's near silence about a bill of rights does not mean that he was unconcerned about the protection of the rights of individuals. It was rather that Madison saw no necessary connection between a bill of rights and the protection of rights. He consistently emphasized the primacy of protecting rights, but he doubted the effectiveness of a bill of rights to do the job.

For example, much of this long letter to Jefferson was devoted to an account of one of the most important setbacks Madison suffered in the convention: the defeat of his proposal that Congress be given a power to veto *state* legislation. He did not speak of it, as we would expect, as a matter concerning federal-state relations. What was at stake, Madison said, was the security of private rights:

> A constitutional negative on the laws of the States seems . . . necessary to secure individuals agst. encroachments on their rights. The mutability of the laws of the States is found to be a serious evil. The injustice of them has been so frequent and so flagrant as to alarm the most steadfast friends of Republicanism . . . . A reform therefore which does not make provision for private rights, must be materially defective.[4]

We have become accustomed to having the federal courts exercise "a constitutional negative on the laws of the states," by virtue of the Supreme Court's interpretation that the Fourteenth Amendment made the first eight amendments applicable to the states. Most students of American constitutional law would be concerned that the security of individual rights would be in jeopardy if the Supreme Court relinquished the power to declare state legislation unconstitutional. Such a "negative on the laws of the States" is what Madison had in mind, except that he intended the power to be in the hands of the Congress rather than of the judiciary. That is probably also what the authors of the Fourteenth Amendment had in mind some eighty years later. As Francis Canavan has argued, "this much is beyond doubt":

59

The evil which sections 1 and 5 of the Fourteenth Amendment were intended to remedy was discriminatory legislation against black people of the kind enacted by the Southern States after the emancipation of the slaves, and the remedy envisioned for this evil was legislation enacted by Congress to override State laws. The Fourteenth Amendment embodied a return, in a limited area of civil rights, to the national negative on State laws that the Constitutional Convention of 1787 had rejected.[5]

As we shall see, Madison had profound theoretical reasons for thinking that the federal legislature would be a better guardian of individual rights than would the state legislatures. But the present point is that while making "provision for private rights" was essential for Madison, that did not mean that he thought a bill of rights was essential. There were other constitutional means available for securing private rights: in Madison's view, more effective means.

Jefferson's Campaign for a Bill of Rights

For Madison, but not for Jefferson, the questionable efficacy of a bill of rights was good reason to do without one. Thus, when Madison wrote that "experience proves the inefficacy of a bill of rights on those occasions when its controul is most needed,"[6] Jefferson conceded *that was true, but* "tho it is not absolutely efficacious under all circumstances, it is of great potency always, and rarely inefficacious."[7] And when Madison wrote that a positive declaration of some essential rights, for example religious freedom, "could not be obtained in the requisite latitude"[8] —meaning that in some states protection of religious freedom was extended only to Christians or even only to Protestants, leaving the religious practices of others in greater jeopardy than if there were no such provision—Jefferson, apparently missing the point of Madison's objection to a partial protection of religious freedom, replied *that was true, but* "Half a loaf is better than no bread. If we cannot secure all our rights, let us secure what we can."[9]

Jefferson, in his reply from Paris to Madison's long letter, praised many of the new features of the Constitution ("I like the organization of the government into Legislative, Judiciary, and Executive"; "I like the power given the Legislature to levy taxes"; and "I am captivated by the compromise of the opposite claims of the great and little states"). But then, in a blunt and abrupt transition—"I will now add what I do not like"—he turned to his chief criticism:

First, the omission of a bill of rights providing clearly and without the aid of sophisms for freedom of religion, freedom of the press, protection against standing armies, restriction against monopolies, the eternal and unremitting force of the habeas corpus laws [by which he meant, as he explained in a later letter, "no suspensions of the habeas corpus"], and trials by jury in all matters of fact triable by the laws of the land.[10]

And then, responding to the contentions of many others, especially Alexander Hamilton, that the states but not the federal government, and monarchies but not republics, may require a bill of rights, Jefferson concluded in his most forceful and quotable style:

Let me add that a bill of rights is what the people are entitled to against every government on earth, general or particular, and what no just government should refuse, or rest on inference.[11]

Jefferson wrote similarly to many others in the weeks and months following, repeating the same list of six articles—religion, press, standing army, habeas corpus, monopolies, and trial by jury—in a letter campaign conducted from Paris obviously intended to influence the deliberations of the state ratifying conventions. He also included in these letters a recommendation that the first nine states be encouraged to ratify the Constitution, but that the last four be advised to withhold ratification until a bill of rights was added. As he put it in a letter to one of his other correspondents:

Were I in America I would advocate [ratification of the Constitution] warmly till nine should have adopted, and then as warmly take the other side to convince the remaining four that they ought not to come into it till the declaration of rights is annexed to it. By this means we should secure all the good of it, and procure so respectable an opposition as would induce the accepting states to offer a bill of rights. This would be the happiest turn the thing could take.[12]

This imprudent suggestion makes one grateful that Jefferson was safely in Paris rather than in Virginia during the ratification struggle. His mischievous plan, which Jefferson communicated to many others before changing his mind and abandoning it when he heard of the Massachusetts formula,[13] would have been less than helpful to Madison and Hamilton in their great struggle to win adoption of the Constitution. New York and Virginia were destined to be among the last four states, and even though nine other states ratified before they did, had they insisted on amending prior to ratifying, the cause of the new Constitution would almost certainly have been lost.

Among those who advocated amendments, some insisted on amending before agreeing to ratification, as we have seen, while others were satisfied to ratify first in the expectation of subsequent amendment, following the amending procedures set forth in the Constitution. Madison had good reason to suspect the motives and intentions of many of those who were insisting on amending the Constitution before giving assent to ratification. Many of the leading advocates of prior amendments were clearly intent on defeating the Constitution or changing it radically. But in his next letter to Jefferson, Madison acknowledged that "not a few" of those demanding prior amendments to the Constitution were acting "from the most honorable & patriotic motives" and that even among the supporters of the Constitution there were "some who wish for further guards to public liberty & individual rights."[14]

Madison Favors a Bill of Rights

Madison then made a prediction about amendments that must have been greatly encouraging to Jefferson: "As far as these may consist of a constitutional declaration of the most essential rights, it is probable they will be added," though he apparently could not refrain from commenting that "there are many who think such addition unnecessary, and not a few who think it misplaced in such a Constitution."[15]

Madison continued with an assertion that ever since has puzzled many, because of his documented record of criticisms and opposition to bills of rights. He said, "My own opinion has always been in favor of a bill of rights."[16] But the statement is less puzzling if we consider the complete paragraph, in which Madison provides an immediate explanation of why, and in what respect, he "always" favored a bill of rights:

> My own opinion has always been in favor of a bill of rights; provided it be so framed as not to imply powers not meant to be included in the enumeration. At the same time I have never thought the omission a material defect, nor been anxious to supply it even by subsequent amendment, for any other reason than that it is anxiously desired by others. I have favored it because I have supposed it might be of use, and if properly executed could not be of disservice.[17]

Madison's careful choice of words here is revealing. He was impressively consistent in the way he spoke about a bill of rights. In his private correspondence and even in his public speeches in support of his own proposals of the amendments that became the Bill of Rights, he was scrupulous in not speaking approvingly of the provisions for their intrinsic worth, or for "any other reason," to use his exact words, than that others thought them important or useful or reassuring. In addition, he regularly added qualifications, such as "if properly executed," and conditional phrasing, such as "it might be of use," and double negatives, such as "could not be of disservice." These two sentences to Jefferson are a typical example of the way Madison spoke of bills of rights, including even his own.

Madison addressed several of Jefferson's points directly, primarily Jefferson's contention that the people are entitled to a bill of rights "against every government on earth." Madison thought that was indiscriminate, that there is an important distinction to be made between monarchical and republican governments, and that a bill of rights is needed in a monarchy in a way that it is not needed where the majority rules—not because a republican government is necessarily less likely to be oppressive than a monarchical government, but because of the different source of probable oppression.

> Wherever the real power in a Government lies [Madison wrote], there is the danger of oppression. In our Governments the real power lies in the majority of the Community, and the invasion of private rights is chiefly to be apprehended, not from acts of Government contrary to the sense of its Constituents, but from acts in which the Government is the mere instrument of the major number of the Constituents. This is a truth of great importance, but not yet sufficiently attended to.[18]

From this factor—that the real danger to individual rights, in a regime where the majority rules, comes not from the legislative or executive branches of the government acting independently of their constituents but from the majority of the people themselves pushing the government to oppressive policy—Madison drew the consequence that in a popular government a bill of rights is likely to be too weak, a mere "paper barrier" that will be least effective when most needed. An impassioned majority will ignore an injunction to restrain itself, and in a republic, what greater force is there than the majority?

Madison suggested to Jefferson that Paris, the seat of the French monarchy in turmoil in 1788, was not the best vantage point for evaluating the efficacy of a bill of rights for the United States. The truth of the distinction he was making, about the oppressive potential of the popular majority,

> is probably more strongly impressed on my mind by facts, and reflections suggested by them, than on yours which has contemplated abuses of power issuing from a very different quarter. Wherever there is an interest and power to do wrong, wrong will generally be done, and no less readily by a powerful and interested party [in a republic] than by a powerful and interested prince [in a monarchy] .... The difference so far as it relates to the point in question—the efficacy of a bill of rights in controuling abuses of power—lies in this: that in a monarchy the latent force of the nation is superior to that of the Sovereign, and a solemn charter of popular rights must have a great effect, as a standard for trying the validity of public acts, and a signal for rousing and uniting the superior force of the community; whereas in a popular Government, the political and physical power may be considered as vested in the same hands, that is in a majority of the people, and consequently the tyrannical will of the Sovereign is not [to] be controuled by the dread of an appeal to any other force within the community.[19]

The Oppressive Potential of a Republican Majority

It seems strange and even startling that at a time when tyrannical monarchs were a commonplace in the world, James Madison, one of the great architects of modern republican government, should insist that a bill of rights would be least effective in a republic, of all forms of government, and that of all oppressive forces, a majority of the people in a republic would potentially be the most dangerous. We must remind ourselves that Madison always argued that experience would be the best teacher in the matters they were deliberating, and that no one in the world had yet had experience in popular national government, or, at the other extreme, experience of the horrors that twentieth-century totalitarian regimes could inflict on mankind. Experience with popular state governments had given rise to much doubt and severe misgivings, and so the question was whether remedies for the flaws of majority rule experienced at the state level could be found at the national level.

The theoretical problem seemed to Madison to be formidable. In a monarchy, oligarchy, or aristocracy, the power of the ruling group is less than the latent power of the majority whenever the people are aroused against the government. In that circumstance, a bill of rights can serve as the rallying "signal for rousing and uniting the superior force" of an angry populace against the oppressive government acting against their wishes and against their rights and interests.

But the situation as Madison saw it in his speculations about a national democratic republic was quite different. The majority would dictate policy to the government, and when it ordered oppressive policies—for example measures severely abusive of the interests of the minority, or of certain groups or individuals—the government would not be acting against the will of the majority but in full accord with it. The danger of republican oppression, of governmental violation of individual rights, would be greater than in other forms of government because it would be more difficult to oppose and stop.

Madison saw little chance that a bill of rights could be the remedy for the problem of restraining an oppressive majority once it had formed. The best chance for justice and security for rights would be to prevent the formation of unjust majorities. And to do that he recommended not a bill of rights but rather structural constitutional arrangements that would encourage the growth of a multiplicity of interests, and devices such as a congressional veto over state legislation. And so Madison was led by this line of reasoning to raise an austere and direct question: "What use then it may be asked can a bill of rights serve in popular Governments?[20]

Madison considered the problem of the oppressive majority the most fundamental of all facing a constitution writer for a republic, for a political society governed ultimately by the will of the majority. The greatest danger to individual rights in any political society is the greatest power in that society. But of all forms of government, the only one where the most powerful latent physical force and the political governing force are identical is a republic, and so popular government presents a unique problem for protecting individual rights.

When Madison, in his first letter to Jefferson in this exchange, recounted the defeat of his proposal to give Congress the power to veto state legislation, he spoke of it not as a question of relations of the federal government to the state governments but as a matter of protection of rights. And he posed the question of why we should think that the federal legislature would be a better guardian of private rights than the state legislatures.

He also added several closely related questions. Under the new Constitution, how will the federal government and the state governments differ in their respect for individual rights? Why should we trust the general government to oversee the state governments? Why should we expect one to have a greater respect for individual rights than the other? Madison put it this way:

> It may be asked how private rights will be more secure under the Guardianship of the General Government than under the State Governments, since they are both founded on the republican principle which refers the ultimate decision to the will of the majority, and are distinguished rather by the extent within which they will operate than by any material difference in their structure.[21]

Madison's argument, familiar to readers of *The Federalist* but at the time of this letter completely new to Jefferson, is this: the greater extent of territory of the Union, made possible by the new Constitution, is what will make the legislature of the general government a superior guardian of the rights of the people. Madison prefaced his explanation to Jefferson of the importance of the extent of territory for a republic with a quietly proud boast of a theoretical innovation of extraordinary significance:

> A full discussion of this question [of extent of territory] would, if I mistake not, unfold the true Principles of Republican Government, and prove in contradiction to the concurrent opinions of the theoretical writers, that this form of Government, in order to effect its purposes, must operate not within a small but an extensive sphere.[22]

Madison began his discourse on the significance of the extent of territory by arguing first that "a simple democracy," direct government by the majority, is based on a fictitious supposition: namely, that the populace is homogenous, and therefore majority rule would not be oppressive, because the majority and the minority would have the same interests. In that case, political decisions would turn on mere differences of "opinion concerning the good of the whole." "We know, however," he said, "that no society ever did or can consist of so homogenous a mass of Citizens."[23]

On the contrary, in all "civilized societies," there will be a multitude of differences of interests. "There will be rich and poor; creditors and debtors; a landed interest, a mercantile interest, a manufacturing interest," and many subgroups of these. In addition to the "natural" differences there will be "artificial" ones "in political, religious, or other opinions," all of which will lead to a diversity of interests and will cause dissension and faction.

And this leads to Madison's dominant concern, whether a majority having a common interest or a common passion "will find sufficient motives to restrain them from oppressing the minority." For example,

> If two individuals are under the bias of interest or enmity agst. a third, the rights of the latter could never be safely referred to the majority of the three. Will two thousand individuals be less apt to oppress one thousand, or two hundred thousand one hundred thousand?[24]

Madison then listed three motives that are ordinarily counted on to restrain the oppressive behavior of individuals—prudent calculation of personal advantage, concern about one's reputation among neighbors and fellow citizens, and religious scruples. These motives for an individual to restrain himself, he argued, are unlikely to be effective restraints of the behavior of large groups, especially of the behavior of a majority. Prudential calculation—for example, that "honesty is the best policy"—will be ineffective because the principle of a majority is more likely to be "what is politic is honest." Next, concern about the public's opinion is often not effective in restraining individuals and will be completely ineffective in restraining a majority, whose opinion *is* public opinion. Finally, Madison dismissed religion as an effective restraint on oppressive mass behavior: "The inefficacy of this restraint on individuals is well known," and experience shows that religion "has been much oftener a motive to oppression than a restraint from it."[25]

Failing to find an effective and reliable restraint to majority oppression once an oppressive majority has formed, Madison summed up the problem and the remedy for Jefferson in one potent sentence:

> If then there must be different interests and parties in society; and a majority when united by a common interest or passion cannot be restrained from oppressing the minority, what remedy can be found in a republican Government, where the majority must ultimately decide, but that of giving such an extent to the sphere, that no common interest or passion will be likely to unite a majority of the whole number in an unjust pursuit.[26]

That sentence tells, in compact form, why Madison thought a bill of rights was too weak a barrier to majority oppression, and why he thought inclusion of a bill of rights in the Constitution was a matter of less than major importance for the purpose of securing the rights of the people. Efforts to restrain an oppressive majority were unlikely to succeed, no matter what the solemn wording on parchment. The best chance to protect rights lay in preventing the formation of an oppressive majority in the first place, and that is why Madison considered the structure of the government and the society fundamental and the provisions of the bill of rights only secondary and supplemental.

The Contents of the Bill of Rights

Madison concluded his discourse on the central importance of the extent of territory and diversity of interests—begging Jefferson's pardon for "this immoderate digression"—and turned from the question of the usefulness of a bill of rights to a second question: If we do have a bill of rights, what articles ought to be included in it?[27]

Of the six articles Jefferson had enumerated as essential for inclusion in a bill of rights, Madison accepted three—freedom of religion, freedom of the press, and jury trials—and rejected three—the prohibition of a standing army, the prohibition of monopolies, and the unlimited privilege of the writ of habeas corpus. He commenced by making a general observation about how to think about what articles to include in a bill of rights if there were to be one.

> I am inclined to think that absolute restrictions in cases that are doubtful, or where emergencies may overrule them, ought to be avoided. The restrictions however strongly marked on paper will never be regarded when opposed to the decided sense of the public, and after repeated violations in extraordinary cases they will lose even their ordinary efficacy.

On the basis of those guidelines, he disposed of two of Jefferson's proposals in rapid fashion:

> Should a Rebellion or insurrection alarm the people as well as the Government, and a suspension of the Hab. Corp. be dictated by the alarm, no written prohibitions on earth would prevent the measure. Should an army in time of peace be gradually established in our neighborhood by Britn. or Spain, declarations on paper would have as little effect in preventing a standing force for the public safety.[28]

Jefferson was advocating, in effect, that the Constitution's habeas corpus clause ("The Privilege of the Writ of Habeas Corpus shall not be suspended, unless when in Cases of Rebellion or Invasion the public Safety may require it"),[29] be amended so that it would say simply, "The privilege of the writ of habeas corpus shall not be suspended." Madison's response was that the effect would be twofold: in emergencies such as rebellion or invasion, when the public would be extraordinarily aroused, habeas corpus would be suspended anyway. Suspected dangerous characters would be detained and held without trial, and the Constitution would become less effective because less respected each time this provision, or any provision, was ignored or disobeyed.

The demand for prohibiting a standing army in time of peace was surprisingly popular at the time. The ratification conventions of six states had proposed amendments to the Constitution, and all six of them had recommended restrictions on a standing army, as compared with only three for protection of freedom of the press, and just one for freedom of speech. This recommended limitation on a standing army was usually coupled with advocacy of state militia as the appropriate means of defense of "a free State." What was at stake was whether the new general government or the several states would control the military power of the nation. Madison did propose, once he was elected to serve in the House of Representatives, an amendment designed to secure the right of the people to bear arms in "a well regulated militia," but he omitted any mention of a limitation on a standing army and fought off repeated efforts in the Congress to enact one. This was consistent with his practice throughout; he picked and chose among the scores of amendments recommended by the state ratifying conventions, omitting, as we shall see, all provisions intended to diminish the powers of the new government.

As for Jefferson's third rejected suggestion, the only monopolies sanctioned by the Constitution are in the so-called copyright and patent clause, which empowers Congress to grant to authors and inventors "the exclusive right"to their products "for limited times."[30] Madison acknowledged that monopolies can be a great "nuisance," but asked whether, nevertheless, "as encouragements to literary works and ingenious discoveries, they are not too valuable to be wholly renounced?" And he added the observation that monopolies are more likely to flourish "where the power is in the few."

Where the power as with us is in the many not in the few
the danger cannot be very great that the few will be thus

favored. It is much more to be dreaded that the few will be unnecessarily sacrificed to the many.[31]

Whether or not we agree with Madison's view of the relative strengths of the few and the many, we see at least the kind of analysis he brought to every aspect of the task of composing a bill of rights. Unlike present-day proponents of civil rights and human rights, who habitually see rights as a problem of morality, Madison approached the problem of securing rights by starting always with questions such as these: Where does the power lie? Whose interests are at stake? Whose interests will be served? And what power is available to prevent the oppression before it occurs, or to curb it if measures to prevent it fail?

As for morality in connection with violations of individual rights, he had a clear-eyed view of human nature: "Wherever there is an interest and power to do wrong, wrong will generally be done."[32] What to do about it? He spent no effort on moralizing about the inclination to do wrong, or on measures to rectify the character of evildoers. His attention was focused instead on devising constitutional arrangements that would keep those with an "interest to do wrong" from acquiring the "power to do wrong."

Madison's answers to Jefferson, however, are far from perfect answers to the problems one confronts in writing a bill of rights, illustrating perhaps why Madison was so reluctant to include one in the Constitution. There are good reasons to doubt that there can be satisfactory answers to the questions he was addressing. Consider, for example, his argument to Jefferson about the privilege of the writ of habeas corpus. If the prohibition is too sweeping, it is unlikely to fit all future circumstances, especially extraordinary circumstances: that is, those unusual occasions when restraints of power are most needed. If, on the other hand, one adds exceptions, in anticipation of unforeseeable future events, they tend to weaken the prohibition and serve as an open invitation to officials to pretend there is an emergency that requires suspension of the writ in order to detain dissidents without trial.

Examples abound. The freedom of the press provisions in many constitutions around the world protect freedom of the press except in emergencies when the national security might be endangered.[33] In some there are so many qualifications and exceptions written into the bill of rights that the state of emergency provision runs several paragraphs, sometimes even several pages. These qualifications allow suspension of the provisions for freedom of the press, and many other protected freedoms, by declaring a state of emergency.[34] Should we be surprised that under such constitutions emergencies are declared often, and that they last sometimes for months and even years?

Allowing for exceptions is prone to intolerable abuse, and yet there are certain emergency situations, especially in time of war, when almost everyone agrees that some restrictions on the press are justified. That necessity becomes obvious to the common sense of the citizenry, and we therefore then accept measures that we would not tolerate in ordinary circumstances, even though the First Amendment says that "Congress shall pass no law . . . abridging the freedom . . . of the press," and makes no mention of exceptions.

Having responded to Jefferson's general and specific suggestions about what should be included in a bill of rights if there is to be one, Madison returned to his own question: "What use . . . can a bill of rights serve in popular Governments?"[35] And, finally, after all his arguments against a bill of rights for republics in general, and for the United States under the new Constitution in particular, he nevertheless found two reasons for adding a bill of rights to the Constitution. These reasons, "though less essential than in other Governments, sufficiently recommend the precaution." One of these reasons, especially, represents a major development in Madison's thought, and explains his advocacy of a bill of rights not as a change of mind but as fully consistent with his long-held views.

His first reason has to do with the effect of a bill of rights on public opinion and the second with the possibility of abuses of power under any form of government. Madison conceded that there could be occasions of abuses of power, or the emergence of an "artful" leader with a hidden ambition to subvert liberty, and then a bill of rights could be the basis for "an appeal to the sense of the community." He also conceded that it is prudent to guard against the danger of such abuses of power, "especially when the precaution can do no injury." But having made those concessions, he apparently could not help adding, "At the same time, I must own that I see no tendency in our Governments to danger on that side." The danger of oppression was greater from "the interested majorities of the people . . . than in usurped acts of the Government."[36]

How Madison Persuaded Himself

Madison was consistent in holding that his sole reason for agreeing to a bill of rights was that others wanted it, but he now gave a new importance to what had previously seemed to be a trivial reason. The public demand for a bill of rights could produce a powerful effect on public behavior and make a bill of rights a mighty instrument in restraining an interested majority. This possibility made this first of his two reasons compelling for Madison:

> The political truths declared in that solemn manner acquire by degrees the character of fundamental maxims of free government, and as they become incorporated with the national sentiment, counteract the impulses of interest and passion.[37]

Here we see the beginning of a theoretical formulation, to be considered at length in the next chapter, that was developed more fully by Madison in his great speech to the House of Representatives introducing the amendments that would become the Bill of Rights. It became an important adjunct to his argument for precautions to inhibit the formation of an all-powerful, persisting majority faction that would be very likely to oppress the minority and endanger the rights of the people.

In a republic of free and independent active citizens, personal liberty depends on a combination and balance of diversity and unity. In *Federalist* 51, Madison described the benefits of a multiplicity of interests and sects:

> In a free government the security for civil rights must be the same as that for religious rights. It consists in the one case in the multiplicity of interests, and in the other in the multiplicity of sects. The degree of security in both cases will depend on the number of interests and sects; and this may be presumed to depend on the extent of country and number of people comprehended under the same government.[38]

But Madison must have known, from experience and observation, as we know, that multiplicity by itself cannot suffice to secure rights. From the many examples of violent disunity around the world, we know that a multiplicity of interests, or of religious sects, or of ethnic groups is not only not enough by itself to ensure personal liberty; it can be the chief cause of internal chaos. In fact, multiplicity works for freedom only in the context of a stable society suffused with a vigorous national unity. Did Madison ignore this? Quite the opposite. When all was said and done, national unity was the chief reason he favored adding a bill of rights, and national unity was the overriding reason why he put so much weight on adding provisions to the Constitution that had no stronger justification, in his opinion, than that others desired them.

Starting almost from the moment the Constitutional Convention ended—first in New York, at the proceedings of the Continental Congress, then in Virginia, in the ratifying convention and in his campaign for a seat in the House of Representatives—Madison grew increasingly aware that there was a genuine constitutional problem to be addressed, a problem that would persist even after the Constitution was ratified. This problem, in his view, was not in the document or in the plan of government, but rather in the widespread public mistrust of the powers of the new government it established.

Madison was confident that this mistrust was unwarranted. But for a constitution establishing popular government, based on consent of the people and majority rule, with powers limited so as to secure the rights of the minority and of individuals—for such a constitution it is not enough to have majority support. Such a constitution, he came to realize, must have the allegiance of "the great mass of the people," of "the whole community." With such universal allegiance, the majority can be expected to restrain itself, by appeal to the Constitution, on those occasions when it is tempted to deny the rights of the minority by the exercise of abusive majority power. Thus Madison found in public opinion another facet of the remedy for the greatest republican danger, the oppressive majority.

Despite his misgivings about the intrinsic merits of bills of rights, Madison saw the necessity to act to gain the support of "the whole community" for the Constitution. He saw a bill of rights, *his* carefully constructed bill of rights, as the most effective solution. If he wrote the amendments, he could win the support of those who were still uneasy, without making any change at all in the constitutional structure. His primary objective was to keep the Constitution intact, to save it from the radical amendments others had proposed; as we shall see, he did it not by opposing all amendments, as many of the most experienced Federalist politicians urged, but rather by proposing in their place his own amendments, taking great care to be certain that they altered nothing in the original Constitution. In place of provisions put forth in the state ratifying conventions and supported by popular demand, he proposed seemingly similar but quite different amendments. To these amendments, as it turned out and as he foresaw, the national citizenry gladly gave its consent. This consent finally established the Constitution as the focus of national unity, to which the whole community, regardless of faction, could pledge its allegiance.

If we think of societies we have seen in advanced stages of chaos and in imminent danger of dissolution from excesses of divisiveness—Lebanon in the 1980s, or Yugoslavia after 1990, or non-Russian provinces and republics of the former Soviet Union after its breakup, to name only a few—we realize that encouraging the development within a society of a multiplicity of competing interests (as well as a multiplicity of ethnic groups and religious sects) cannot promote the stability that Madison saw as the bedrock of political liberty unless other equally powerful, countervailing factors are at work. These countervailing factors must be capable of moving the hostile groups in other directions, promoting the unity of the whole community. When we consider the many nations in the world on the brink of self-destruction because of domestic divisions, we see that an undesirable diversity can lead to violent strife and deprivation of all rights, especially the basic and essential right to physical safety under lawful authority.

The desirable diversity sought by Madison, based on a multiplicity of interests and a multiplicity of religious sects, can be the basis of personal liberty only if there is a solid underlying foundation of unity in support of the fundamental principles of the regime. In the American case, those principles include limited government and security of individual rights. Just how Madison sought to use his proposed amendments to promote national unity, encourage diversity of interests and religious sects, provide protection for private rights, and secure the limited powers of the central government from the efforts of the Anti-Federalists to emasculate it—all these aims were made emphatically evident to those who heard and, very soon after, read his historic speech to the House of Representatives.

5

"To Introduce the Great Work": Congressman Madison Takes the Floor

The speech that James Madison delivered on the floor of the House of Representatives early in the first session of the First Congress, on June 8, 1789, proposing the first amendments to the new Constitution of the United States, was one of the most consequential political orations in American history. The speech itself may not be remarkable for eloquence or rhetorical flourishes, but it stands as an extraordinary example of democratic statesmanship in action. It would be well worth our careful study for its abundance of political sagacity even if it had not produced the profound and far-reaching results from which we and the rest of the freedom-loving world have benefited ever since.

Madison's Surprising Role

How did Madison get to the point of delivering the speech that made him the Father of the Bill of Rights? We know that he did not start out as a supporter of a bill of rights, and even after he became an advocate of the amendments he did not express enthusiasm for them. Madison made no secret of his reservations about the efficacy of a bill of rights as an instrument to secure the rights of the people. He expressed these reservations on numerous occasions both public and private, in political speeches he made in Virginia,[1] and in his letters to Thomas Jefferson[2] and others. He was thus an unlikely candidate for the role of initiator of the amendments that are now known as the Bill of Rights, and yet that is the role he undertook. The explanation of how and why it happened is of much more than historical interest. And much of the explanation, if not all, can be found in his June 8 speech.

The Bill of Rights was produced by the collaborative efforts of many members of the First Congress, and yet Madison is called the Father of the Bill of Rights, deservedly, because so much of the task was exclusively his doing. Although many changes of wording and many deletions were made by the Congress, what was included in the amendments and, equally important, what was excluded were determined almost entirely by Madison's legislative leadership. Moreover, the amendments came before the House for deliberation only because of Madison's stubborn persistence. Federalists as well as Anti-Federalists in the House, albeit for different reasons, were almost unanimously opposed to commencing any discussion of amendments so early in their first session, and they told Madison so in terms that were caustic, scornful, and even derisive. Madison had to use all his determination and legislative skill to persevere in the business.

The Threat of a Second Convention

On May 4, 1789, just four weeks into the first session of the First Congress, Madison gave notice to the House that he intended "to bring on the subject of amendments" before the end of the month.[3] His timing for delivering this warning that day was surely related to the fact that the next day his fellow congressman from Virginia, Theodoric Bland, following procedures set forth in Article V of the Constitution, was scheduled to present an application to Congress from the Virginia legislature calling for a second constitutional convention. It asked

> that a convention be immediately called, of deputies from the several States, with full power to take into their consideration the defects of this constitution that have been suggested by the State Conventions, and report such amendments thereto as they shall find best suited to promote our common interests.[4]

Bland read the full text of the Virginia application to the House on May 5, and concluded by moving that it be referred to a committee of the whole.[5] This motion led to an immediate discussion of how the provisions of Article V would work and what Congress must do when states sought to use the convention method to amend the Constitution. Madison and others contended that there was no constitutional basis for responding to Bland's motion to refer the application to a committee, because there was nothing for Congress to deliberate. Article V requires the Congress to call a convention when two-thirds of the state legislatures apply for one, but until Congress has received the applications from two-thirds of the states, no congressional action is required or permitted, other than to file the applications and keep count of them. And when applications have been received from two-thirds of the states, there is still nothing for Congress to deliberate. Article V is imperative: With no alternative, Congress "shall call a convention for proposing amendments."

With these arguments, Madison and the other Federalists turned away Bland's effort to bring the Virginia legislature's Anti-Federalist amendments, instead of the ones Madison planned to present, before the House as the basis of discussion of amendments. After Bland made a few more futile attempts to get the House to accept the Virginia amendments as "a guide to the deliberations of the committee on the subject of amendments," he withdrew his motion and the House filed away Virginia's application. On the following day, May 6, John Laurance of New York presented an application from the New York legislature for a second constitutional convention, "which being read, was ordered to be filed."

Two major states had now taken decisive steps toward calling a second constitutional convention, which would have taken the matter of amendments out of the hands of the overwhelming Federalist majorities in both houses of Congress. Madison had long considered this possibility a serious threat to the existence of the new government, but most other members of Congress seemed less concerned. They were caught up in the demanding business of establishing the several departments of the new government and passing other essential legislation, and they did not conceal their annoyance at Madison's efforts to get them to discuss his proposals for amendments, or even to hear them.

Madison did not get to "bring on the subject of amendments" before the end of May, as he had hoped. But on June 8 he sought to get the action started, announcing that he intended to make this "the day . . . for bringing forward amendments to the constitution," and he moved that the House resolve itself into a committee of the whole to receive his proposals.[6] This motion generated an immediate storm of complaint and opposition. One member after another rose to object to any delay of their important legislative business. "Are we going to finish it in an hour; believe not; it will take us more than a day, a week, a month—it will take a year to complete it!"[7] Even members who said they favored amending at an appropriate time voiced the objection that consideration of amendments now was "premature." Would it not be more sensible to wait until they had some experience of the defects of the Constitution before attempting to correct them?

In response to this barrage, Madison, intent on taking some prompt action in order to head off the threat of a second convention, tried to deal with the complaint of taking too much time and interrupting urgent legislative business:

> I only wish to introduce the great work, and . . . I do not expect it will be decided immediately; but if some step is taken in the business it will give reason to believe that we may come to a final result. This will inspire a reasonable hope in the advocates for amendments. . . . I hope the House will not decline my motion for going into a committee.[8]

But the complaints from members continued unabated: "The executive part of the Government wants organization; the business of the revenue is incomplete, to say nothing of the judiciary business. . . . I have strong objections to being interrupted in completing the more important business"; "I hope the House will not spend much time on this subject"; "however desirous this House may be to go into consideration of amendments, . . . yet the important and pressing business of the Government prevents their entering upon that subject at present." "I hope the House will not go into a Committee of the whole . . . . The wheels of the national machine cannot turn, until the impost and collection bill are perfected; . . . are not vessels daily arriving, and the revenue slipping through our fingers?"

John Page of Virginia, trying to support Madison, pointed out to his colleagues, so desirous of using their time well, that "if no objection had been made to his motion, the whole business might have been finished before this."[9] And he reminded them that if Congress did not at least get started on amendments, the matter would soon enough be decided by others:

> I venture to affirm, that unless you take early notice of this subject, you will not have power to deliberate. The people

will clamor for a new convention . . . . Those, therefore, who dread the assembling of a convention, will do well to acquiesce in the present motion . . . . I do not think we need consume more than half an hour in the Committee of the whole.[10]

Page's argument fell on deaf ears. It was followed immediately by a lengthy speech by John Vining of Delaware, repeating many of the objections and complaints previously brought forth by several others against going into committee of the whole. But Madison, undaunted, brought this heated procedural controversy to an abrupt end by simply ignoring it. He withdrew his motion to go into a committee of the whole, moved instead that a select committee be appointed, and then, seemingly oblivious to the numerous objections to taking the time of the House to hear amendments, and without waiting for any decision on which kind of committee would consider his proposals, launched directly into the momentous speech "to introduce the great work."

Why Consider Amendments Now

Madison divided the speech into three parts: first, an explanation of why it was timely and prudent for Congress to consider amendments without delay; second, the presentation of the amendments themselves; and third, the arguments in support of the amendments.

Following this scheme, he began by giving several reasons why the Congress, in their first session, despite other urgent legislative business of major importance, ought to take the time to propose amendments to send to the state legislatures for ratification.[11] The first, he said, was to offer evidence to the Americans who did not yet support the Constitution that those who do support it are as devoted to liberty as they are, by showing that they "do not disregard their wishes." Prudence dictates that advocates of the Constitution take steps now to make it "as acceptable to the whole people of the United States, as it has been found acceptable to a majority of them."

The fact is, Madison said, there is still "a great number" of the American people who are dissatisfied and insecure under the new Constitution. So, "if there are amendments desired of such a nature as will not injure the constitution, and they can be ingrafted so as to give satisfaction to the doubting part of our fellow-citizens," why not, in a spirit of "deference and concession," adopt such amendments? For it is also a fact that "a great body of the people" are inclined to support the Constitution if only they can be "satisfied on this one point" of private rights.

Madison concluded this part of the argument by urging on the House members a direct and simple remedy for the widespread dissatisfaction. "We ought not to disregard their inclination, but, on principles of amity and moderation, conform to their wishes and expressly declare the great rights of mankind secured under this constitution." Madison, as in this last sentence, seemed to be urging his colleagues to do nothing more nor less than add to the Constitution an explicit declaration of protection of rights that were, in his opinion and probably also in the opinion of his congressional colleagues, already "secured under this constitution." And he was urging them to do so not so much for some intrinsic reason, but rather for the sake of dispelling dissatisfaction.[12]

Two purposes are consistently linked and given equal weight in Madison's argument: first, to reassure those uneasy Americans who needed reassurance, and second, to avoid changing anything in the Constitution. And the terms in which he cast his argument—"caution," "deference," "concession," "amity," "moderation," "prudence"—were clearly chosen to invite reconciliation with the opposition, mutual respect, and national unity.

After touching briefly on another "motive" for prompt consideration of amendments, that of bringing into the Union the two states, North Carolina and Rhode Island, that had not yet ratified the Constitution, Madison moved on to a substantive point he said he ranked "over and above all these considerations." Keeping in mind that all power can be abused, he said,

> it is possible the abuse of the powers of the General Government may be guarded against in a more secure manner than is now done, while no one advantage arising from the exercise of that power shall be damaged or endangered by it. We have in this way something to gain, and, if we proceed with caution, nothing to lose.

Madison's Strategy

Thus Madison began a line of argument reassuring the old friends of the Constitution that they could introduce amendments that do not "open a door" for reconsideration of the constitutional structure, while at the same time gaining new friends by opening a different door, for "provisions for the security of rights," amendments of such a moderate nature that they would be likely to get the approval of the constitutionally mandated two-thirds majority of both houses of Congress and three-fourths of the state legislatures. As an additional substantive bonus, "it is possible" that they "may" even do some good.

Madison's strategy begins to become clear at this point, as he turns to consideration of the "objections of various kinds made against the constitution," revealing his analysis of the opposing forces. On the one hand, he sought to persuade the supporters of the Constitution that the adversaries are formidable and that action is therefore urgently required. On the other hand, he sought to show that the adversaries, though formidable, are definitely not invincible. In fact, he argued, not only could the adversaries be thwarted; "the great mass" of those withholding their approval could be won over and recruited as new friends of the Constitution by efforts that would cost little, if anything.

Leading opponents of the Constitution—Madison called them "respectable characters"—were critical of it because of the structure it established and the broad powers it delegated to the government of the United States, especially over taxes, commerce, elections, and the military. These were the Anti-Federalist leaders in the state governments and in the Congress. But Madison believed that their followers in the public at large, "the doubting part of our fellow-citizens" still dissatisfied with the Constitution, were not dissatisfied for the same reasons. He perceived that "the great mass of the people who opposed it, disliked it because it did not contain effectual provisions against encroachments on particular rights."

Madison's analysis of those opposed to the Constitution, and of their efforts to convene a second constitutional convention, was this: while the opposition's political leaders and spokesmen (the "respectable characters") might want profound structural changes, their followers were indifferent to such matters and were deeply engaged only on the issue of provisions relating to their private rights. Madison thus perceived that the movement to call a second constitutional convention seeking to make radical changes in the Constitution could be undercut by offering instead his moderate, cautious, and less-than-consequential additions to the Constitution:

> It is a fortunate thing that the objection to the Government has been made on the ground I have stated, because it will be practicable, on that ground, to obviate the objection, so far as to satisfy the public mind that their liberties will be

perpetual, and this without endangering any part of the constitution which is considered as essential to the existence of the Government by those who promoted its adoption.

It is important to note to whom Madison addressed his arguments as he pursued this dual line of reasoning. He was *not* speaking to those one would think of as his opponents in the Congress, nor was he seeking to convert the Anti-Federalist members of Congress to becoming friends of the unamended Constitution. He addressed, instead, those who one would think would be his allies in the Congress—those who, in agreement with him, supported the original Constitution and opposed efforts to alter it. He sought to explain to them that their opponents, those who wanted to make changes in and additions to the Constitution, could be divided. A few of these opponents—the Anti-Federalist leaders in the Congress and in the state legislatures—would be frustrated in their desires to make fundamental changes, but the rest, most of their followers— "the great mass of the people"—could be won over as new and loyal supporters of the Constitution.[13] His analysis was that the popular support could be stripped away from the Anti-Federalists by offering not what their spokesmen sought—radical alterations in the Constitution—but rather only explicit assurances on "the great rights of mankind," and that that could be accomplished without altering in any way the powers of the new government.

Madison's rhetoric was not aimed at the Anti-Federalists, the vocal minority in the House, because he was in the act of stealing their following, stripping them of their popular support by acceding, in part, to their demands for a bill of rights in the Constitution. To succeed in this effort he needed to persuade not his opponents, but his adherents, supporters of the Constitution who were opposed to amending it in any way, especially at such an early date.

Madison's Proposed Amendments

Having explained why he thought it timely and prudent to consider amendments now, at least certain kinds of amendments, Madison proceeded to the second part of his speech, the presentation of the amendments themselves. The whole substance of the Bill of Rights as we have it now in the Constitution was included in Madison's initial list of proposed amendments. Some of them now appear in the Constitution word for word as he first proposed them; others were modified, some extensively, some only slightly.[14] But there is nothing in the ten amendments as finally ratified that was not first included, in some form, in Madison's proposals.

We will consider at length in subsequent chapters (part three) the amendments that were adopted by Congress and subsequently ratified. But we can better appreciate what Madison was trying to accomplish in this speech by focusing our attention instead on two of Madison's proposals that were rejected by the Congress. First was his plan to "interweave" the amendments into the body of the Constitution instead of placing them at the beginning, as in many of the state constitutions, or appending them at the end of the document, as we have them now. Second was his curious proposal that several sentences be inserted before the Preamble—what I choose to call the pre-Preamble.[15] In addition, we ought to consider Herbert Storing's contention, fully supported by the statements of members of the First Congress, that what Madison kept out of the Bill of Rights was as important as what he put into it.[16]

First, the plan to interweave: Madison proposed ten articles to insert in Article I, section 9, between clauses 3 and 4, containing all of what are now the First, Second, Third, Fourth, Eighth, and Ninth Amendments and parts of the Fifth and Sixth Amendments. Placed thus, his new clauses would have followed two clauses in the original text that have the character of provisions of a bill of rights, so that the sequence of clauses, starting with clause 2 in section 9 of Article I, would have read this way:[17]

2. The privilege of the writ of habeas corpus shall not be suspended, unless when in cases of rebellion or invasion the public safety may require it.

3. No bill of attainder or ex post facto law shall be passed.

And then the ten new articles, if interwoven as Madison proposed, would have followed, starting with these four:

4. The civil rights of none shall be abridged on account of religious belief or worship, nor shall any national religion be established, nor shall the full and equal rights of conscience be in any manner, or on any pretext, infringed.

5. The people shall not be deprived or abridged of their right to speak, to write, or to publish their sentiments; and the freedom of the press, as one of the great bulwarks of liberty, shall be inviolable.

6. The people shall not be restrained from peaceably assembling and consulting for their common good; nor from

applying to the Legislature by petitions, or remonstrances,
for redress of their grievances.

7. The right of the people to keep and bear arms shall
not be infringed; a well armed and well regulated militia
being the best security of a free country; but no person
religiously scrupulous of bearing arms shall be compelled
to render military service in person.

In that style and sequence, most of the new articles would have
continued in the Legislative Article, in that place in Article I, section
9. What is now the Seventh Amendment, providing for jury trials,
would have been added to Article III, the Judiciary Article, along
with most of what are now the Fifth and Sixth Amendments. And,
finally, a provision that "The powers not delegated by this constitution, nor prohibited by it to the States, are reserved to the States respectively," almost the same as the Tenth Amendment, would have
been added as part of an entirely new article.[18]

Interwoven into the original Constitution in this fashion, these
provisions—although substantially the same as the ones we have
now appended in a group at the end of the Constitution—would
have been much less visible, though not necessarily less important
or effective. If the House of Representatives had gone along with
Madison's proposal to insert the new articles in the body of the Constitution, it would have been difficult to think of them collectively as
a body to be called the Bill of Rights, or any other collective name.
They would more likely have been seen as integrally part of the Constitution, in no way unlike the rest of the text, and thus less likely to
be considered as some sort of corrective of a defective original, or of
a different character, or as pointing in a different direction. With no
substantive difference from what we have now, they would nevertheless have blended in and become part and parcel of the original
text, instead of seeming to stand separate and apart.

It would also then have been clearer that these new articles were
not, in one strict sense of the word, amendments. That is, it would
have been clearer that they added to but changed nothing in the text
of the Constitution. This was a clear distinction in the minds of the
congressmen. When they decided, after many votes, not to interweave
the new articles but instead to place them at the end of the original
text, as an appendage after the signatures, they composed a heading
for the twelve proposed articles, commencing as follows:

Articles in addition to, and amendment of, the Constitution of the United States of America.[19]

This heading distinguishes two kinds of articles, one kind adding to the original text, the other amending it. Of the twelve proposed articles, one was an article "in . . . amendment of" the Constitution, and the rest were articles "in addition to" it. But the one amending article, changing the size of congressional districts, which would have altered the wording of Article I, section 2, clause 3, was not ratified by the requisite number of states. All the articles that were ratified were additions, not amendments. That is, when the ten amendments became part of the Constitution, not one word in the original text was changed. The heading, referring to two kinds of articles, was therefore not an appropriate one until the subsequent ratification of articles that do amend the Constitution.

Two important consequences followed from the scheme to interweave the new articles into the original text: all the formulations are imperative, and almost all are negative. One might reasonably contend that they would have had that form in any case, but the intention of placing them where Madison indicated required that they be negative and imperative or else stand out as badly misplaced, clumsily patched rather than artfully interwoven. As we have seen, the new articles would have been placed after Article I, section 9, clause 3, and before the eight remaining clauses of that Article. Madison chose the perfect spot to interweave negative, imperative provisions: Every one of those nine clauses where Madison sought to insert them in the original Constitution begins with the word "No" and includes the word "shall."[20] To appreciate fully Madison's design of the Bill of Rights, we must never lose sight of its negative and imperative character.

The amendments, especially as revised by Congress, make no grants of power to the government to protect or guarantee rights. Instead, they consistently set forth negations, denials of power to the government, beginning with those five sovereign words of negative command: "Congress shall make no law." As for the imperative "shall" in every one of the first nine amendments, one need only compare it with the pervasive "ought" in the bills of rights of the state constitutions to appreciate that a major change was made from what had previously been understood to be the characteristic form of a bill of rights. In the state constitutions, bills of rights usually came at the head of the constitution; it seems very likely, therefore, that the new form of the proposed articles was influenced by the initial expectation of placement in the body of the text, and that, reciprocally, the intention of designing negative and imperative articles dictated Madison's choice of placement.

No Guarantees

It is common usage for many who are otherwise knowledgeable about the Constitution, including civil rights activists, journalists, political scientists, law school professors, other lawyers, judges, and even Supreme Court Justices, to speak of "our First Amendment guarantees" of freedom of religion, speech, press, assembly, and petition. But in fact there are no guarantees in the First Amendment; there cannot be a guarantee if there is no grant of power but only a denial of power. The one time the word "guarantee" occurs in the Constitution is in the aptly named "guarantee clause" (Article IV, Section 4), in which the United States guarantees to every state a republican form of government. That is a clear, affirmative guarantee.

The First Amendment would have a very different meaning and mode of enforcement if it were affirmative and provided that "Congress shall make laws" to guarantee the freedom of speech, press, and religion. The affirmative form, as opposed to a denial, would result in an accretion, not a diminution, of governmental power. The affirmative form would call for agencies of government with affirmative powers to deal with the press and religious institutions, with consequences very different from what Americans are accustomed to. Awareness of the difference that the negative and imperative character of the Bill of Rights makes, in large part a consequence of the initial interweaving intention, is an essential step in perceiving how Madison, as the sole author of this aspect of the Bill of Rights, thought rights are truly made secure.

Interweaving was one proposal of Madison's that was rejected by his congressional colleagues; the pre-Preamble was another. The very first addition proposed by Madison in the June 8 speech, before any of the provisions protecting specific rights that were to be inserted in Article I, was "that there be prefixed to the constitution a declaration"

> That all power is originally rested in, and consequently derived from, the people.

> That government is instituted and ought to be exercised for the benefit of the people; which consists in the enjoyment of life and liberty, with the right of acquiring and using property, and generally of pursuing and obtaining happiness and safety.

> That the people have an indubitable, unalienable, and indefeasible right to reform or change their Government,

whenever it be found adverse or inadequate to the purposes of its institution.[21]

As proposed by Madison, this declaration, with its heavy emphasis on "the people," was meant to become the new opening of
the Constitution, preceding the Preamble. It was soon revised and
condensed by the Select Committee to which the amendments were
referred into less than one sentence, an introductory clause to the
opening of the Preamble. In the process it was made less fitting and
more awkward than the original. We should not be surprised at the
fate of this one-of-a-kind pre-Preamble, which would have had the
effect of stripping the Preamble of its splendid rhetorical forceful-
ness. As it came from the Select Committee, the amended Preamble
would have read as follows:

> Government being intended for the benefit of the people,
> and the rightful establishment thereof being derived from
> their authority alone, we the people of the United States,
> in order to form a more perfect union, establish justice,
> insure domestic tranquillity, etc.

In subsequent debate the proposal to alter the Preamble was
denounced, reviled, ridiculed, and rejected. We can concur gratefully
with the decision of the members of the First Congress in rejecting
its "intolerable grammatical cumbersomeness"[22] and thus preserv-
ing the Preamble, and yet we can be instructed by grasping what
Madison was attempting to do.

The most obvious thing about Madison's original pre-Preamble
is its seeming resemblance to the Declaration of Independence. But
there are interesting differences. Although Madison's passage and
the Declaration of Independence both speak of "the people,"
Madison's formulation does not speak of individual persons, as does
the Declaration ("that all men are created equal, that they are en-
dowed with certain unalienable rights"), either as the source of political power or as the possessors of rights. In Madison's pre-Preamble,
the source of all power and the possessor of rights is "the people."
This is doctrine for a society already formed, already "one people,"
now in the act of constituting government. One might argue that the
power of the people had its origin in the natural powers of each individual person, but most individual powers are surrendered up to
the society when it is formed. Forming individuals into a people,
that is, forming a society that can be considered one body, is an ante-
cedent step on the way to establishing a constitution. Individuals do
not establish a constitution; we, the people, do.

One other point of difference is worth noticing: "the . . . right to reform or change their Government" is a much modified version of the Declaration's "right of the people to alter or abolish it." The Constitution, it seems, is no place for a permanent and emphatic reminder of the ultimate consequence of the natural right to resist tyranny, however much it might be an underlying principle of the Constitution.

A comparison closer than one with the Declaration of Independence is to be seen with a typical state bill of rights of the time, such as the Massachusetts State Constitution of 1780.[23] It includes these passages, all very similar to the formulations in Madison's proposed pre-Preamble:

> All power residing originally in the people, and being derived from them. . . .

> Government is instituted for the common good; for the protection, safety, prosperity and happiness of the people . . . .

> Therefore, the people alone have an incontestable, unalienable, and indefeasible right to institute government; and to reform, alter, or totally change the same, when their protection, safety, prosperity and happiness require it.

Madison was willing to have the new bill of rights say, as did the Massachusetts bill of rights, that the people are the original source of political power, but he was unwilling to include an explicit assertion, as part of the Constitution, that the people have the right to "alter, or totally change" the government. He used, instead, the words "reform or change," but even this milder formulation was deleted by the Select Committee, of which Madison was a member, when they condensed the pre-Preamble. The Massachusetts bill of rights had other features that illustrate one reason why Madison was leery of state bills of rights. Its religion provisions, for example, authorized the use of public funds to promote religion and limited such support not only to Christians but to Protestants.[24]

The Purpose of the Pre-Preamble

Why did Madison propose this pre-Preamble? "The first of these amendments [that is, the pre-Preamble]," Madison said, "relates to what may be called a bill of rights." We, now, are accustomed to thinking of the first ten amendments as not only *a* bill of rights, but as *the* Bill of Rights. But that was not the state of things at the moment of this speech. In fact, as we shall see, a good part of Madison's commentary was devoted to an inquiry into the question of just what Americans meant when they spoke of a bill of rights. One of his chief motives was to ease the minds of those who wanted a bill of rights. If the pre-Preamble was what, in the public mind, "may be called a bill of rights," then we can see that, as a constitutional provision, it would have been at once useful and innocuous, reassuring to the public without really changing anything.

Interweaving the new articles in the body of the text would have made them little visible; what would have been visible, even prominent, would have been this pre-Preamble, "what may be called a bill of rights." The combination of the pre-Preamble and interweaving would have well served Madison's dual purposes: first, to protect the Constitution against significant change; and second, to reassure those who were uneasy because of the absence of the kind of bill of rights to which Americans were accustomed in their state constitutions and felt properly belonged in any constitution.

As we have seen, several state ratifying conventions, most prominently Virginia's and New York's, had urged the addition of structural amendments as well as amendments securing individual rights. These conventions had enjoined their representatives in Congress to do all that was reasonable and legal to achieve the approval of these amendments in Congress. The scores of amendments proposed by state ratifying conventions were abundant enough to supply Madison and his colleagues in the Congress with all the material for a bill of rights. There is nothing in the final Bill of Rights as we have it that was not already present in amendments proposed by one or another of the state ratifying conventions. But there was far more recommended by the state conventions that is not included in the Bill of Rights. Here we come to the importance of what Madison left out.

The Significant Selection

Madison took advantage of the fact that several of the conventions, including especially Virginia and New York, had made two distinct, separate lists of recommended amendments, one seeking to secure civil and legal rights, the other seeking to alter the distribution of powers between the states and the government of the United States. Madison drew heavily from one list, and almost not at all from the other. He included protection for "the great rights of mankind," and he excluded every provision that would diminish the powers of the new government, despite the repeated complaints of Anti-Federalist representatives that he was omitting those they considered most important.

These Anti-Federalists looked less at what was in the text of the amendments and much more at what had been omitted. What was omitted, they thought, was the heart of the matter. Patrick Henry and the Anti-Federalist congressmen were much more concerned about the amendments relating to a standing army, the power of Congress to levy direct taxes, and congressional control over elections than about paper assurances of security for the rights of religion, speech, and press—not because they did not care about those rights but because they did not think that these new words, by themselves, in the wrong kind of constitution, were powerful enough to provide security for those rights. To the Anti-Federalists, the threat to religion, speech, and press, and to all liberty, came from a powerful central government that was able to tax from a great distance, was in control of elections, and had a standing army at its disposal. Such a government would be able to exert too much intrusive power over the lives of the citizenry while rendering state and local governments relatively powerless.

Both sides were in agreement on one fundamental point. The opponents and proponents of the Constitution, caring deeply about rights, thought rights were best secured by preventing a concentration of political power. That was why the Framers in Philadelphia gave so much attention to providing checks and balances, a bicameral legislature, separation of powers, and the federal structure, and why they built complexity into the constitutional structure at every opportunity. Patrick Henry and his Anti-Federalist colleagues, not trusting the efficacy of those constitutional checks and balances and the other "auxiliary precautions," and alarmed at what they considered to be the imbalance of state and federal powers, feared the concentration of power in the new government. They, like the Federalists, thought the security of individual rights depended on the structure of government; but unlike the Federalists, they considered Madison's proposals inadequate to the task of securing private rights. They sought, therefore, a return to old, familiar constitutional dispersals of power, as under the Articles of Confederation.

The Anti-Federalists in Congress initially pressed for amendments, while the Federalists determinedly opposed taking them up. Once it became clear, however, that Madison's amendments could prevail and that all structural amendments would be excluded, the sides reversed. When it became apparent to everyone that Madison's amendments would change nothing at all in the Constitution, the Federalists began to vote for amendments, the Anti-Federalists against them.

Consideration of the final part of Madison's speech, his arguments in favor of his amendments, can be confined to a few main points: his list of what is said in favor of bills of rights; his own view of "the great object" of bills of rights; and a list of the objections made to bills of rights, followed by his responses to them.[25]

Madison began the arguments in favor of his proposals with some remarkably faint praise of bills of rights. He was aware, he said, that "a great number of the most respectable friends to the Government, and champions for republican liberty," have thought a bill of rights "not only unnecessary" and "improper," but "even dangerous." Madison did not say he disagreed; instead, his rejoinder was simply that it was a fact that among the general public "a different opinion prevails." He cited the prevalence of state bills of rights as evidence that the American people generally considered bills of rights proper and necessary. But aside from the factor of public opinion, Madison said little in support of bills of rights, and that little was conspicuously tepid. He was "inclined to believe" that "although some of them [that is, state bills of rights] are rather unimportant, yet, upon the whole, they will have a salutary tendency." With that not-quite-rousing tribute out of the way, Madison turned to the question: What is a bill of rights intended to do?

The Goal of a Bill of Rights

The state bills of rights have a variety of objectives. They declare "the perfect equality of mankind"; or they assert the rights of the people in establishing a government; or they list the rights retained by the people when others are surrendered to the legislature; or they specify positive rights under government, like trial by jury; or they lay down "dogmatic maxims," such as affirming the principle of separation of powers. Madison did not say so at this point, but his own proposals in this speech do all of the above, except for explicitly proclaiming equality. Madison concluded, however, that "the great object in view" in every bill of rights, no matter what its form, is to "limit and qualify the powers of Government."

Madison then turned to a thesis familiar to us from his correspondence with Jefferson: that the people themselves are the greatest danger to personal liberty and private rights in a nation ruled, ultimately, by public opinion. Under other forms of government, the executive usually poses the greatest threat to liberty and the problem is how to impose restraints on it. "In our Government," that is, the United States, it is more important to restrain the legislature than the executive, and most important to restrain "the community," that is, the people. He warned that,

> in a Government modified like this of the United States, the great danger lies rather in the abuse of the community than in the legislative body. The prescriptions in favor of liberty ought to be levelled against that quarter where the greatest danger lies, namely, that which possesses the highest prerogative of power. But it is not found in either the executive or legislative departments of Government, but in the body of the people, operating by the majority against the minority.[26]

This had long been a sticking point for Madison; how can any "paper barrier" restrain the power of the majority of the people, the greatest danger because the greatest force in a popular government, when that majority is determined to "operate against the minority"? In short, where the majority rules, what power can control a bad majority? The answer Madison gave here, somewhat tentatively, and not without reservations, is that public opinion may be strengthened in support of the rights proclaimed in a bill of rights, so that "the whole community" may be able to restrain the majority.

> as they [bills of rights] have a tendency to impress some degree of respect for them, to establish the public opinion in their favor, and rouse the attention of the whole community, it may be one means to control the majority from those acts to which they might be otherwise inclined.

This profound but tentative endorsement of bills of rights, composed of "tendency," "some degree," "may be," and "might be," was Madison's response to the first of a list of objections. He then set out and responded to several more, which objections, taken together, added up to an indictment that a bill of rights in the Constitution would be ineffective, unnecessary, or dangerous.

The indictment ran this way: A bill of rights is unnecessary in a republican government; it is especially unnecessary in the Constitution of the United States, because the states have bills of rights; it would endanger rights, since it cannot enumerate every right, and thus would disparage those not mentioned; and, finally, bills of rights have not been successful in securing rights in the states. Madison then gave a brief response to each count of the indictment. First, even in a republican form of government there can be abuses of power in the means used to carry out constitutional powers, especially given the "necessary and proper" clause in this Constitution, which many feared gave Congress sweeping, unspecified powers. Second, not all the states have bills of rights, and some of those that do have inadequate and even "absolutely improper" ones. Next, the problem of the disparagement of unenumerated rights is taken care of by one of his proposed amendments ("The exceptions . . . made in favor of particular rights, shall not be so construed as to diminish the just importance of other rights retained by the people").[27] Finally, granting that there have been "few particular states in which some of the most valuable articles have not, at one time or other, been violated; . . . it does not follow but they may have, to a certain degree, a salutary effect against the abuse of power," because the courts can use a bill of rights to make themselves a bulwark against abuses of the executive and legislative branches.

Madison had, of course, expressed most of the objections in this indictment as his own personal opinion in private correspondence over the years, which may explain why he was now so restrained in refuting them. In fact, his objections to a bill of rights were stated much more forcefully and persuasively than were his responses in favor of one. Right to the end of his comments on what are now the first ten amendments, Madison's emphasis was on the expected favorable public reaction, not on the intrinsic merits of the amendments. The most positive word he used in speaking of the substance of the proposals is that they were "proper"; he had much more to say about the beneficial effects on "the tranquillity of the public mind" and consequently on "the stability of the Government."

> I conclude . . . that it will be proper in itself, and highly politic, for the tranquillity of the public mind, and the stability of the Government, that we should offer something, in the form I have proposed, to be incorporated in the system of Government, as a declaration of the rights of the people.

Madison's effort throughout the speech was not to persuade his listeners by praising the excellence of the provisions, or to argue that the Constitution was defective without them, or that it would be improved in any significant way by their addition. His emphasis was on their substantive harmlessness, that they would make no meaningful change in the Constitution.

For example, several state ratifying conventions were "particularly anxious that it should be declared in the constitution, that the powers not therein delegated should be reserved to the several states." That fact was the basis of Madison's advocacy of an article that might otherwise, he said, on its merits, be considered "superfluous" and "unnecessary"; "the powers not delegated by this constitution, nor prohibited by it to the States, are reserved to the States respectively."[28] He did not urge the substance of the declaration as a reason for adding it, but only that there would be a beneficial effect on a significant part of the public, and that there was "no harm" in it:

> Perhaps words which may define this more precisely than the whole of the instrument now does, may be considered as superfluous. I admit they may be deemed unnecessary: but there can be no harm in making such a declaration, if gentlemen will allow that the fact [that several states were "particularly anxious" to add it to the Constitution] is as stated.

Almost all of Madison's affirmative argument on behalf of his proposals concerned the beneficial political consequences. The real change to be hoped for was greater public acceptance. That is the theme on which Madison concluded:

> I believe every gentleman will readily admit that nothing is in contemplation, so far as I have mentioned, that can endanger the beauty of the Government in any one important feature, even in the eyes of its most sanguine admirers. I have proposed nothing that does not appear to me as proper in itself, or eligible as patronized by a respectable number of our fellow-citizens; and if we can make the constitution better in the opinion of those who are opposed to it, without weakening its frame, or abridging its usefulness, in the judgment of those who are attached to it, we act the part of wise and liberal men to make such alterations as shall produce that effect.

This self-appraisal does less than full justice to what Madison was about to accomplish. Despite the setbacks he experienced in the lengthy subsequent debates, as one or another of his proposals was voted down, consider his approaching successes. He designed for the nation a bill of rights superior to and quite different from any the world had seen before; he accurately assessed the one great obstacle to universal acceptance of the new Constitution and found the way to reassure those among the general public who had been uneasy about it; by his determination to take timely action, he saved the

Constitution from every contemplated radical amendment aimed at regaining sovereign powers for the states and diminishing essential powers of the general government; and he gave an instructive display of a new kind of democratic statesmanship on the national scene—political wisdom artfully joined to popular consent. This last, an impressive display of the working of a "combining mind," especially deserves our attention and admiration. As we shall see, the immediate consequence of this one speech was the elimination, once and for all, of the movement for a second constitutional convention.

Reflections on Part Two

"Madison made a mistake at the Federal Convention" by opposing George Mason's effort "to graft a bill of rights onto the Constitution," according to Robert Rutland, the eminent Madison editor and scholar, and his "tactical error had almost immediate repercussions." It resulted in "a groundswell of public opinion" demanding a bill of rights, which "forced the supporters of the Constitution to acknowledge that they had erred."

> Once back in his home county, Madison realized that he must support a bill of rights to win election to the House of Representatives. He redeemed his campaign pledge by offering a bill of rights at the first session of the new federal Congress. Public opinion? No one knew its might more than Madison. . . . The people had spoken; Madison listened and made his pledge. Thus it was that at a most critical stage in our nation's history public opinion forced some able politicians to revise their views about what Madison called our "parchment barriers."[1]

There can be no quarreling with Rutland over his factual account of the sequence of events, but I think his explanation of the facts, that Madison's support for a bill of rights was forced by the pressure of public opinion, is far off the mark. A truer explanation emerges from paying close attention to Madison's words and thoughts. It is a complex explanation, and a much more enlightening account of how and why Madison, perhaps the most penetrating and perceptive critic of bills of rights, became the Father of the Bill of Rights.

Throughout the process of making the Constitution, first in the Constitutional Convention and subsequently in his correspondence with Jefferson, in the writing of *The Federalist*, and in the debates in the First Congress, Madison struggled with one problem above all others: how to protect private rights from an oppressive majority in a political society in which the majority, ultimately, decides everything. This fundamental concern, security for private rights, gave shape and direction to all his constitution-making actions. Thus, the first thing we must take notice of is that Madison's coolness to a bill of rights did not indicate a lack of concern for private rights, but exactly the opposite. The threat he saw to private rights was too powerful to be restrained by a mere declaration. As he wrote to Jefferson,

> experience proves the inefficacy of a bill of rights on those occasions when its controul is most needed. Repeated violations of these parchment barriers have been committed by overbearing majorities in every State.[2]

Madison was cool to a bill of rights not because he was indifferent to private rights, but rather because he was devoted to them and thought declarations of rights had proven to be ineffective in protecting them. He sought something else, therefore: something with greater power, something commensurate with the threat to the security of the rights of the people, something sturdier than a "parchment barrier."

Apparently other political leaders did not see the problem as he did, or did not consider it as significant as he did, and so he had little or no help in addressing it. But how to secure private rights was the preeminent problem he set forth in his letters to Jefferson and in *The Federalist*. He asked Jefferson,

> If then . . . a majority when united by a common interest or passion cannot be restrained from oppressing the minority, what remedy can be found in a republican Government, where the majority must ultimately decide?"[3]

In *Federalist* No. 51 he argued that, because an oppressive majority "cannot be restrained," the best protection is to keep an oppressive majority from forming in the first place, and there he prescribed his arguments for "extent of territory" and "multiplicity of interests" as the cure for this greatest danger to majority-rule regimes:

> It is of great importance in a republic not only to guard the society against the oppression of its rulers, but to guard

one part of the society against the injustice of the other part. Different interests necessarily exist in different classes of citizens. If a majority be united by a common interest, the rights of the minority will be insecure.[4]

The Constitution, he explained, was designed to prevent the formation of oppressive majorities "by comprehending in the society so many separate descriptions of citizens as will render an unjust combination of a majority of the whole very improbable, if not impracticable." Because of the great extent of territory made possible by the Constitution,

> the society itself will be broken into so many parts, interests and classes of citizens, that the rights of individuals, or of the minority, will be in little danger from interested combinations of the majority. In a free government the security for civil rights must be the same as that for religious rights. It consists in the one case in the multiplicity of interests, and in the other in the multiplicity of sects. The degree of security in both cases will depend on the number of interests and sects; and this may be presumed to depend on the extent of country and number of people comprehended under the same government.[5]

In short, Madison argued, the best way to prevent an oppressive majority from doing its dirty work is to prevent it from forming in the first place, and this protection is provided by the Constitution without a bill of rights.

But in that same paper of *The Federalist*, where Madison set out his argument for preventing the formation of oppressive majorities, he spoke of that method as one of two possibilities; there was also another way of avoiding the consequences of an oppressive majority.

> There are but two methods of providing against this evil: the one by creating a will in the community independent of the majority—that is, of the society itself . . . . [This] method prevails in all governments possessing an hereditary or self-appointed authority. This, at best, is but a precarious security; because a power independent of the society may as well espouse the unjust views of the major as the rightful interests of the minor party, and may possibly be turned against both parties.[6]

Madison did not mention this method again, a method not attractive to constitution makers for a republic. But I think there are sound reasons, grounded in Madison's own words, to believe that something like it grew in Madison's mind as a possible additional safeguard of private rights, a possibility made more attractive by popular support for a bill of rights.

The disadvantage of a hereditary monarch, a powerful "will . . . independent . . . of the society itself," is that too much depends on the unpredictable vagaries of the person wearing the crown. An unreliable prince, himself above the law and powerful enough to restrain an oppressive majority, might have his own corrupt reasons to align himself with the unjust cause. Can this disadvantage be avoided? Can there be a republican version of "a will in the community independent of the majority" that is powerful enough to restrain an oppressive majority and unlikely to "espouse the unjust views" of that majority?

With that question in mind, consider Madison's description of the power to do good of a properly drawn bill of rights:

> The political truths declared in that solemn manner acquire by degrees the character of fundamental maxims of free Government, and as they become incorporated with the national sentiment, counteract the impulses of interest and passion.[7]

That is what Madison wrote to Jefferson, in answer to his own question, "What use then it may be asked can a bill of rights serve in popular Governments?" At this climactic moment in his exchange of views with Jefferson, at a late date, months after all of *The Federalist* papers had been published, he finally came to the point of persuading himself that a bill of rights had a possibly useful function in a constitution for the United States. To the best of my knowledge, this sentence is the only statement by Madison, in public speeches or private correspondence, in which he spoke favorably of a bill of rights without any qualifications, without conditionals, without double negatives. And in this sentence we see that he is describing a force independent of, and superior to, the majority; a force, unlike a hereditary monarch, that is appropriate to a republic, in which public opinion ultimately decides everything. Most important, it is a force potentially more powerful than any majority because it involves a profound commitment of "the whole people of the United States."

How does it work? We know the answer from our own experience of living under the Constitution. If these "maxims become incorporated with the national sentiment," then ordinary citizens say to themselves, when the occasion presents itself, something like this: "Even if that person's speech, or book, or religious doctrine is obnoxious to me and to the majority of my fellow-citizens throughout the nation, bizarre and distasteful and contrary to my own opinions and cherished beliefs, and detrimental to my interests; and even if a majority in the Congress and in the public at large would be glad to see him silenced and fined or jailed or exiled or even executed, nevertheless, the Constitution forbids us, even though we are an overwhelming majority, from silencing him. And I am for the Constitution, first and above all else."

That is how it works; to the extent that these principles of free government have become a part of our "national sentiment," they do, indeed, often enable us, the majority, to restrain ourselves, the majority, from oppressive actions. That is the import of the first five words of the Bill of Rights: "Congress shall make no law" that attempts to accomplish certain prohibited things. It means that even if a majority in Congress, representing a majority of us, the people, wants to make a law that the Constitution forbids it to make, we, all of us, superior to any majority, say it must not be done, because the Constitution is the will of all of us, not just a majority of us.

From Madison's effort to introduce a bill of rights in Congress, and the opposition of his fellow congressmen to it, we see that he thought the process of constitution making was still going on—and they thought it was over. Members of Congress, understandably, thought the facts were clear. The Constitution was ratified, the Congress was in session and legislating actively, the president was elected and signing bills into law. Supporters of the Constitution, the overwhelming majority in Congress, saw no need for yielding to the demands of the minority clamoring for amendments. But Madison was still engaged in constitution making, because he saw the task as still unfinished. Opposition continued to be widespread, two states had not yet ratified, and there were persisting efforts to call another convention to enact amendments to change the Constitution radically. In these circumstances, Madison saw the popular demand for a bill of rights not only as itself a grave problem, but also as the way to solve all these problems.

By proposing his amendments, which in the end did not change one word in the text of the Constitution, Madison blocked the adoption of all the structural amendments of the Anti-Federalists. That is, he used the public demand for a bill of rights to thwart all efforts to weaken the Constitution. His proposed amendments resembled sufficiently those the public were most attached to; they won enthusiastic support as soon as they became known, long before they were finally ratified, and so, most important of all, he gained devoted allegiance to the Constitution from "the great mass of the people." And finally, by generating a strong "national sentiment" in support of the Constitution, he took the decisive step toward establishing an independent force in the society, a devotion to the Constitution powerful enough to restrain a malevolent majority. Madison saw that the proposed amendments could make the Constitution universally revered. But he saw the Constitution itself, not the amendments, as the sturdy barrier to fend off majority oppression and defend private rights. A bill of rights added to the intact Constitution would bring to it the only thing it presently lacked—the support of the whole people.

Rutland, in my opinion, does not give enough attention to how much the amendments Madison proposed differed from the amendments being called for by the opposition leaders who claimed to be the spokesmen of the public. Madison showed that he knew something about public opinion that is vital to leadership in a democracy. Lesser democratic politicians try to satisfy public opinion by following the lead of the crowd, seeking out and doing whatever is calculated to be popular. Madison was the exemplar of the truer democratic leader. Without ignoring the demands of public opinion—in fact, paying close heed to them—he had the ability to discern the difference between the unwise measures the public was asking for and the much wiser measures they could be persuaded to accept. In presenting his amendments, he chose to do only what he considered "proper in itself." What he offered was not what the people were asking for, and yet it was something they willingly accepted, in fact embraced enthusiastically, as if their own.

Did public opinion force Madison to revise his views? I don't think so. His actions throughout were consistent with his long-standing criticisms of reliance on a bill of rights for the security of private rights. Since his amendments would leave the original Constitution unchanged, proposing them left unchanged his conviction that the greatest security for rights resides in a well-designed structure of society and government. A sound constitution is what truly secures the rights of the people. That is what Alexander Hamilton meant when he wrote, in *Federalist* No. 84, that without amendments, "the Constitution is itself, in every rational sense, and to every useful purpose, a BILL OF RIGHTS."[8] But Madison had come to see that one critical thing was lacking; he saw that no matter how sound the Constitution might be, it could not be effective in securing the rights of the people unless it commanded the devoted allegiance of the whole people.

Rutland may be right in saying of Madison and public opinion that "no one knew its might more than Madison." Madison did say often that in a republic such as ours, public opinion ultimately decides everything. Rutland is right when he says that "the people had spoken; and Madison listened," but wrong when he includes Madison as one of the politicians "public opinion forced . . . to revise their views." What led Madison to revise his view about making additions to the Constitution was his own solution to his own greatest theoretical problem. The problem was how to restrain an oppressive majority in a democratic republic. His solution was to make the Constitution more powerful than any majority by making it the accepted sovereign instrument of the whole people. And he accomplished that by inducing Congress to pass his amendments.

The significant truth about Madison and public opinion and the Bill of Rights is that when Madison spoke, the people listened. And *they* revised *their* views.

PART THREE

Closing the Parenthesis

6
"Rats and Anti-Rats": The Debate Begins

Madison's momentous speech to the House of Representatives on June 8, 1789, in which he set forth the entire content of what was to become the Bill of Rights, was followed by a discussion of it that had nothing to do with rights. Madison had made a motion at the end of the speech that his proposed amendments be referred to a select committee, so that "the subject may be going on in the committee, while other important business is proceeding to a conclusion in the House."[1] That procedural motion required just a few brief sentences in Madison's lengthy speech; yet as far as we can tell from the record of the proceedings, that was all his fellow congressmen were willing to discuss. Not one congressman said anything at all that day about any part of any one of the proposed amendments. What they did say, emphatically, one after another, was that they did not want to consider amendments, certainly not now; and that if they ever should be required to consider amendments, they wanted them referred to a committee of the whole, not to a select committee. They discussed timing and procedure, and nothing else.

Procedural Inertia

Madison, understandably exasperated at the protracted procedural wrangling, reminded them that he had initially proposed referring the amendments to a committee of the whole, but the objections had been so numerous and vigorous that he had changed his motion and proposed a select committee instead. Now, he said, he would willingly switch again, just so long as they would move the project forward. But they continued to discuss at great length the least time-consuming way to rid themselves of this vexing problem, which Madison would not let them evade. In the end they voted to refer his proposed amendments not to a select committee but to a committee of the whole—without, however, setting a date. And then, with that procedural matter settled, the House turned to other business. There would be no further mention of the amendments in the House for six more weeks.

But while the House was inactive on the amendments, there was effective, purposeful activity elsewhere. Madison's June 8 speech was published within days, in the New York *Daily Advertiser* of June 12 and the *Gazette of the U.S.* of June 13.[2] Copies were sent to correspondents everywhere,[3] to build support for the amendments among influential political leaders and the general public. Madison began receiving reports that the public's reaction was strongly favorable and that the speech was having the hoped-for effect of stealing away public support from the opposition leaders. One correspondent wrote that "of the opposition . . . those who are honest are well pleased . . . .Those who are not honest . . . are stript of every rational, and most of the popular arguments they have hitherto used."[4] Another reported that "your proposition of amendments . . . gives general Satisfaction, and I trust if adopted will shut the mouths of many."[5]

On July 21, with still no congressional action, Madison "begged the House" to take up consideration of the amendments. He reminded them that on June 8 they had voted to refer the proposals to a committee of the whole, and he moved that they now do so. Whereupon the House, consistent in its erratic pursuit of legislative efficiency, switched once again. On the motion of Fisher Ames, opposed strenuously by his Massachusetts colleague, Elbridge Gerry, the House rescinded its previous decision in favor of a committee of the whole and voted instead to refer the amendments to a select committee, composed of one member from each of the eleven states. This Committee of Eleven, with John Vining of Delaware as chairman and Madison, Roger Sherman of Massachusetts, and Aedanus Burke of South Carolina most prominent among its members, was charged to consider all the proposed amendments, Madison's and also those proposed by the various state conventions, and to report their recommendations back to the House.

One week later, now July 28, the committee submitted its report, with Madison's proposed amendments rewritten but **substantively unchanged**. As Bernard Schwartz has observed, the report was "a virtual restatement of the amendments proposed by Madison."[6] Conspicuous by their absence from the committee's report were all traces of the "radical amendments" proposed by one or another of the state ratifying conventions.

Madison Gets Things Started

On August 13, more than two months after Madison's speech and the vote to refer his amendments to a committee of the whole,[7] Richard Bland Lee of Virginia moved that "the House now resolve itself into a Committee of the whole, on the report of the committee of eleven," but it soon appeared doubtful that the motion would be agreed to. Instead the wrangling over how best to proceed resumed. One optimist sought to persuade his colleagues that the business would not take much time; "it was impossible," he said, "that much debate could take place" because of "the simplicity and self-evidence" of the proposed amendments. On that point, not surprisingly, he was immediately proved to be very much in error.

The next speakers resumed rehearsing all the familiar objections. This was the wrong time, they said, to be considering amendments, when they had more important legislative business before them: impost and tonnage laws, the bill for registering and clearing vessels, the bill establishing a land office for the disposal of the vacant lands in the Western Territory, and especially the judiciary bill. Without the judiciary, "not a single part of the revenue system can operate; no breach of your laws can be punished; illicit trade cannot be prevented."

In addition, of course, some members did not consider the amendments quite so simple and self-evident as advertised. There were even some new objections. Since the report of the Committee of Eleven did not include amendments proposed by the state ratifying conventions, someone would surely bring them up in the course of the deliberations, and that would make the process even longer. Finally, John Laurance of New York pointed out that "few, if any, of the State Assemblies are now in session," and so the ratification of constitutional amendments by the state legislatures could not go forward "even if Congress had already done their part."

In short, the House was reluctant, to put it mildly, to turn its attention to these amendments. Only some sort of flogging could drive them to take up the report of the Committee of Eleven. Madison let them know that he was more than willing to snap the whip. In the face of the barrage of objections, his counterattack was brief and effective. He told his colleagues, in effect, to get on with it. If they put off dealing with the amendments until all their other business was done, he said, their "patience and application will be so harassed and fatigued, as to oblige them to leave it in an unfinished state until the next session." With that, they agreed to Lee's motion, voting to resolve themselves into a committee of the whole. And this time, at long last, they actually did begin deliberations, right then, on the report of the Committee of Eleven—although, as we shall see, their discussion was to be, at first, and for most of the time thereafter, tangential to the amendments, to say the least.

The Pre-Preamble

They started with the first proposed amendment, the new version of Madison's pre-Preamble, now severely truncated by the Committee of Eleven, but definitely not improved:

> Before the words "We the people," add "Government being intended for the benefit of the people, and the rightful establishment thereof being derived from their authority alone."

But instead of discussing the proposed pre-Preamble, they turned at once to something else. Sherman, despite his being one of the members of the Committee of Eleven, renewed his previous objection to amending by interweaving the new clauses into the text of the Constitution, insisting that the right way was to add them at the end, as a supplement to the Constitution. Madison disagreed but seemed willing to compromise; "there is a neatness and propriety in incorporating the amendments into the constitution itself," he said. "I am not, however, very solicitous about the form, provided the business is but well completed." Sherman's position was bolstered by a new argument: placing anything in the text of the original Constitution before the signatures would make it seem that "George Washington, and the other worthy characters who composed the convention," had signed their names to provisions that were in fact written subsequently by others.

A brief digression from Sherman's digression was the first comment that came close to touching on the question before the committee, the pre-Preamble, although it was really more a statement about the original Preamble:

> As for the alteration proposed by the committee to prefix before "We the people," certain dogmas, I cannot agree to it; the words, as they now stand, speak as much as it is possible to speak; it is a practical recognition of the right of the people to ordain and establish Governments, and is more expressive than any other mere paper declaration.[8]

Sherman, unrelenting on his subject of where to put the amendments, returned immediately to it and argued that whether amendments were incorporated or appended was much more than a matter of form, as Madison had intimated, because incorporating the new articles into the body of the text was tantamount to replacing the original Constitution with a new one. This led to a lengthy exchange between Sherman and Gerry on whether amendments, any amendments, would have the same legitimacy as the original Constitution. Their discussion went on so long that members complained that if they were to discuss abstract subjects such as this, too much time would be spent on this debate. Vining, the chairman of the Committee of Eleven, who had in previous weeks objected strenuously to taking any time at all to discuss amendments, now replied that this question of the constitutional validity of amendments was so important that he, for one, "was not displeased with the discussion that had taken place." With this encouragement, Gerry undertook to counter Sherman's point, at equal length, insisting on the legitimacy of amendments.

But when Sherman's motion—to add the amendments as a supplement at the end of the Constitution, after the signatures, rather than incorporating them into the body of the text—was finally put to a vote, it was defeated. And so, after an entire day of debate, in which the committee of the whole did not get to the point of voting on the pre-Preamble, the first proposal referred to them by the Committee of Eleven, and in fact hardly even touched on the substance of it in debate, they adjourned.

The next day's debate, however, started out more promisingly;[9] the House, sitting again as a committee of the whole, did get directly to the unfinished subject, the proposed pre-Preamble. Gerry objected to adding the words "government being intended for the benefit of the people" to the Preamble, because he said he did not believe "that one out of fifty" of the governments of the world were "intended for any such purpose." The maxim did not seem to be true and therefore should not be in the Constitution. Thomas Tudor Tucker of South Carolina chimed in with another kind of objection; why should they even consider amending the Preamble, since, he said, it was "no part of the constitution"? John Page of Virginia said he agreed that it was no part of the Constitution,

> but if it was, it stood in no need of amendment; the words "We the people," had the neatness and simplicity, while its expression was the most forcible of any he had ever seen prefixed to any constitution.

Madison defended his proposal that the Constitution be prefaced with a statement of principle, but his defense was based not so much on how the addition would improve the Preamble, but more on how it would serve the political purpose of "promoting harmony":

> If it be a truth, and so self-evident that it cannot be denied; if it be recognized, as is the fact in many of the State constitutions; and if it be desired by three important States, to be added to this, I think they must collectively offer a strong inducement to the mind desirous of promoting harmony, to acquiesce with the report.

He then went on, as he had in his June 8 speech, to state the best arguments in opposition to his own proposal, not saying he agreed with them, but also, conspicuously, not denying their validity:

> My worthy colleague says, the original expression is neat and simple; that loading it with more words may destroy the beauty of the sentence; and others say it is unnecessary, as the paragraph is complete without it. Be it so, in their opinion; yet, still it appears important in the estimation of three States, that this solemn truth should be inserted in the constitution.

"Be it so," as Madison would say, that inserting this "solemn truth" into the Preamble was "important in the estimation of three States"; but was it important in the estimation of James Madison? There is reason to suspect that it was not.[10] His defense of the pre-Preamble was not what one could call spirited, forceful, or persuasive. He repeated the best arguments of others against his position without even responding to them, let alone refuting them, and the strongest advocacy he then put forward in support of the pre-Preamble, other than that the principle it set forth was a true one and three states had proposed it, was another marvelous example of his faintly praising double negatives: "For my part, sir," he said, "I do not think the association of ideas anywise unnatural." But it could not be denied that he had kept his pledge to his constituents in Virginia; he had put forward and argued for, if not enthusiastically, at least dutifully, "what may be called a bill of rights."

In contrast, Sherman's plea to his colleagues to keep hands off the Preamble was vigorous, affirmative, and direct. In the Preamble as it stands, he said,

> the truth is better asserted than it can be by any words whatever. The words "We the people" in the original constitution, are as copious and expressive as possible; any addition will only drag out the sentence without illuminating it; for these reasons it may be hoped the committee will reject the proposed amendment.

The vote on the Committee of Eleven's text of the pre-Preamble, nevertheless, was carried in the affirmative, at least for the time being, narrowly: twenty-seven votes for, twenty-three against.[11]

The rest of the legislative day was spent in debating and approving the two amendments that would, in the end, fail to be ratified by enough state legislatures to become part of the Constitution. One concerned compensation for members of Congress,[12] the other the size of congressional districts and the size of the House of Representatives. Each of these amendments also mustered just twenty-seven affirmative votes.

The House met the next day, August 15,[13] a Saturday, resolved itself at once into a committee of the whole, and commenced consideration of the special committee's proposed amendment concerning religion:

> Article I. Section 9. Between paragraphs two and three insert "no religion shall be established by law, nor shall the equal rights of conscience be infringed."

Criticisms abounded: that the first clause could be read to abolish religion altogether, that the two parts of the sentence should be reversed, that it should read "no religious doctrine" shall be established, and even that the amendment was "altogether unnecessary." Madison said he understood the words to mean

> that Congress should not establish a religion, and enforce the legal observation of it by law, nor compel men to worship God in any manner contrary to their conscience.

This provision was indeed necessary, he said, because there were some who feared that the "necessary and proper" clause of the Constitution gave Congress sweeping powers that might be used as an instrument to establish a national religion. He recommended that the word "national" be inserted, so that the amendment would read, "no national religion shall be established by law." He believed that the people feared one sect might obtain a preeminence, or that two sects might combine and establish a religion to which they would compel others to conform. He thought if the word "national" were introduced, it would point the amendment directly to the object it was intended to prevent.

Samuel Livermore of New Hampshire, who railed against wasting the time of the House on the business of amending every time he spoke, now broke in to make a suggestion of lasting value: he

> was not satisfied with that amendment; but he did not wish them to dwell long on the subject. He thought it would be better if it was altered, and made to read in this manner, that Congress shall make no laws touching religion, or infringing the rights of conscience.

The discussion veered away from the subject of rights almost immediately thereafter, but despite Livermore's hostility to the project of amending, the opening words of his proposal, "Congress shall make no laws," became firmly fixed in the minds of his colleagues.

Elbridge Gerry's Rancor

Judging from the course the debate was now about to take, and how easily and often it was deflected into discussions of other matters only remotely related to the question before the committee, it seems that a declaration of the rights of the people was not the subject uppermost in the minds of many of the members, not the subject they most wanted to talk about or act on. Personal animosities related to old controversies concerning the allocation of powers, lingering from the ratification struggles, were still terrible irritants to many of the former combatants, especially to one who had suffered as many setbacks as Elbridge Gerry had.

Gerry had experienced one defeat after another, not only for his ideas and issues, but also personally. For example, although he was probably his state's most knowledgeable authority on the Constitution, he had been defeated in the elections for delegate to the Massachusetts ratifying convention (because he had to run in his home district, Cambridge, which was heavily Federalist), and he had been allowed to participate only in the humiliating role of nonvoting information resource.[14] This was the sequel to his series of defeats in the Constitutional Convention and his self-inflicted injury of depriving himself of the enduring honor of being a signer of the Constitution. He continued to nurse resentment over the fact that the supporters of the Constitution appropriated for themselves the name Federalists, and left those, like him, who sought to amend the Constitution to strengthen the powers of the states before agreeing to ratify it, to be called Anti-Federalists, to their great disadvantage. And now, as a minority member of Congress, he knew that he faced a continuation of defeats, and that somehow it was his fate to carry on as the principal spokesman of minority views that were doomed to lose. His rancor now erupted, understandably, as he pounced on Madison's proposal to prohibit establishment of a national religion.

Gerry's fury focused on the word "national." He said the ideas of *national* government and *federal* government were opposed to each other. He and other Anti-Federalists had complained in the state ratifying conventions that the new form of government "consolidated the Union," but the Federalists had denied it and had derided him and other Anti-Federalists for having said it. Madison, by seeking now to introduce the word "national" into the Constitution, was tacitly admitting that he "considers it in the same light."

> Those who were called antifederalists at that time complained that they had injustice done them by the title, because they were in favor of a Federal Government, and the others were in favor of a national one; the federalists were for ratifying the constitution as it stood, and the others not until amendments were made. Their names then ought not to have been distinguished by federalists and antifederalists, but rats and antirats.

Though denounced by Gerry as perhaps the leading "rat" of the ratification process, Madison did not allow himself to be provoked by this punning insult into a retrospective discussion of the labels Federalist and Anti-Federalist, nor did he enter into a debate on the issue of the *national* versus the *federal* character of the Constitution.[15] He simply denied that prohibiting a "national religion" would imply that "the Government was a national one." And then he drew back from that particular controversy and yielded to Gerry by withdrawing his motion to insert the word "national." Whereupon the attention of the members returned to the business at hand, the amendment securing religious freedom and prohibiting an establishment.

Samuel Livermore's Contribution

Livermore's substitute wording was adopted by a vote of thirty-one for, twenty against. It commenced with the powerful negative command, an explicit denial of power, that "Congress shall make no laws touching religion, or infringing the rights of conscience," in place of the form of the amendment as proposed by the special committee: "no religion shall be established by law, nor shall the equal rights of conscience be infringed." Throughout the many subsequent revisions of the religion clauses, except for changing the word "laws" from plural to singular, no alteration was ever after made in that phrase. And so, by the unplanned eventuality that the first two amendments submitted to the states by the Congress failed to get ratified, those five words, "Congress shall make no law," became the magisterial opening of the Bill of Rights.

From the example of Livermore's profound contribution, we see that even those members who were opposed, for one reason or another, to taking up the task of amending were nevertheless responsibly attentive to the business of formulating sound and worthy constitutional provisions. Good suggestions from the other side, like Livermore's, were considered respectfully, and sometimes accepted. But the erratic course of the debate shows that the attention of many of the members was focused more on issues that had divided them throughout the ratification, most especially the question of the powers of the new government of the United States relative to the states. While they were discussing the wording of the religion clauses, there was a cooperative spirit underlying their debate, with no harsh lines drawn, as they strove to find the best way to say what they agreed they meant. But when the subject matter was deflected to the character of the new government and the scope of its powers, the tone and spirit became markedly different. Then it would turn intense and bitter, and Anti-Federalist resentment of the way the Federalists had achieved victory in the ratification campaigns could erupt in the form of angry denunciations of the "rats" by the "antirats."

The Right to Instruct Representatives

Something similar occurred when they proceeded to the discussion of the next proposed amendment in the report of the special committee:

The freedom of speech and of the press, and the right of

the people peaceably to assemble and consult for their common good, and to apply to the Government for redress of grievances, shall not be infringed.

The debate on this amendment was to be lengthy and at times profound, but not what one might have expected. The digressions began at once, quickly moving to topics other than "the freedom of speech and of the press." First there was lengthy quibbling about whether it was necessary to include the word "assemble," since it was clear that the people could not consult unless they first assembled. In the midst of this digression, Tucker of South Carolina digressed further, saying he wanted to point out something that had been left out, "the most material part" of the proposed amendment, "which was, a declaration that the people should have a right to instruct their representatives." He moved to insert the words, "to instruct their Representatives." The ensuing debate, over the meaning and consequences of declaring the right to "instruct" representatives, once again revivified bitter old controversies.

The exchange of ideas on the subject of instructing representatives was learned and thoughtful, at least at first, concerning how much elected representatives should be governed by public opinion "under a democracy." Thomas Hartley of Pennsylvania said he "wished the motion had not been made."

> When the passions of the people are excited, instructions have been resorted to . . . and although the public opinion is generally respectable, yet at such moments it has been known to be often wrong; and happy is that Government composed of men of firmness and wisdom to discover and resist popular error. . . .
>
> Sir, I have known within my own time so many inconveniences and real evils arise from adopting the popular opinions on the moment, that although I respect them as much as any man, I hope this Government will particularly guard against them, at least that they will not bind themselves by a constitutional act, and by oath, to submit to their influence.

The issue, as John Page of Virginia saw it, was democracy, specifically the role of public opinion in a democracy.

> [U]nder a democracy, whose great end is to form a code of laws congenial with the public sentiment, the popular opinion ought to be collected and attended to. . . . Our Government is derived from the people, of consequence the people have a right to consult for the common good;

but to what end will this be done, if they have not the power of instructing their representatives?

George Clymer of Pennsylvania hoped they would not adopt Tucker's proposal. "Do gentlemen foresee the extent of these words?" he asked.

> If they have a constitutional right to instruct us, it infers that we are bound by those instructions. . . . I presume we shall be called upon to go further, and expressly declare the members of the Legislature bound by the instruction of their constituents. This is a most dangerous principle, utterly destructive of all ideas of an independent and deliberative body.

Gerry supported Tucker's proposal. Instructions need not be binding, he argued, but whether they were binding or not was not the main point; the main point, he said, is that the people are sovereign.

> Now, though I do not believe the amendment would bind the representatives to obey the instructions, yet I think the people have a right both to instruct and bind them. . . ; the friends and patrons of this constitution have always declared that the sovereignty resides in the people. . . ; to say the sovereignty vests in the people, and that they have not a right to instruct and control their representatives, is absurd to the last degree. . . . But the amendment . . . only declares the right of the people to send instructions; the representative will, if he thinks proper, communicate his instructions to the house, but how far they shall operate on his conduct, he will judge for himself.

Once embarked on this theme, that sovereignty resides in the people, Gerry seemed to be carried away by his own oratory, one grand thought leading to another. He foresaw that declaring "the right of the people to instruct their representatives" would give a great encouragement to the development of public opinion.

> Much good may result from a declaration in the constitution that they possess this privilege; the people will be encouraged to come forward with their instructions, which will form a fund of useful information for the Legislature. We cannot, I apprehend, be too well informed of the true state, condition, and sentiment of our constituents, and perhaps this is the best mode in our power of obtaining information. I hope we shall never shut our ears against that information which is to be derived from the petitions and instructions of our constituents.

Then, unstoppably warming to his subject, he launched into a glowing tribute to the qualities of mind of the common man, praising this paragon as the richest source of political wisdom and the most reliable guide for political leaders such as themselves. It was important to declare the right of the people to instruct their representatives not just for the sake of the people, but even more for the lofty purpose of enlightening the representatives, who would benefit immensely from hearing the superior knowledge of the common man, if only they "would descend to listen to it."

> I hope we shall never presume to think that all the wisdom of this country is concentred within the walls of this House. Men, unambitious of distinctions from their fellow-citizens, remain within their own domestic walk, unheard of and unseen, possessing all the advantages resulting from a watchful observance of public men and public measures, whose voice, if we would descend to listen to it, would give us knowledge superior to what could be acquired amidst the cares and bustles of a public life; let us then adopt the amendment and encourage the diffident to enrich our stock of knowledge with the treasure of their remarks and observations.

This time, Madison did not back away from direct confrontation. He ignored Gerry's windy, almost comical flight of oratory and, in a carefully reasoned and methodical style, in sharp contrast to Gerry's, focused instead on the uncertain meaning of a declaration that the people have a right to instruct their representatives. The declaration is true, he said, if we mean nothing more than that the people have a right to "communicate their sentiments and wishes." That right, he said, will be secured by putting the rights of freedom of speech and press "beyond the reach of this Government." But,

> if gentlemen mean to go further, and to say that the people have a right to instruct their representatives in such a sense as that the delegates are obliged to conform to those instructions, the declaration is not true. Suppose they instruct a representative, by his vote, to violate the constitution; is he at liberty to obey such instructions? Suppose he is instructed to patronize certain measures, and from circumstances known to him, but not to his constituents, he is convinced that they will endanger the public good; is he obliged to sacrifice his own judgment to them? . . . Suppose he refuses, will his vote be the less valid. . . ? If his vote must inevitably have the same effect, what sort of a right is this in the constitution, to instruct a representative

who has a right to disregard the order, if he pleases? In this sense the right does not exist; in the other sense it does exist, and is provided largely for.

Madison also responded briefly to Gerry's other main contention, on the question of the sovereignty of the people. "My idea of the sovereignty of the people is, that the people can change the constitution if they please; but while the constitution exists, they must conform themselves to its dictates."[16]

Attack and Counterattack

Several members, irritated at being made a captive audience for this extended theoretical exchange on the fundamentals of representative government, and impatient at the length of the debate, now called for a vote on the question. But before the chairman could act, Gerry protested that the majority were trying to rush matters through to silence those who sought to consider amendments other than Madison's:

Gentlemen seem in a great hurry to get this business through. I think, Mr. Chairman, it requires a further discussion; for my part I had rather do less business and do it well, than precipitate measures before they are fully understood. . . . Is not the report [of the Committee of Eleven] before us for deliberation and discussion, and to obtain the sense of the House upon it; and will not gentlemen allow us a day or two for these purposes, after they have forced us to proceed upon them at this time? I appeal to their candor and good sense on the occasion, and am sure not to be refused; and I must inform them now, that they may not be surprised hereafter, that I wish all the amendments proposed by the respective states to be considered. . . . [A]nd why it [Tucker's amendment on instructing representatives], with others recommended in the same way, were not reported, I cannot pretend to say; the committee know this best themselves.

Vining counterattacked at once on both counts, of rushing matters and of ignoring the states' proposed amendments. The trouble was not that anyone was rushing matters, he said, but rather that Gerry was intentionally dragging out the discussion. He accused him of

unnecessary delay and procrastination [that was] improper

and unpardonable. . . . Is it not inconsistent in that honorable member to complain of hurry, when he comes day after day reiterating the same train of arguments, and demanding the attention of this body by rising six or seven times on a question.

As for Gerry's complaint that the special committee had not reported out the amendments proposed by the state ratifying conventions, Vining's response was brief and harshly blunt:

The gentleman . . . has insinuated a reflection upon the committee for not reporting all the amendments proposed by some of the State conventions. I can assign a reason for this. The committee conceived some of them [to be] superfluous or dangerous, and found many of them so contradictory that it was impossible to make any thing of them; and this is a circumstance the gentleman cannot pretend ignorance of.

Vining concluded this passionate and directly personal blast by expressing the hope that debate hereafter would be "conducted in a laconic and consistent manner." Gerry could not resist responding that Vining had indeed "given him an example of moderation and laconic and consistent debate that he meant to follow." He then unapologetically resumed his discussion of instructing representatives by commenting on an argument made earlier that binding representatives by instructing them would change the government "from a representative one to a democracy, wherein all laws are made immediately by the voice of the people." The proponents of the Constitution, he said, had always given assurances that it provided for a democracy, "but perhaps he was misled, and the honorable gentleman was right in distinguishing it by some other appellation; perhaps an aristocracy was a term better adapted to it."

Anger at Gerry was evidently running strong at this point, as he persisted in continuing his time-consuming digressions. But he and his fellow Anti-Federalists were equally vexed by their conviction that debate was about to be cut short in order to deny them a fair hearing. Increasingly harsh criticisms mingled with increasingly feeble attempts to continue the discourse. When "several members now rose, and called for the question," this time it was Page who complained, bitterly; he said he "was sorry to see gentlemen so impatient; the more so, as he saw there was very little attention paid to any thing that was said; but he would express his sentiments if he was only heard by the Chair."

The Anti-Federalists Accuse

From this point on, the underlying concerns came fully to the surface and became the dominant ones. Thomas Sumter of South Carolina offered a few sentences to the effect that instructions would not be binding, but quickly turned to what was really on his mind. Although he spoke in calm and civil phrases, he delivered a mixed and somewhat menacing message. He hinted a threat to break off consideration of amendments, while at the same time urging that they take all the time necessary, even if it should take a year, rather than rush their deliberations:

> I rose on this occasion, not so much to make any observations upon the point immediately under consideration, as to beg the committee to consider the consequences that may result from an undue precipitancy and hurry. . . . If gentlemen are pressed for want of time, and are disposed to adjourn the session of Congress at a very early period, we had better drop the subject of amendments, and leave it until we have more leisure to consider and do the business more effectually. For my part, I would rather sit till this day twelve-month, than have this all-important subject inconsiderately passed over. The people have already complained that the adoption of the constitution was done in too hasty a manner; what will they say of us if we press the amendments with so much haste?

Now just about all pretense of substantive debate about the proposed amendment before them disappeared, and the real cause of anger and animosity emerged, brimming with resentment and scornful accusations. Aedanus Burke spoke very briefly in favor of the right to instruct representatives and then switched to the real issue. The amendments that Madison and the Committee of Eleven had proposed were insignificant, he said. The amendments they had left out were the truly significant ones. Further, he accused the proponents of these amendments of parliamentary improprieties, devious maneuvering, and wasting the time of the Congress:

> I do not mean to insist particularly upon this amendment: but I am very well satisfied that those that are reported and likely to be adopted by this House are very far from giving satisfaction to our constituents; they are not those solid and substantial amendments which the people expect; they are little better than whip syllabub,[17] frothy and full of wind, formed only to please the palate; or they are like a tub thrown out to a whale,[18] to secure the freight of a

ship and its peaceable voyage. In my judgment, the people will not be gratified by the mode we have pursued in bringing them forward. There was a committee of eleven appointed; and out of the number I think there were five who were members of the convention that formed the constitution. Such gentlemen, having already given their opinion with respect to the perfection of the work may be thought improper agents to bring forward amendments. Upon the whole, I think it will be found that we have done nothing but lose our time, and that it will be better to drop the subject now, and proceed to the organization of the Government.

Now annoyance was expressed on all sides. "Mr. Sinnickson [of New Jersey] inquired of Mr. Chairman what was the question before the committee, for really the debate had become so desultory, as to induce him to think it was lost sight of altogether." And Laurance of New York added that "if gentlemen would confine themselves to the question when they were speaking, the business might be done in a more agreeable manner."

Madison Responds

Madison apparently did not think these admonitions applied to him; he responded directly to Burke's barrage. What was included and what was left out of the Committee of Eleven's set of proposed amendments was now, for Madison as much as for Gerry and Burke, the question before the committee of the whole. Speaking as one whose personal honor had been questioned by the thinly veiled accusations of rigging and bad faith, Madison first responded to the charges that he was trying unfairly to rush the business through, and especially that he and those on his side were "not acting with candor."

He denied that the amendments proposed by the states had been ignored and argued instead that the Committee of Eleven had considered them, starting with the fact that the states had proposed two significantly different kinds of amendments; Madison was taking tactical advantage of this opportunity the Anti-Federalists had imprudently presented. The Virginia convention, for example, had recommended forty articles for inclusion in the Constitution and had neatly divided them into two distinct sets. The first set of twenty dealt fairly strictly with individual political and legal rights, the second set of twenty with the structure of the Constitution and the distribution of powers between the federal government and the states. They had entitled the first list of twenty articles "a Declaration or Bill of Rights asserting and securing from encroachment the essential and unalienable Rights of the People"; the second set came under a separate heading, "Amendments to the Body of the Constitution." Madison drew his own proposed amendments, selecting and abridging with care, almost entirely from the first set of articles; he took hardly anything from the second set.

In short, Madison had done just what he kept telling everyone he would do: he culled from the long list of proposed Anti-Federalist amendments only those parts that addressed "the great and essential rights"; were overwhelmingly popular and noncontroversial and therefore likely to win approval by two-thirds of both houses of Congress and three-fourths of the state legislatures; were "plain, simple, and important"; would not change any aspect of the new government; and were "proper" in themselves. The rest he left out.

The first kind, he now reminded Burke, were the ones the Anti-Federalists had insisted were "most strenuously required." These the Committee of Eleven had recommended:

> It was wished [by the people] that some security should be given for those great and essential rights which they had been taught to believe were in danger. I concurred, in the convention of Virginia, with those gentlemen, so far as to agree to a declaration of those rights which corresponded with my own judgment.... I appeal to the gentlemen on this floor who are desirous of amending the constitution, whether these proposed are not compatible with what are required by our constituents? Have not the people been told [by the Anti-Federalists] that the rights of conscience, the freedom of speech, the liberty of the press, and trial by jury, were in jeopardy? that they ought not to adopt the constitution until those important rights were secured to them?

Thus Madison insisted that the amendments the Committee of Eleven had presented were just what the advocates of a bill of rights had been calling for, and that as far as amendments of that sort were concerned he had done what he had pledged to do, and what they had insisted on. But the other kind of amendments, he said, were a different matter. The Committee of Eleven had not favored amendments that would alter the structure of the government or that had no chance of adoption. He would oppose, he said, the consideration at this time of such as are likely to change the principles of the Government, or that are of a doubtful nature; because I apprehend there is little prospect of obtaining the consent of two-thirds of both Houses of Congress, and three-fourths of the State Legislatures, to ratify propositions of this kind; therefore, as a friend of what is attainable, I would limit it to the plain, simple, and important security that has been required.

Because many of the state conventions had proposed two different sets of amendments, clearly labeled, Madison and the Committee of Eleven had found an easy solution. The amendments in one set were clear, broad, popular, and, in Madison's eyes, not dangerous; the others were technical, detailed, dubious, not especially interesting or appealing to the public, and a threat to the foundations of the new constitutional structure. They drew heavily from the first and almost not at all from the second. The factual question, then, whether Madison and the Committee of Eleven had put forth amendments that were "compatible" with those proposed by the states, or had ignored them, was easily answered. They had done both.

Burke, in response, did not in any way soften his accusations and complaints about what had been left out of the proposed bill of rights. But he did attempt, not very successfully, to minimize the question of candor, Madison's or anyone else's, by making a distinction with little if any difference. He said he

> never entertained an idea of charging gentlemen with the want of candor, but he would appeal to any man of sense and candor, whether the amendments contained in the report were anything like the amendments required by the States of New York, Virginia, New Hampshire, and Carolina; and having these amendments in his hand, he turned to them to show the difference, concluding that all the important amendments were omitted in the report.

After one more exchange on how the amendments now being considered differed from those that had been proposed by the states, the Congressional Register tells us that

> The question was now called for from several parts of the House, but a desultory conversation took place before the question was put; at length the call becoming very general, it [that is, Tucker's motion on the right of the people to instruct their representatives] was stated from the chair,

123

and determined in the negative, 10 rising in favor of it, and 41 against it.

Voting without Discussing

And so Tucker's amendment, which never had had the slightest chance of being adopted, was overwhelmingly defeated, four to one. There was no surprise in that outcome, but the very next sentence in the record is more than surprising; it is astonishing. It reads, simply, "The question was now taken on the 2d clause of the 4th proposition, as originally reported and agreed to." What was "the 2d clause of the 4th proposition as originally reported"? It was the early form of most of what is now the First Amendment:

> The freedom of speech and of the press, and the right of the people peaceably to assemble and consult for the common good, and to apply to the Government for redress of grievances, shall not be infringed.

And why is it astonishing that at this point the committee of the whole agreed to it? Because in all the debate there had been no discussion whatsoever of the proposal itself! Madison had spoken the words "freedom of speech and of the press" twice in the course of the deliberations, but just in passing. No one else had so much as uttered those words, let alone discussed them, at any time. The entire debate had been devoted to one proposed deletion, of the word "assemble," and one proposed addition, the right of the people to instruct their representatives. When those proposals were voted down, the amendment itself was adopted without debate. No one spoke about the importance of a free press in a democratic republic and whether there might have to be any measures to control or protect the press; no one discussed the advantages, or the dangers, or the limits of freedom of speech, or indeed what they meant by "speech"; that is, whether speech was limited to spoken words or could be extended, as it has since been extended, to include such nonverbal "expressions" of opinion as picketing,[19] flag-burning,[20] and nude dancing.[21]

There was, in fact, no discussion of any of the issues that have become so important in First Amendment and Fourteenth Amendment constitutional law. On all these great themes, the authors of the First Amendment were completely silent. The question was simply "taken . . . and agreed to." The lack of probing deliberation on a subject such as this is striking. Had Jefferson been a member of the House, for instance, the deliberations (and perhaps also the First Amendment) might have been different. He would have provoked consideration of a number of clarifications, qualifications, and even limitations on the freedoms of speech and press. As he wrote to Madison, he would have favored this wording:

> "The people shall not be deprived or abridged of their right to speak to write or *otherwise* to publish any thing but false facts affecting injuriously the life, liberty, property, or reputation of others or affecting the peace of the confederacy with foreign nations."[22]

But Jefferson was in Paris, and nothing like that was proposed by anyone sitting that day in the House of Representatives.

Just as the legislative day was nearing its end, a parliamentary maneuver was abruptly introduced with somewhat puzzling motivation. Fisher Ames "moved to discharge the committee from any further proceeding." He gave two reasons: too much time was being devoted to "unnecessary debate"; and motions were being agreed to by simple majority in the committee of the whole, whereas the Constitution required a two-thirds majority of the House, and so the decisions of the committee "might be set aside for the want of the constitutional number to support them in the House."[23]

As we have seen, many members had been opposed to taking up the business of amendments, not all for the same reasons. Some saw no need to amend; some were willing to consider amendments, but not now when other business was urgent; some wanted amendments, but not the ones Madison was proposing, and they indicated they would be willing to postpone deliberations now in hopes of faring better at a later time; and some who wanted amendments other than Madison's were anxious to continue so that they could present their own amendments for consideration, fearful that any discontinuation of deliberations might end their chance, perhaps forever. Madison, almost alone, was determined to push through his amendments, and no others, without delay. He was true to his plan to win universal public support for the Constitution while simultaneously protecting it from any major alteration.

Gerry accused Ames of having a hidden motive for terminating the deliberations of the committee of the whole. The real purpose, he said, was to prevent thorough discussion. He recalled that on July 21 Ames had persuaded the House to rescind its vote to refer Madison's amendments to a committee of the whole House and assign them instead to a select committee. He saw this as the beginning of a sinister plan by his Massachusetts colleague to stifle debate, to push through Madison's amendments, and to block consideration of the amendments of others.

> Mr. Gerry thought that the object of the motion was to prevent such a thorough discussion of the business as the nature of it demanded. He called upon gentlemen to recollect the consistency of his honorable colleague, who had proposed to refer the subject to a select committee, lest an open and full examination should lay bare the muscles and sinews of the constitution. He had succeeded on that occasion, and the business was put into the hands of a select committee. He now proposes to curtail the debate, because gentlemen will not swallow the propositions as they stand, when their judgment and their duty require to have them improved. Will this House, said he, agree that an important subject like this shall have less consideration than the most trifling business yet come before us? I hope they will not. If they are tired of it, let it be postponed until another session, when it can be attended to with leisure and good temper. Gentlemen now feel the weather warm, and the subject is warm; no wonder it produces some degree of heat. Perhaps, as our next will be a winter session, we may go through more coolly and dispassionately.

Now there were pleas from all sides for less heat and more tolerance and patience. Burke "begged gentlemen to treat the subject with fairness and candor, and not depart from their usual mode of doing business." Smith of South Carolina, who had initially supported Ames's motion, withdrew his support. Livermore, too, urged Ames to withdraw his motion and not "leave the business in the unfinished state it now stood." Ames thereupon did withdraw his motion "to discharge the committee from any further proceeding" and, on that note, the House adjourned.

Thus ended a long, hot Saturday's work. In its deliberations filled with meandering discourses, long-winded digressions, angry exchanges of insults, name-calling, accusations and counter-accusations of deceit and bad faith, and, intermittently, marvelous explications and demonstrations of the splendors of deliberative democracy, accompanied by admirable displays of restraint and civility, the House had completed the first steps of a wondrous achievement. The members had erected a simple but sturdy barrier of explicit protection against governmental invasions of the freedoms of religion, speech, press, assembly, and petition. They had earned a day of rest.

7
"Those Solid and Substantial Amendments," All Defeated

When the House met, once again as a committee of the whole, on the following Monday, August 17, to resume deliberations on the amendments proposed by the Committee of Eleven, it was evident that they were determined not to follow their own bad example of the preceding Saturday; that is, they were going to try to restrain Elbridge Gerry.

The Second Amendment

The first amendment on their agenda was the one that became the Second Amendment, containing not only the familiar phrases, "a well regulated militia," and "the right of the people to keep and bear arms," but also a conscientious objector clause:

> A well regulated militia, composed of the body of the people, being the best security of a free state, the right of the people to keep and bear arms shall not be infringed; but no person religiously scrupulous shall be compelled to bear arms.[1]

The first member to speak, surely to no one's surprise, was Elbridge Gerry, who launched into one of his characteristic discourses. First he explored the purpose of a declaration of rights; then he explained that the purpose of a militia is "to prevent the establishment of a standing army, the bane of liberty"; and finally he gave a historical account of how Great Britain, "at the commencement of the late revolution," had sought to prevent Massachusetts from establishing an effective militia.

The immediate response had all the marks of a preplanned resolve to keep Gerry under control this day, in hopes of making more rapid progress:

> Mr. Seney [of Maryland] wished to know what question there was before the committee, in order to ascertain the point upon which the gentleman was speaking.

Gerry, undeterred, replied that he "meant to make a motion" to improve the proposed amendment. He considered it dangerous to grant "a discretionary power to exclude those from militia duty who have religious scruples," because the authorities "can declare who are those religiously scrupulous, and prevent them from bearing arms." Gerry and all the others who spoke to this amendment clearly took the phrase "to bear arms" to refer to "militia duty." In other words, he was concerned that the authorities could use this amendment to label numbers of individuals as religiously scrupulous, deny them the right "to bear arms" (that is, the right to serve in the militia), and by that practice prevent the establishment of an effective militia, as the British had once done in Massachusetts.

His proposed remedy was to apply the exemption to members of a religious sect that was "scrupulous of bearing arms" rather than the more vague "person religiously scrupulous." The debate that ensued revealed considerable disagreement about this, or any, "religiously scrupulous" provision, with several members urging that it be deleted, that dealing with conscientious objectors should be left to legislatures. When they voted, Gerry's motion was defeated very narrowly, 22 for, 24 against, and then the amendment as proposed by the Committee of Eleven was adopted, without change.

As we shall see, this was not the last discussion by its congressional authors of what is now the Second Amendment. They discussed the "religiously scrupulous" provision, which was subsequently deleted, and they discussed the purpose of a militia; but what was not mentioned at all, by anyone, was any private use of arms. In short, there is no reason to believe that the authors of the Second Amendment thought it had anything to do with private ownership of arms or the personal uses of guns, such as hunting or defense of the home. This does not mean that they denied or even doubted the right of citizens to own a gun for such purposes, but it does indicate that that is not the subject matter of the Second Amendment.[2] If the congressional debate among its authors provides any guidance, the intention of the amendment was to ensure that the states would continue to have a significant share of the military forces, and that the principle be sustained that citizen armies would be relied on, rather than a standing army, to the extent possible, for defense against foreign enemies.

Madison and the Committee of Eleven had been careful to omit any words limiting or banning a standing army under the control of the general government of the United States, as several state ratifying conventions had recommended. This omission was immediately addressed by Aedanus Burke of South Carolina. He proposed adding a standing army provision to the militia amendment:

> A standing army of regular troops in time of peace is dangerous to public liberty, and such shall not be raised or kept up in time of peace but from necessity, and for the security of the people, nor then without the consent of two-thirds of the members present of both Houses; and in all cases the military shall be subordinate to the civil authority.

But after the briefest possible discussion, this limit on a standing army was defeated, and they moved on to the next provision, what is now the Third Amendment, the ban on quartering soldiers in private homes. From this point on, the committee of the whole proceeded rapidly. The Federalist majority defeated almost every motion to add, delete, or alter the wording of the amendments as proposed by the Committee of Eleven, making some, but very few, changes. They covered in one day the Second and Third Amendments plus all or significant parts of what are now the Fourth, Fifth, Sixth, Seventh, Eighth, and Ninth Amendments.

On the following day, Tuesday, August 18, before the House could resolve itself into a committee of the whole, Gerry once again was the first to take the floor, this time to make a determined effort to get the Anti-Federalist amendments referred to a committee of the whole for deliberation. He moved

> That such of the amendments to the constitution proposed by the several States, as are not in substance comprised in the report of the select committee appointed to consider amendments, be referred to a Committee of the whole House; and that all amendments which shall be agreed to by the committee last mentioned be included in one report.[3]

Tucker, but no one else, spoke in support of Gerry's motion. When it came to a vote, it was defeated, yeas 16, nays 34. Whereupon the House again resolved itself into a committee of the whole and resumed, doggedly, consideration of the amendments reported by the Committee of Eleven.

Portions of what are now the Fifth and Seventh Amendments were quickly agreed to without changes, but when they came to what is now the Tenth Amendment, Tucker moved that the word *expressly* be added to the Committee of Eleven's version, so as to read, "The powers not expressly delegated by the constitution, nor prohibited by it to the States, are reserved to the States respectively." Madison objected to including the word *expressly* because, he argued,

> it was impossible to confine a Government to the exercise of express powers; there must necessarily be admitted powers by implication, unless the constitution descended to recount every minutia.

Tucker's motion was defeated, but that was not the end of the effort to add the word "expressly." The proposal would be brought up several more times in the days to follow, always with the same negative result.[4]

Before they left this amendment, however, a different addition was proposed, by Daniel Carroll of Maryland, to add to the end of the amendment the words *or to the people,* so that it would read,

> The powers not delegated by the constitution, nor prohibited by it to the States, are reserved to the States respectively, or to the people.

This addition was agreed to, with the result that the last two words of the Bill of Rights, as finally ratified and made part of the Constitution, are *the people*. And with that significant affirmation, the work of the committee of the whole was completed. "The committee then rose," and the amendments of the Committee of Eleven, as amended, were reported to the House.

What the Anti-Federalists Were For

Only then was Thomas Tudor Tucker of South Carolina finally able to make his long-delayed presentation of the amendments drawn from the state ratifying conventions. These amendments provide a clear and authoritative picture of what the congressional Anti-Federalists were for, what they had in mind when they spoke of "all the important amendments [that] were omitted in the report," evidence of what they considered to be "those solid and substantial amendments which the people expect." As such, Tucker's amendments give us a detailed picture of how the Anti-Federalists wanted America to be constituted.

Tucker moved that a set of seventeen amendments he was about to present to the House be referred to a committee of the whole. Of these seventeen articles, as we shall see, only one dealt expressly with a subject appropriate to a bill of rights. That one had to do with religion, and it was drawn directly from one of the amendments proposed by the South Carolina ratifying convention. But none of Tucker's sixteen other amendments made explicit mention of speech, press, assembly, searches and seizures, warrants, trial by jury, cruel or unusual punishments, or any similar matters of rights of persons.

These "solid and substantial" Anti-Federalist amendments dealt instead with such matters as the length of terms of office for representatives, senators, and the president; congressional control of elections; congressional powers of taxation; various powers of the presidency; and the organization and jurisdiction of the federal judiciary. The intention was to alter radically the structure of government established under the Constitution, and the thrust of the proposed provisions was to transfer power from the several branches of the federal government back to the states. What these alterations were thought to have to do with the security of the rights of individuals is an important clue to understanding the fundamentals of the Anti-Federalist position.

Not content with the influence that state political leaders had already secured by the constitutional provision that senators were to be chosen for six-year terms by the legislatures of the states, one of the first of Tucker's amendments would have made the senators even more subservient to the state legislatures by altering the terms of office so that

> the election of Senators for each State shall be annual, and
> no person shall be capable of serving as a Senator more
> than five years in any term of six years.

The change from six-year terms to one-year terms was clearly designed to make the senators little more than errand boys and mouthpieces of their respective state legislatures. In that circumstance, any senator who might show some independence of judgment and do other than the bidding of his state legislature could be put out of office within a year at most, differing little, if at all, from being subject to recall by the legislature. The Senate, under this rule, could not be a deliberative body; rather it would be a place where the different states would make known their positions on pending legislation through senators who would speak and vote in accord with instructions received from their respective state legislatures. They would be in the situation of delegates in international bodies like the General Assembly of the United Nations, who may send information and recommendations to their ministries and in that fashion seek to influence policy, but who speak and vote in accord with the instructions they receive from their capitals. Such delegates therefore cannot use their own judgment when deliberating on pending resolutions, based on facts and arguments presented in debate. They can do no more than negotiate, within the limits of their instructions, with other delegates who are also acting under instructions. With one-year–term senators, the Senate with which the House of Representatives and the president would have had to deal would have been a sham deliberative legislative assembly, with its members under the control of dispersed and diverse state legislatures.

Tucker's next proposed amendment addressed an important power of the Congress, the power to control congressional elections; Article I, section 4 of the Constitution provides that

> The times, places and manner of holding elections for senators and representatives, shall be prescribed in each State by the legislature thereof; but the Congress may at any time by law make or alter such regulations, except as to the places of chusing Senators.

Tucker sought to free the legislatures from any trace of congressional control by proposing to strike out all the words following the semicolon, thus depriving Congress of any control over elections.[5] Election laws and their enforcement, and even the dates for holding elections, could then have varied from state to state, and the possibilities for abuses greatly increased. And that was not all.

This assault on the powers of Congress to make sure that congressional elections were conducted in a fair and uniform manner throughout the United States was continued in Tucker's next amendment. Article I, section 5, clause 1 of the Constitution provides that "Each House shall be the judge of the elections, returns and qualifications of its own Members." Tucker proposed to transfer this power, too, to the States:

> Sect. 5. clause 1. amend the first part to read thus, "Each State shall be the judge (according to its own laws) of the election of its Senators and Representatives to sit in Congress, and shall furnish them with sufficient credentials."

Having proposed this destruction of Congress's power over congressional elections, Tucker next moved on to address Congress's taxing powers, considered by many of the Anti-Federalists to be the single most vexing issue in the new Constitution. Article I, section 8 of the Constitution provides that

> The Congress shall have power to lay and collect taxes, duties, imposts and excises . . . ; but all duties, imposts and excises shall be uniform throughout the United States.

Duties, imposts, and excises must be uniform, but not taxes. The constitutional provisions dealing with one species of tax, "direct taxes," provide restraints on the congressional power other than uniformity. Article I, section 2, clause 3 provided that "direct taxes shall be apportioned among the several states which may be included within this Union, according to their respective numbers . . . . The actual enumeration shall be made within three years after the first meeting of the Congress." And Article I, section 9, clause 4 provided that "No capitation, or other direct, tax shall be laid, unless in proportion to the census or enumeration herein before directed to be taken." That was the congressional taxing power that Tucker now proposed to modify by adding these words:

> No direct tax shall be laid, unless any state shall have neglected to furnish, in due time, its proportion of a previous requisition; in which case Congress may proceed to levy, by direct taxation, within any State so neglecting, its proportion of such requisition.

The Anti-Federalist expectation, apparently, was that states would, by means of this amendment, be the primary authorities to exercise the power of levying direct taxes, and that the Congress would be blocked from exercising this power except when a state was delinquent in providing its apportioned share.

The Issue of Direct Taxation

Despite the apportioning protections already in the Constitution in Article I, sections 2 and 9, the Anti-Federalists had a powerful dread of conceding to Congress a power to levy direct taxes. Their emphasis on the issue of direct taxes is difficult to exaggerate. Patrick Henry is reported to have said when he first saw the twelve amendments as finally approved by the Congress that a ban on the congressional power to levy direct taxes would be "worth all the rest" of these amendments,[6] as if he thought that limiting that one congressional power would do more for the cause of liberty and the protection of the rights of individuals than would the whole Bill of Rights.

It is not a simple matter to explain what distinguishes a direct

133

tax from an indirect tax. During the Constitutional Convention, when the matter was first being deliberated, "Mr King asked what was the precise meaning of direct taxation? No one answd."[7] In the first case in which the Supreme Court considered the question, in 1796, the Court held that only taxes on the value of land and capitation taxes are direct taxes.[8] The issue of direct taxes then lay dormant for the next century, because the federal government levied very few taxes other than customs duties.[9] But when, in 1894, Congress levied a flat tax of two percent on all annual incomes above $4,000, the Court held, in a five-to-four decision, that an income tax was a direct tax and unconstitutional because not apportioned.[10] It was in reaction to that controversial split decision that a movement began that resulted, eighteen years later, in the passage of the Sixteenth Amendment.[11] It authorized a federal income tax, without deciding whether it was a direct tax or not:

> The Congress shall have power to lay and collect taxes on incomes, from whatever source derived, without apportionment among the several States, and without regard to any census or enumeration.

One possible explanation of the fear of a congressional power to levy direct taxes is its connection to slavery, a fear that taxes on land and slaves would put a disproportionate burden on the southern states. In the Virginia state ratifying convention, Madison had argued at length to demonstrate to the opposition that this fear was irrational, but he failed to persuade them.[12] It is evident from Tucker's efforts, and Patrick Henry's never-ending complaints about direct taxation, that the fear was real and persistent.

Tucker's assault on federal powers was not restricted to the Congress, but reached to the other branches as well. The federal judiciary would have been almost completely eliminated in two simple steps. One amendment proposed to change Article I, section 8, clause 9, granting Congress the power "to constitute tribunals inferior to the Supreme Court"; Tucker would have erased mention of "tribunals inferior to the Supreme Court" and would have had it read instead, "to constitute courts of admiralty." A second Tucker amendment would have completed the demolition of the federal judiciary by striking out the words "inferior courts" in Article III, section 1 and inserting instead the words "courts of admiralty," thus eliminating almost the entire federal court system and the presence of federal courts within the states, leaving the Supreme Court as the only court of law of the United States, except for admiralty courts.

The Issue of Executive Powers

Nor did the executive power escape Tucker's attention. He proposed a presidential term limit, that no one be allowed to serve as president for "more than eight years in any term of twelve years." The next amendment addressed Article II, section 2, which provides that "The President shall be Commander in Chief of the Army and Navy." Tucker proposed to strike the words *be Commander in Chief* and insert a quite different phrase, so that the provision would read as follows:

> The President shall have power to direct (agreeable to law) the operations of the Army and Navy of the United States, and of the militias of the several States, when called into the actual service of the United States.

Aside from taking away from the president the title of commander in chief, it is likely that the words *agreeable to law* were intended to place a congressional restraint on the actions of the president, requiring that he obtain prior congressional authorization for any military action, and perhaps also continuing congressional oversight, very much as hoped for by the proponents of the 1973 War Powers Resolution.

No president has acknowledged the constitutionality of the War Powers Resolution, and the Congress has not pressed to have its validity tested, but if Tucker's amendment had been in place there would be little doubt of the constitutional validity of congressional war powers. Tucker's amendment would have enhanced congressional power at the expense of the executive power, and considering the influence of state legislatures over the United States Senate prior to the Seventeenth Amendment and popular election of senators (even without the additional control that Tucker's annual-election amendment would have provided), it would also have greatly enhanced the power of the states at the expense of the federal government, giving state legislators a significant role in major national concerns, national security, and the conduct of war.

Just where the Constitution places the control of foreign policy and the issues of war and peace, whether in the Congress, and especially in the Senate, or in the executive, has been an unsettled matter of dispute from the very beginning.[13] But there is no basis for questioning where the Constitution assigns control of foreign trade. The power "to regulate commerce with foreign nations" was granted expressly to the Congress (Article I, section 8, clause 3). As one of the ways to implement this power, Congress was granted power "to lay

135

and collect . . . duties, imposts and excises," provided only that "all duties, imposts and excises shall be uniform throughout the United States." And the exclusive grant of powers to the Congress to regulate foreign trade was complemented and strengthened by the imposition (Article I, section 10, clause 2) of restraints on the powers of the states:

> No State shall, without the consent of the Congress, lay any imposts or duties on imports or exports, except what may be absolutely necessary for executing it's [sic] inspection laws: and the net produce of all duties and imposts, laid by any State on imports or exports, shall be for the use of the Treasury of the United States; and all such laws shall be subject to the revision and controul of the Congress.

Under this provision, a state could not levy duties except to cover inspection costs. If the revenue from such levies as the Congress might consent to should happen to produce a surplus, that surplus would go to the United States, not to the state. And as if that were not sufficiently restrictive, Congress was given the power to change, as it wishes, any state law on the subject.

Tucker sought to alter this combination of congressional power and state powerlessness in foreign trade by amending "the first sentence" of the section (actually, the entire section is just one sentence) to read thus:

> No State shall lay any duties on imports or exports, or any duty of tonnage, except such as shall be uniform in their operation on all foreign nations, and consistent with existing treaties, and also uniform in their operation on the citizens of all the several States in the Union.[14]

Thus, in an artful display of the legislative draftsman's skill, a negative prohibition on the states is transformed into an affirmative grant of power to the states. Without changing the opening words *No State shall*, the sentence is completed by imposing almost no restraints on the power of the states to lay duties, except that they not discriminate among the foreign nations with which they trade. The congressional role would be completely abolished simply by not mentioning it.

The Issue of Religion

But perhaps the most striking example of clever legislative draftsmanship was the last of Tucker's amendments, the only one of the seventeen to deal with a subject we expect in a bill of rights. This one was designed to amend the Constitution's ban on religious tests, changing it into its opposite by the addition of one innocent word. Article VI, section 3 of the Constitution provides that:

> The Senators and Representatives before mentioned, and the Members of the several State Legislatures, and all executive and judicial Officers, both of the United States and of the several States, shall be bound by Oath or Affirmation, to support this Constitution; but no religious test shall ever be required as a Qualification to any Office or public Trust under the United States.

The ban on religious tests was a remarkable and controversial feature of the new Constitution, the only mention of religion in the original document. This provision had been variously criticized in several state ratifying conventions as opening the door to "Jews, Turks, and infidels" and to "pagans, deists, and Mahometans," or as "an invitation for Jews and pagans of every kind," but the objections did not garner enough support in any state convention to make the issue a barrier to ratification.[15]

Eleven of the thirteen states had religious tests in their constitutions or statutes as a requirement for holding state office. Maryland, for example, required an oath of belief "in the Christian religion" as a barrier to Jews, Muslims, and nonbelievers, but many of the other state religious tests did not have Jews and "Turks" as their main target. The purpose often was to bar Catholics from holding public office, appointed or elective, in predominantly Protestant states, and to bar members of certain Protestant sects in others.[16]

And so when South Carolina ratified the Constitution it is not especially surprising that they recommended that this provision be amended, but the method of amending is what is noteworthy. Tucker proposed the insertion of one word: "Between the word *no* and the word *religious*, insert the word *other*." A provision requiring all executive, legislative, and judicial officers of the states and of the United States to take an oath to support the Constitution, followed by the words *but no* other *religious test shall ever be required*, would obviously sanction transforming the oath to support the Constitution into a religious test. Thus the ban on religious tests, by the addition of one innocuous word, would become its opposite, an authorization to make the oath of office into a religious test, even if the only religious test to be allowed thereafter under the Constitution.[17]

There were number of other amendments in Tucker's motion,

but these suffice to make it abundantly clear that the issue of the security of private rights, for him and his Anti-Federalist colleagues, was determined by the structure of the government under the Constitution and especially the assignment of powers to the federal and state governments. Even when the subject matter was what we now expect in a bill of rights, the Anti-Federalist thrust was the same. This had been evident in the earlier efforts of the Anti-Federalists when they sought to alter two of Madison's amendments. One attempt, as we have seen, sought to use the protection of the "right of the people peaceably to assemble" as the means to subject representatives to binding "instructions," thus weakening fundamentally the strength and independence of the national legislature. The other sought to insert the word *expressly* into the provision concerning the delegation of powers to the United States, seeking to eliminate any implied powers, thus enhancing the reserved powers of the states.

We know what Madison and his colleagues thought of these amendments and why they opposed them so strenuously. Madison had explained many times how he had maneuvered to defeat them, by separating the provisions having to do with "those great and essential rights," "the rights of conscience, the freedom of speech, the liberty of the press, and trial by jury," from efforts to restructure the government. He had taken as his own the popular proposals, those that could win the support of two-thirds of the Congress and three-fourths of the states, and he had left Tucker and his colleagues with technical, overly clever, and sweepingly radical revisions that aroused no enthusiasm among the public, however important they may have been in the eyes of Anti-Federalist political leaders.

It is important to notice and acknowledge that in these congressional debates, and in the ratification conventions that preceded them, the Anti-Federalists had identified at the very beginning many of the great issues of American constitutional politics that have persisted ever since: the congressional power over taxes and foreign trade, the presidential war powers, the role of the federal judiciary, and the character and balance of American federalism. The Anti-Federalists, and their heirs in American politics, have lost one political battle after another down through the decades, but their causes persist. Though they have lost repeatedly, they have never quit the field.

Perhaps their greatest setbacks, more than a century after their defeats in the First Congress, have been two amendments, both ratified in 1913. The first gave Congress the power to levy a federal income tax. [18] The other provided for popular election of senators, thus depriving the state legislatures of their power to choose, and thereby to influence, if not control, senators.[19] An additional development of great consequence for the Anti-Federalist cause was the Supreme Court's interpretation of the Fourteenth Amendment, starting in the 1920s, applying the Bill of Rights to the states, thus giving the Court that veto over state legislation that Madison failed to obtain as a congressional power when his "most valuable amendment" was rejected.

How did the members of Congress respond to Tucker's proposed amendments when, after so long a waiting period, they were finally introduced? The record reveals no discussion of them whatsoever. Immediately after his presentation of them, the record reports, simply and starkly:

> On the question, Shall the said propositions of amendments be referred to the consideration of a Committee of the whole House? it was determined in the negative.

And so on August 18, 1789, almost two-and-a-half months after Madison's speech introducing "the great work," as the finale of the committee's deliberations, the Anti-Federalists were made to suffer a decisive and crushing defeat. The very next day, the House of Representatives would begin consideration of the proposed amendments as reported to them by the committee of the whole.

8

"Kill the Opposition, Every Where"

As the months passed following Madison's June 8 speech, the nature of the project to amend the Constitution changed drastically. Prior to that speech, much of Madison's attention had been focused on the kinds of questions he and Thomas Jefferson explored in their correspondence: questions such as where the dangers to liberty lurk in a democratic republic and what kinds of safeguards to individual rights might be effective in a society ruled, ultimately, by majority public opinion. After the speech was delivered, however, the questions were of a markedly different sort: how to persuade, cajole, conciliate, coerce, and compromise with a wide variety of political allies and foes to produce, in the end, the constitutionally required number of votes to pass the amendments and give the Constitution the firm foundation of public acceptance it presently lacked.

From the start of the process of constitution making, Madison had had a vision—a grand and lofty vision of a nontyrannical, majority-ruled, democratic republic governed by a constitution that was universally accepted and even revered. Such a constitution could be a restraining force more powerful than the majority because it would be the voice and the will not just of the majority but of the whole people. A constitution with such universal support could provide security for individual and minority rights and a barrier against the gravest danger to liberty in a democratic republic—government abuse stemming from, and supported by, an oppressive majority.

Madison also had a strategy for transforming this vision into a reality: his proposed amendments would win the allegiance and affection of the great mass of the people for the Constitution without weakening it or, in fact, altering it in any way. Up to June 8, the amending project had been Madison's alone; he formulated the thoughts, composed the arguments, and planned the legislative program. But, now, to implement the plan—that is, to achieve passage of the amendments by a two-thirds majority of both houses of Congress and ratification by three-fourths of the state legislatures—would involve scores, and eventually hundreds, of other elected officials. A project that had been directed by one mind and a solo voice would now become, at best, a numerous chorus and more often a confusing, discordant babble. Madison conceived the strategy for advancing his amendments, but to carry it out he had to devise tactics to contend with fifty strong-willed, vocal, independent-minded politicians in the House of Representatives. Many of them misunderstood what he was attempting to do and therefore opposed him, and others of them understood him all too well and therefore also opposed him. If Madison succeeded in winning the support of two-thirds of the representatives, the same would have to be achieved with two-thirds of the senators, and after that a majority of both houses of three-fourths of the state legislatures. These daunting challenges were what Madison was referring to when he complained to a colleague about "the difficulty of uniting the minds of men accustomed to think and act differently."[1]

Of course, as the numbers increased of those whose minds had to be united, and the distances grew that separated them, so also did the need increase for Madison to find and persuade allies in every state to assist him in the project. To recruit supporters, he had to develop arguments properly accommodated to winning their support. He was not now contending with the elegant intellect of Thomas Jefferson, but with state and local politicians and their constituents. In short, the project of advancing the amendments became an immense and complex political enterprise, very different from the lofty and theoretical vision with which it began.

Where to Place the Amendments

On August 19, the House of Representatives began consideration of the amendments they had reported to themselves when they concluded their deliberations as the committee of the whole House. Before the first of the amendments could be brought up, Roger Sherman of Connecticut moved, as he had more than once before in the committee of the whole, that the amendments be added at the end of the Constitution, "by way of supplement," rather than by "interweaving" them into the text, as Madison and the Committee of Eleven had proposed. Sherman had been unsuccessful in this same attempt just a week earlier, but now, although no new arguments were introduced, the outcome was different. The account in the Congressional Register is succinct: "Hereupon ensued a debate similar to what took place in the committee of the whole but on the question, Mr. Sherman's motion was carried by two-thirds of the house, of consequence it was agreed to."[2]

Ironically, those who advocated the supplementary form thought that setting the amendments off separately, at the end, after the signatures, would emphasize their inferiority in relation to the original Constitution. As George Clymer of Pennsylvania, a signer of both the Declaration of Independence and the Constitution, had observed a week earlier when placement was being debated in the committee of the whole,

> the amendments ought not to be incorporated in the body
> of the work, which he hoped would remain a monument to
> justify those who made it; by a comparison, the world would
> discover the perfection of the original, and the superfluity of
> the amendments; he made this distinction because he did
> not conceive any of the amendments essential.[3]

Sherman's denunciation of interweaving and the amendments was even more disparaging: "We might as well endeavor to mix brass, iron and clay, as to incorporate such heterogeneous articles; the one contradictory to the other."[4] We know now that setting the amendments off separately, all in a group that can be identified as a separate entity with its own revered appellation, made it possible to give them a prominence and status that they could not have had had they been dispersed in several places and woven imperceptibly into the original fabric of the Constitution.

The Right to Bear Arms

But though the consequences of this vote and several others proved to be momentous, the discussions that produced them were not. In fact, with few exceptions, the debates were mostly repetitions of what had been said before, in committee of the whole, and hardly even interesting.

An exception of considerable interest was the renewed discussion of the proposed conscientious-objector clause of what became the Second Amendment: "No person religiously scrupulous shall be compelled to bear arms." This clause, which was, of course, destined to be deleted from the militia amendment, received more discussion than any other part of the amendment. And that discussion was important because it provides the clearest indication of what the authors of the amendment meant by the phrase *to bear arms*.

Thomas Scott of Pennsylvania initiated the discussion by objecting that if there were such an exemption from military service written into the Constitution, "you can never depend on your militia," and as a consequence "you must have recourse to a standing army."

> I know there are many sects religiously scrupulous in this respect: I am not for abridging them of any indulgence by law; my design is to guard against those who are of no religion. It is said that religion is on the decline; if this is the case, it is an argument in my favour; for when the time comes that there is no religion, persons will more generally have recourse to these pretexts to get excused.

Elias Boudinot's response directly opposed Scott except in one significant respect: for both of them, the phrase *to bear arms* meant to serve in the militia, and had nothing to do with private ownership or personal uses of guns.[5] "What justice can there be," Boudinot asked Scott,

> in compelling them to bear arms, when, if they are honest men they would rather die than use them? . . . In forming a militia we ought to calculate for an effectual defence, and not compel characters of this description to bear arms. . . . If we strike out this clause, we shall lead such persons to conclude that we mean to compel them to bear arms.

After this brief exchange, two words—*in person*—were added at the end of the clause. It read, "No person religiously scrupulous shall be compelled to bear arms in person," and the amendment was adopted.

The Declaration and the Constitution

One might have expected that the final stage of the deliberations that produced the Bill of Rights would be distinguished and perhaps even inspiring, or at the very least enlightening, but with only a few intermittent exceptions such was not the case. There were no discussions of the nature, or origins, or history of "the great rights of mankind"; no discourses on the political importance of the freedoms of religion, speech, press, and assembly; no speeches on the jurisprudential consequences of the right of trial by jury, or any other of the essential legal protections.

The explanation for this lack can probably be traced to the nature of the disagreements and agreements among the congressmen. There were sharp disagreements, as we have seen, about whether these amendments were necessary or efficacious and about what distributions of political powers within a republican form of government would best secure rights, but there were no disagreements about the importance of "the great rights of mankind" and the need to secure them. None of the members disagreed with the founding principle enunciated in the Declaration of Independence, "that to secure these rights, governments are instituted among men." But they did disagree about the need to say so in the Constitution.[6] And so the focus was not on lofty discourse or philosophical inquiry but on what did and did not belong in a constitution, and then on getting on with the voting.

Two-Thirds of Both Houses

The outcome of that voting, on most but certainly not on all questions, was foreordained by the partisan composition of the Congress. This First Congress was overwhelmingly Federalist; in the House, Anti-Federalists held ten seats out of fifty-nine, and in the Senate, two out of twenty-two.[7] These five-to-one and ten-to-one Federalist majorities guaranteed the defeat of the whole collection of Anti-Federalist amendments, as in the case of Tucker's amendments. But their minority position did not stop the Anti-Federalists from seeking passage, repeatedly, of their favorite provisions concerning instructing representatives, powers not "expressly" delegated, controlling elections, levying direct taxes, abolishing inferior courts, and restoring religious test-oaths. These Anti-Federalist amendments were all voted down, every one of them failing to achieve even a simple majority, let alone the two-thirds majority required for passage of a constitutional amendment.

The big Federalist majority, however, did not guarantee the passage of all of Madison's proposals. As we have seen, many of the amendments had been approved in the committee of the whole by less than a two-thirds majority, and some of them by a margin of only two or three votes. As a consequence, Madison now faced a formidable political task. The constitutional requirement that an amendment must be approved by "two thirds of both houses" meant that he had to pick up the votes of members in the House that he did not get initially when the same members were sitting as the committee of the whole. The political arithmetic was simple, stark, and troubling: because he could not count on any support from Anti-Federalists, Madison needed the votes of a minimum of forty of the forty-nine Federalists in the House and fifteen of the twenty Federalist senators.

Federalist members, many of whom were far from enthusiastic supporters of the amendments, were able to exact a price for their votes. For example, Madison, by his own account, saw that the additional votes he needed to reach a two-thirds majority for some of his amendments would be gained only by giving up "interweaving." This was a loss that, in his judgment, though important, was not vital; and, in any case, it was "unavoidable." He so informed a correspondent in a letter written after the voting had been completed in the House and almost all of the propositions "ha[d] been agreed to by two thirds of the House":

> The substance of the report of the Committee of eleven has not been much varied. It became an unavoidable sacrifice to *a few* who knew their concurrence to be necessary, to the despatch if not the success of the business, to give up the form by which the amendts. when ratified would have fallen into the body of the Constitution, in favor of the project of adding them by way of appendix to it.[8]

Other Committee of Eleven provisions were also either unavoidably "sacrificed" or simply defeated for the lack of the additional votes needed to reach two-thirds. The pre-Preamble, which had been opposed passionately in the early debates and approved only narrowly in the committee of the whole, was defeated, a sacrifice that Madison probably did not much regret.

The Federalist majority was not enough to assure Madison of the necessary two-thirds vote, primarily because so many Federalists were critical of his initiative in proposing amendments in the first place.[9] They thought he was yielding unnecessarily to opposition pressures and that it was wrong to be making any concessions to Anti-Federalists, who were, after all, a minority in the Congress, easily rebuffed any time they sought to assert themselves. This opinion, prevalent among Federalists in and out of Congress, endangered the prospects for passage and ratification of the amendments.

Many of Madison's fellow Federalists were not in sympathy with efforts to conciliate Anti-Federalists; they did not make the distinction that ruled Madison's analysis, the distinction between Anti-Federalist leaders and their followers. These Federalist politicians failed to see what Anti-Federalist politicians saw only too clearly—that Madison was not making concessions to them but rather was enfeebling them. Bypassing and even ignoring the leaders, he was instead intent on stealing their followers. To succeed, however, he had to gain the additional votes of Federalists who did not understand his strategy, which was to "detach" the misled followers from the misleading leaders, and not just to detach them but to convert them into devoted supporters of the Constitution. Madison, therefore, concentrated on persuading, and where that was not possible, compromising with his uncomprehending fellow Federalists, but not with the Anti-Federalists.

An instructive example of this effort to explain and to gain the support of an influential Federalist state legislator is to be found in Madison's exchange of letters with Richard Peters, the speaker of the Pennsylvania Assembly. Peters's letters to Madison were friendly, admiring, humorous, and respectful; they show clearly that he was well aware of Madison's great importance and heavy responsibilities. His literary style was rather labored and excessively metaphorical, but he was a skillful state politician, and when he disagreed with Madison, as he did about his handling of the amending process, he could be bluntly critical. While always serious in purpose and to the point, he seemed to consider it his duty to amuse Madison, as if somehow to lighten his burdens; his hard-hitting letters of political argument were accompanied by enclosures of long, humorous, rhyming fables of his own composition. Madison gave every evidence of enjoying these unusual letters, and one of them even inspired this profoundly prosaic man to try his hand at a brief verse of his own.[10]

Peters had initiated the exchange of letters a few weeks after Madison's June 8 speech. While the House was active on other legislative matters and still inactive on the amendments, Peters had written to Madison in his usual half-comical, all-serious style:

> I see you have been offering Amendments to the Machine
> before it is known whether it wants any. After these shall
> be added[,] the Ingenuity of those who wish to embarrass
> its Motions will find out some Things that it wants & so

after making it as complicated as a Combination of Dutch Stocking Looms they will alledge it to be too intricate for Use.[11]

Madison could not have given much weight to Peters's two complaints: that he was seeking amendments before it was known that the Constitution needed changing, and that he was thereby opening the door for Anti-Federalists to add amendments of their own. As he had explained repeatedly in public speeches and private correspondence, his amendments would change nothing in the Constitution, and they would head off the amendments of others that would change it a great deal. But Peters was an intelligent and experienced political leader, and if he misunderstood what Madison was trying to accomplish, it was very likely that others misunderstood, too.[12] Peters was, after all, the kind of political leader whose support would be needed if the amendments were to be ratified by state legislatures. Madison sought, therefore, to persuade him and also to supply him with effective arguments he could use to persuade others.

The "Nauseous Project"

And so, on the same day that the House commenced debate and voting on the report of the committee of the whole, Madison wrote a letter to Peters beginning with the statement that "the nauseous project of amendments has not yet been either dismissed or dispatched." His use of that adjective—*nauseous*—in speaking of the Bill of Rights has been the subject of much comment by those who consider it an indication of his privately held, true judgment of the amendments he had proposed. Many authors since have wondered what could have prompted Madison to speak of the project of amendments as he did.[13] After Madison had spent so much time and effort just to get the House to take up the matter of the amendments, and then so much more in disputes over the legislative procedure—such as whether to refer the amendments to a special committee or to a committee of the whole, with the House reversing itself repeatedly, meanwhile complaining throughout about how much time the process was taking—it would seem that Madison had ample reason to speak of "the nauseous project."

Consider the procedural history of the amending process. On May 4, on Madison's motion, the House reluctantly agreed to debate the subject of amendments on May 25. But on May 25 there were so many expressions of annoyance at being asked to consider amendments, the best Madison could do was to win approval of a new motion to commence consideration of amendments on June 8. On June 8, despite renewed and lengthy objections to considering amendments then, they did submit to listen to Madison's speech proposing amendments and voted, after contentious debate, to refer them to a committee of the whole (without then doing so). Six weeks later, on July 21, after Madison "begged the House" to commence consideration of the amendments, they rescinded their decision to refer them to a committee of the whole and voted instead to appoint a special committee. One week later, on July 28, the House received the report of the special committee, the Committee of Eleven, but did nothing with it until August 3, when, again prodded by Madison, they voted to begin consideration of it on August 12.

At last, on August 13, they formed themselves into a committee of the whole to consider the report of the Committee of Eleven, commencing a week of intense and often acrimonious debate.[14] This debate ended, as we have seen, with the defeat of Tucker's set of Anti-Federalist amendments and the approval of Madison's amendments, substantially intact, as revised first by the Committee of Eleven and then by the committee of the whole House. Finally, on August 19, after these fifteen weeks of stop-and-go legislative action and inaction, the full House was about to begin consideration of the amendments as reported by the committee of the whole.

From this sequence of events, as well as from the text of the letter to Peters, it seems quite clear that it was not the amendments themselves that Madison found so offensive, as some authors have assumed,[15] but rather the *"project of amendments"*—that is, the frustratingly slow legislative process, and the demanding and sometimes stormy debate that he had had to persevere in managing, almost single-handedly, throughout those hot summer months.

That Madison was not speaking of the substance of the amendments seems clear also from similar comments he made about the process in letters written to others; in one he described "the last 8 or 10 days . . . spent on the subject of amendts" as "extremely difficult and fatiguing," and in another as "exceedingly wearisome."[16] *Nauseous* is, no doubt, a more vivid word than *wearisome* or *fatiguing*, and Madison himself, on second thought, may have thought the word excessive. The letter to Peters begins and ends with an apology; perhaps with the word *nauseous* in mind, he concluded the letter with this sentence: "I set out with an apology for not writing sooner, I must conclude with one for writing so much, & still more for writing so scurvily."[17]

Whether the word *nauseous* or something else in the letter was weighing on Madison's mind as worthy of an apology, the point remains that he was complaining of the process of amending, not the content of the amendments. Madison did not want Peters to be confused about the subject of his apology; he went out of his way to emphasize that he was not apologizing for pushing the amendments through Congress:

> We are so deep in them now, that right or wrong some thing must be done. I say this not by way of apology, for to be sincere I think no apology requisite.

Persuading a State Legislator

The letter had two purposes: to persuade Peters to support the amendments and to provide him with arguments for persuading others. The substance of the letter is given in seven numbered reasons why no apology is needed for advancing the amendments. "I think no apology requisite," he wrote,

> [1.] because a constitutional provision in favr. of essential rights is a thing not improper in itself and was always viewed in that light by myself.

We see here again, even in private correspondence, the same double-negative, faint-praise formulation—*not improper in itself*—that Madison had employed in his June 8 speech to the House and that he continued to use consistently throughout the debates whenever he spoke substantively about the amendments. He concedes that such a constitutional provision "may be less necessary" in a federal republic than in a monarchy, but "it is *in some degree* rational in every Govt., since in every Govt. power may oppress, and declarations on paper, *tho' not an effectual restraint*, are *not without some* influence" (emphasis added).

After this brief, carefully formulated, and emphatically qualified justification of amendments "in favor of essential rights," in the rest of the letter Madison says nothing more about the amendments themselves. The remaining six arguments are of a markedly different character, all designed to appeal directly to the inclinations and needs of a practical politician:

2. Many states ratified the Constitution with a tacit understanding that such provisions would be pursued, and they would not have ratified otherwise.

3. If Madison, and other Virginia congressional candidates like him, had not taken a stand in the elections in favor of amendments, Virginia would have been represented by Anti-Federalists "instead of the *federal* reps now in Congs."

4. If he had not proposed the amendments in Congress when he did, "the proposition would have come *within three days*, from the adverse side." It is much better that they be initiated by Federalists and that they appear to be given freely rather than extorted.

5. Adoption of his proposals "will kill the opposition every where," meaning, of course, the opposition to the Constitution that derived its strength from the widespread public support for amendments protecting rights.

6. If amendments had not been proposed, it is easy to imagine the likely "language of antifedl. leaders to the people." Madison, displaying his skill as a ghost speechwriter, then composed for Peters the main arguments of the speech that Anti-Federalist leaders would have delivered:

> We advised you not to adopt the Constn. witht. previous amendts. you listened to those who told you that subsequent securities for your rights would be most easily obtained—we urged you to insist on a Convention as the only effectual mode of obtaing. these—You yielded to the assurances of those who told you that a Convention was unnecessary, that Congs. wd. be the proper channel for getting what was wanted. &c &c.

This is what would be heard, Madison wrote, from those who want to revive the Anti-Federal cause, who had been planning "to blow the trumpet for a second Convention" in the forthcoming fall sessions of the state legislatures.[18]

7. And, finally, to get North Carolina to ratify the Constitution, some amendments are necessary.

The Practical Politician and the Constitution Maker

There we have, in compact form, Madison's political justification for pressing for amendments and the arguments he thought would be most useful in persuading his fellow pro-Constitution adherents to support his amending endeavors. But Peters remained unconvinced. In a prompt reply to Madison he acknowledged that "some of your Reasons are the best that can be given," but, he continued,

> many of them are founded on Apprehensions which for-

give me for saying I think too highly wrought. I believe that a Firmness in adhering to our Constitution 'till at least it had a longer Trial would have silenced Antifederalists sooner than magnifying their Importance by Acknowledgements on our Part & of ourselves holding up a Banner for them to rally to. All you offer comes not up to their Desires & as long as they have one unreasonable Wish ungratified the Clamour will be the same. I know there are among them good characters but many of those who lead do it not from other Motives than to make or keep themselves Head of a Party.[19]

This was a shrewd politician's analysis, one that makes good political sense if the matter is viewed as most politicians would view it, as a contest in which the primary objective is to prevail over opponents, decisively if possible, to subdue or silence them. Peters's reply helps make clear why Madison had so much trouble with his Federalist colleagues: they saw Madison making concessions that were politically unnecessary. After all, if the Federalist majorities ensured that the Anti-Federalists could be outvoted on all constitutional issues, without any need for compromise, why make concessions to Anti-Federalist weakness? Why not use the Federalist majority to defeat the "radical" Anti-Federalist amendments, keep Federalist hands off the Constitution as well, and get on with the urgent legislative business of raising revenue and establishing the institutions of the new government?

In Peters's view of the situation, Madison should have been concentrating his efforts on silencing the Anti-Federalists, avoiding "magnifying their importance," not making concessions to those whose motives are "to make or keep themselves Head of a Party." Because Madison's amendments fell far short of their desires, Peters contended that the Anti-Federalists would not be satisfied and their "Clamour" would persist, so that nothing would be accomplished by conciliatory concessions.

Madison saw the amending project in an entirely different light, as transcending partisan political struggle, as something more fundamental than a conflict between two parties striving for dominance. He saw it as an opportunity to diminish divisions and generate unity and therefore as an essential part of the constitution-making process. The Constitutional Convention had been the first phase in constitution making and ratification the second. In this third phase, the task was not only to defend the vulnerable young Constitution against those who would weaken or transform it but also to strengthen it by

151

converting the numerous opponents in the general public into devoted supporters of the Constitution. Stealing away, by conciliation, the Anti-Federalists' public following would transform a divided populace into one that was unified in its patriotic support of the Constitution.

Well before the congressional session began, in a letter to Jefferson, Madison had spelled out with unmistakable clarity the approach he intended to take; he described to Jefferson the overwhelming majorities the Federalists would enjoy in both houses of Congress, and then went on to say that

> Notwithstanding this character of the Body, I hope and expect that some conciliatory sacrifices will be made, in order to extinguish opposition to the system, or at least break the force of it, by detaching the deluded opponents from their designing leaders.[20]

Other Federalists may have wanted to extinguish those "designing leaders"; Madison wanted to "extinguish opposition" to the Constitution. There was nothing meek or weak about Madison's position; he wanted "to kill the opposition, every where." But he did not seek to "kill" the opponents. The target of Peters's partisan ire was the Anti-Federalist leadership; he wanted to bring down those who sought to "keep themselves Head of a Party." Madison's target was their followers; he wanted to ignore or bypass those "designing leaders" and instead to aim at "detaching" their "deluded" followers. The leaders would be of no consequence if he could win away their followers and convert them, transform them into supporters who would happily pledge their allegiance to the Constitution. Madison meant to give them sufficient reason to make that conversion.

Peters rebuked Madison for exaggerated "apprehensions," meaning that Madison was somehow overestimating the strength of the Anti-Federalists and the need to make concessions to them. Peters might have had in mind the example of Madison's own congressional election experience. The Anti-Federalist majority in the Virginia legislature had denied Madison a seat in the Senate, and then, under the leadership of Patrick Henry, had drawn a congressional district designed to defeat him in his bid for a seat in the House of Representatives. Nevertheless, even in Virginia, with its strong Anti-Federalist representation, running against a very respectable opponent, James Monroe, in a district drawn to Madison's great disadvantage, he had won election to Congress with 57 percent of the vote. Was this not evidence on Peters's side that Madison's "apprehensions" of Anti-Federalist strength were unwarranted?

Madison's response would be twofold. First, he almost certainly would not have been elected in Virginia had he not pledged his support of amendments, as a key element of his campaign. Second, his purpose in seeking election to the First Congress was not to crush political opponents but to participate in the building of the new government and to be in a position to continue and complete the work of constitution making. His amending project was not aimed against certain persons but was conceived as a positive effort to strengthen support of the Constitution by increasing the popular support for it—without his altering it or allowing others to do so. "Too highly wrought Apprehensions" thus had nothing to do with it.

But Madison included none of this thinking in his letter to Peters. He gave him only such reasoning as Peters could use with other legislators and with constituents. The letter to Peters was as well suited to the recipient and to the still unfinished project, as had been Madison's earlier letters to Thomas Jefferson, exploring the uncertain theoretical aspects of bills of rights.

Additional support was still needed for adoption of the amendments, first in the Congress, then in the state legislatures. Madison would find the task of "uniting the minds" of men like Peters, and others much less friendly, "a nauseous project," indeed.

9

Fisheries, Post Roads, and Ratifications

When the Constitutional Convention was nearing its end, back in Philadelphia, in mid-September 1787, George Mason had tried to persuade his fellow delegates that it would not take them long to preface the Constitution with a bill of rights. "With the aid of the State declarations," Mason had said, "a bill might be prepared in a few hours." This forecast, as we have seen, was not one it would have been wise to rely on. Now, two years later, in New York City, near the end of August 1789, after nearly three months of stop-and-go legislative efforts, the House of Representatives was still several days of deliberation away from the vote that would finally send on to the Senate their proposals for a bill of rights to be appended to the Constitution.

During those last days of deliberation in the House, the Anti-Federalists persisted in bringing forward almost their entire list of radical amendments, despite their repeated defeats throughout the time when the House was sitting as the committee of the whole. They sought to add the phrase *to instruct their representatives* to the provision for peaceable assembly; to insert *expressly* into what is now the Tenth Amendment, so that "the powers not expressly delegated to the United States" would be reserved to the states; to strip Congress of its control over congressional elections "except when any state shall refuse or neglect, or be unable, by invasion or rebellion, to make such election"; to prevent Congress from levying direct taxes "until congress shall have made a requisition upon the states to assess, levy, and pay their respective proportions of such requisitions"; to abolish all federal courts except the Supreme Court and admiralty courts by deleting all mention in the Constitution of "tribunals inferior to the Supreme Court"; and to transform the constitutional ban on religious tests into an authorization of a religious test as a qualification for public office.[1]

These well-rehearsed Anti-Federalist amendments, designed to diminish the power of the government of the United States in favor of the states, were all voted down by the House, every one of them failing to achieve even a simple majority, let alone the two-thirds majority required for passage of a constitutional amendment. The strength and the impatience of the majority were both clearly demonstrated by their contrasting reactions to proposals offered by Anti-Federalists and Federalists to amend the amendments. When Elbridge Gerry moved that the word *expressly* be inserted in what became the Tenth Amendment, the motion was promptly and overwhelmingly defeated. In contrast, when Roger Sherman moved to amend the same provision by adding the phrase "or to the people" so as to make it read "The powers not delegated to the United States, by the Constitution, nor prohibited by it to the states, are reserved to the states respectively, or to the people," the Congressional Register reported that "this motion was adopted without debate."[2]

The House Concludes Debate

Saturday, August 22, the last day of deliberations in the House on the amendments, was devoted to an intense and extended debate of Tucker's proposed amendment to limit or deny the power of Congress to levy direct taxes. It developed into one of the lengthiest debates of the entire session, despite the lateness of the hour, with impassioned pleas on the part of the Anti-Federalists to give serious attention to those who considered this an issue of paramount importance. But it was obvious that the patience of the House had finally been exhausted; "the question . . . being called for from every part of the House, the yeas and nays were taken," and Tucker's direct-tax amendment was defeated by a margin of more than four-to-one, yeas 9, nays 39. Undeterred, the minority forces, seemingly indefatigable, pressed on in their hopeless program. Tucker proposed two more of his previously defeated amendments, and Gerry proposed two more of his own; all four "passed in the negative," without debate.

This final phase of the business of amending had now clearly reached its end. A committee was named "to arrange the said amendments and make report thereof," and when the House met again on the following Monday, they ordered "that the clerk of this House do carry to the Senate a fair engrossed copy of the said proposed articles of amendment, and desire their concurrence." Three months of congressional deliberation were now all reduced to a resolution communicating to the Senate the text of seventeen "Articles in addition to, and amendment of," the Constitution:

House Resolution and Articles of Amendment[3]

August 24, 1789

Congress of the United States

in the House of Representatives

RESOLVED, BY THE SENATE AND HOUSE OF REP-RESENTATIVES OF THE UNITED STATES OF AMERICA IN CONGRESS ASSEMBLED, two thirds of both Houses deeming it necessary, That the following Articles be proposed to the Legislatures of the several States, as Amendments to the Constitution of the United States, all or any of which Articles, when ratified by three fourths of the said Legislatures, to be valid to all intents and purposes as part of the said Constitution—Viz.

Articles in addition to, and amendment of, the Constitution of the United States of America, proposed by Congress, and ratified by the Legislatures of the several States, pursuant to the fifth Article of the original Constitution.

Article the First

After the first enumeration, required by the first Article of the Constitution, there shall be one representative for every thirty thousand, until the number shall amount to one hundred, after which the proportion shall be so regulated by Congress, that there shall be not less than one hundred representatives, nor less than one representative for every forty thousand persons, until the number of representatives shall amount to two hundred, after which the proportion shall be so regulated by Congress, that there shall not be less than two hundred representatives, nor less than one representative for every fifty thousand persons.

Article the Second

No law varying the compensation to the members of Congress, shall take effect, until an election of representatives shall have intervened.

Article the Third

Congress shall make no law establishing religion or prohibiting the free exercise thereof, nor shall the rights of conscience be infringed.

Article the Fourth

The freedom of speech, and of the press, and the right of the people peaceably to assemble, and consult for their common good, and to apply to the government for a redress of grievances, shall not be infringed.

Article the Fifth

A well regulated militia, composed of the body of the people, being the best security of a free state, the right of the people to keep and bear arms, shall not be infringed, but no one religiously scrupulous of bearing arms, shall be compelled to render military service in person.

Article the Sixth

No soldier shall, in time of peace, be quartered in any house without the consent of the owner, nor in time of war, but in a manner to be prescribed by law.

Article the Seventh

The right of the people to be secure in their persons, houses, papers and effects, against unreasonable searches and seizures, shall not be violated, and no warrants shall issue, but upon probable cause supported by oath or affirmation, and particularly describing the place to be searched, and the persons or things to be seized.

Article the Eighth

No person shall be subject, except in case of impeachment, to more than one trial, or one punishment for the same offence, nor shall be compelled, in any criminal case, to be a witness against himself, nor be deprived of life, liberty or property, without due process of law; nor shall private property be taken for public use without just compensation.

Article the Ninth

In all criminal prosecutions, the accused shall enjoy the right to a speedy and public trial, to be informed of the nature and cause of the accusation, to be confronted with the witnesses against him, to have compulsory process for obtaining witnesses in his favour, and to have the assistance of counsel for his defence.

Article the Tenth

The trial of all crimes (except in cases of impeachment, and in cases arising in the land or naval forces, or in the militia when in actual service in time of war or public danger) shall be by an impartial jury of the vicinage, with the requisite of unanimity for conviction, the right of challenge, and other accustomed requisites; and no person shall be held to answer for a capital, or otherways infamous crime, unless on a presentment or indictment by a grand jury; but if a crime be committed in a place in the possession of an enemy, or in which an insurrection may prevail, the indictment and trial may by law be authorized in some other place within the same state.

Article the Eleventh

No appeal to the Supreme Court of the United States, shall be allowed, where the value in controversy shall not amount to one thousand dollars, nor shall any fact, triable by a jury according to the course of the common law, be otherwise re-examinable, than according to the rules of common law.

Article the Twelfth

In suits at common law, the right of trial by jury shall be preserved.

Article the Thirteenth

Excessive bail shall not be required, nor excessive fines imposed, nor cruel and unusual punishments inflicted.

Article the Fourteenth

No state shall infringe the right of trial by jury in criminal cases, nor the rights of conscience, nor the freedom of speech, or of the press.

Article the Fifteenth

The enumeration in the Constitution of certain rights,

shall not be construed to deny or disparage others retained by the people.

Article the Sixteenth

The powers delegated by the Constitution to the government of the United States, shall be exercised as therein appropriated, so that the legislative shall never exercise the powers vested in the executive or judicial; nor the executive the powers vested in the legislative or judicial; nor the judicial the powers vested in the legislative or executive.

Article the Seventeenth

The powers not delegated by the Constitution, nor prohibited by it to the states, are reserved to the states respectively.[4]

The Senators as Copy Editors

With the passage of this resolution by the House of Representatives, the continuing project of "uniting the minds of men accustomed to think and act differently" moved on to the Senate. During the next two weeks the senators worked on these amendments like a team of diligent copy editors, making many changes, some of them, but not all, significant improvements.[5] But the record of their proceedings tells us only what editing decisions they made, not what their reasons were for doing so, because at this time the Senate's proceedings were closed to the public and not reported. One skimpy first-hand description of their deliberations has survived, from the diary of Senator William Maclay of Pennsylvania—but for only one day, August 25, the day the House amendments were introduced in the Senate. Maclay fell ill the next day and was not present for any subsequent deliberations on the amendments.

His diary entry for that first day describes the unwelcoming reception some of the senators accorded the amendments:

> [T]hey were treated contemptuously by Z [Senator Ralph Izard of South Carolina], [John] Langdon [of New Hampshire] and Mr. [Robert] Morris [of Pennsylvania]. Z moved they should be postponed to next Session Langdon seconded & Mr. Morris got up and spoke angrily but not well. they however lost their Motion and Monday was assigned for the taking them up.[6]

The gist of what Senator Morris probably said, "angrily but not well," we can surmise from a letter he wrote the previous day to Richard Peters, the prominent Pennsylvania politician:

> Poor Madison took one wrong step in Virginia by publishing a letter, respecting *Amendments* . . . . He in consequence has been obliged to bring on the proposition for making Amendments; The Waste of precious time is what has vexed me the most, for as to the Nonesense they call Amendments I never expect that any part of it will go through the various Trials which it must pass before it can become a part of the Constitution. . . . [O]ur Friends Clymer & Fitzsimmons [both of Pennsylvania] . . . said Yesterday that the business of Amendments was now done with in their House & advised that the Senate should adopt the whole of them by the Lump as containing neither good or Harm being perfectly innocent. I expect they will lie on our Table for some time.[7]

In the ensuing weeks, fellow senators visited the sick man, and Maclay recorded what they told him about Senate business, but either they said nothing about the amendments, or Maclay did not consider what they might have said about them important enough to include in his diary. In either case, after that one entry, the diary never again mentions the amendments, and all we can learn about them from the Senate Journal is the editing decisions the senators made—revising the wording of some amendments, tightening and combining several of them, deleting parts of others, and deleting two of them completely.

The Senate combined the House's Articles Three and Four, joining the protections for religion to those for speech, press, assembly, and petition, beginning to come closer to the final form as we have it in the First Amendment, except for their version of the establishment clause. Senate Records for September 9 provide an example of their methodical editing of the amendments received from the House, recording the revision and combining of the amendments on religion, speech, and press:

> To erase from the 3d. Article the word *"Religion"* & insert— *articles of faith or a mode of worship.*

> And to erase from the same article the words *"thereof, nor shall the rights of Conscience be infringed"* & insert—*of Religion; or abridging the freedom of speech, or of the press, or the right of the people peaceably to assemble, & to petition to the government for a redress of grievances.*

> To erase the 4th. article, & the words *"Article the fourth."*[8]

When they moved on to the *well regulated Militia* amendment, Article Five, they deleted the much-disputed *religiously scrupulous* clause, as well as the phrase *composed of the body of the people*; the remaining text was reworded to make it read exactly as we have it now in the Second Amendment: "A well regulated Militia, being necessary to the security of a free State, the right of the people to keep and bear arms, shall not be infringed."

Articles Eight and Ten, dealing with legal protections relating to indictment, double jeopardy, self-incrimination, due process, and just compensation, were rewritten and combined to form what became the Fifth Amendment.

When the senators were finished, they had reduced the House's seventeen amendments to twelve and, like good editors, had tightened and mostly improved the text without significantly altering the work of the authors, the members of the House of Representatives, and, for the most part, without attempting to interject their own ideas. There were a few efforts, almost all defeated, to introduce some new provisions, some that would have been significant. For example, the senators defeated a motion to qualify the protection of the freedom of the press by adding the words "in as ample a manner as hath at any time been secured by the common law."

The senators also defeated, just as their colleagues in the House had, several of the persistent Anti-Federalist efforts to alter the amendments by insertions: "to instruct their representatives," in what is now the First Amendment; "that no standing army or regular troops shall be raised in time of peace, without the consent of two thirds of the Members present in both Houses," in what is now the Second Amendment; and, yet again, the word "expressly" in what is now the Tenth Amendment.[9]

The senators deleted completely Article Fourteen, the one Madison had called "the most valuable amendment on the whole list,"[10] providing that

> No State shall infringe the equal rights of conscience, nor the freedom of speech, or of the press, nor of the right of trial by jury in criminal cases.

And they also erased Article Sixteen, the cumbersome and redundant amendment on separation of powers:

> The powers delegated by the Constitution of the United States, shall be exercised as therein appropriated, so that the Legislative shall never exercise the powers vested in the Executive or the Judicial; nor the Executive the pow-

ers vested in the Legislative or the Judicial; nor the Judicial the powers vested in the Legislative or the Executive.

The stark reportage of the Senate Journal provides not the slightest clue to the Senate's reasons for these deletions:

On Monday, the 7th, the subject [of amendments] being again before the Senate, . . . [t]he thirteenth article was then agreed to as it came from the House of Representatives: and the fourteenth article was rejected. . . .

The fifteenth article of amendment was then agreed to; and the sixteenth article was rejected.[11]

When the House received back from the Senate the amended amendments, now reduced to twelve in number, they would not accept some of the changes the Senate had made, especially the clauses dealing with religion. They called for a committee of conference "on the subject matter of the amendments disagreed to." This conference committee—three representatives (including Madison, of course) and three senators—was quickly able to make several changes, the most important one being the final revision of the establishment clause.

The Evolution of the Establishment Clause

The establishment clause had been debated at relatively great length in the House, and there had been many versions of it. Madison's original proposal for an establishment clause was, "nor shall any national religion be established." But when it came out of the Committee of Eleven it read, "No religion shall be established by law." The objection was immediately raised that that wording "might be thought to have a tendency to abolish religion altogether." Madison, in response, had said he thought it meant that "Congress should not establish a religion," but for some reason he never proposed that simple and unambiguous wording, using the indefinite article to clarify what it is that Congress must not do. At that moment in the debate, Livermore had proposed new wording: "The Congress shall make no laws touching religion." The Committee of the Whole House, preferring that form to the previous version, modified it and finally agreed to wording moved by Fisher Ames (but reportedly written by Madison): "Congress shall make no law establishing religion." It was that version the House of Representatives then submitted to the Senate.

Madison and most other members of the House, it seems safe to conclude from the arguments they advanced, would have agreed that the purpose of the clause was to keep Congress from favoring one religion in preference to others, but not to indicate hostility or opposition to religion, or anything but approval of it, as consistent with, and even essential to, the well-being of a secular society.[12]

We can study the debates in the House and make judgments, on the basis of the substantive arguments, about the intentions of the various speakers. But when we turn to the Senate and the conference committee we can do no better than speculate on the reasons for their actions, because there is no record of their debates. We know that they must have been uneasy about the establishment clause they received from the House, because they made so many attempts to find other acceptable wording. In fact, the Senate seemed to have even more trouble than the House had had in finding wording of the establishment clause that satisfied them.

In place of the amendment sent to them by the House, they proposed and rejected several substitutes in the course of a week of deliberation. The first version they produced, "Congress shall make no law establishing one religious sect or society in preference to others," was defeated when first proposed, but then agreed to on reconsideration. Later the same day, two similar versions were proposed and defeated: "Congress shall not make any law ... establishing any religious sect or society" and "Congress shall make no law establishing any particular denomination of religion in preference to another." They ended that legislative day by abandoning all their own attempts at an establishment clause and adopting instead the very same wording that the House had submitted to them: "Congress shall make no law establishing religion." Whatever the uncertainties among them that led the senators to consider and reject and reconsider and adopt so many revisions, this last version did not settle the matter; several days later, they produced a wholly new one all their own: "Congress shall make no law establishing articles of faith, or a mode of worship." This formulation, the third one to be adopted within the same week, was the establishment clause the Senate sent to the House, which the House promptly refused to accept.

Without being able to know what arguments were brought forth in the deliberations, it is difficult to understand what great differences of meaning were seen in these various versions. We can be reasonably sure that members wanted to prohibit Congress from establishing "a" religion, but the indefinite article was never used. We can also be sure that they did not want to express hostility to religion as such; that much we can derive from the earliest debate in the

House. There is solid additional evidence that this Congress looked favorably on a general sort of government aid to religion, so long as it was not preferential or discriminatory. This same Congress voted to reenact the Northwest Ordinance of 1787, which provided grants of federal land for schools that were expected to promote religion and morality, as expressed in the Ordinance's famous pronouncement, "Religion, morality, and knowledge, being necessary to good government and the happiness of mankind, schools and the means of learning shall forever be encouraged."[13]

Finally, the Anti-Federalists were surely not the only ones concerned that nothing be enacted to enable Congress to interfere with the powers of the states with regard to religion; after all, several states had established churches, and no one in the First Congress ever expressed an intention to use this amendment to abolish those establishments.

The quest for an acceptable establishment clause had to cope with those three concerns: no preference among religions; openness to nondiscriminatory encouragement of religion; and no interference in state establishments. The final version—"Congress shall make no law respecting an establishment of religion"—produced by the conference committee and promptly concurred in by both House and Senate, can be understood as dealing with all three concerns: it prohibits Congress from establishing *a* religion, it simultaneously prohibits Congress from interfering with any existing state establishment of religion, and it leaves open the possibility of general, nondiscriminatory government encouragement of religion.[14] All of these have been the subject of much dispute ever since.

The Anti-Federalists Vote No

The House and the Senate approved the conference committee's report, and at last all deliberations about text and wording were done with. No decision remained except approval or disapproval—take it or leave it—by three-fourths of the state legislatures. The final resolution, with a new preamble added to the text of the amendments, was adopted by more than the required two-thirds majority in both houses of the Congress and sent to President Washington, requesting him to transmit copies of it to the governors of the states that had ratified the Constitution and the two that had not:

Resolution
September 24, 1789[15]

RESOLVED, That the President of the United States be requested to transmit to the executives of the several states which have ratified the Constitution, copies of the amendments proposed by Congress to be added thereto; and like copies to the executives of the states of Rhode-Island and North-Carolina.

Proposed Amendments to the Constitution

The conventions of a number of the states having, at the time of their adopting the Constitution, expressed a desire, in order to prevent misconstruction or abuse of its powers, that further declaratory and restrictive clauses should be added; and as extending the ground of public confidence in the government will best ensure the beneficent ends of its institution—

Resolved by the Senate and House of Representatives of the United States of America, in Congress assembled, two-thirds of both houses concurring—That the following articles be proposed to the legislatures of the several states, as amendments to the Constitution of the United States, all or any of which articles, when ratified by three-fourths of the said legislatures, to be valid, to all intents and purposes, as part of the said Constitution, viz:

Articles in addition to, and amendment of, the Constitution of the United States of America, proposed by Congress, and ratified by the legislatures of the several states, pursuant to the fifth article of the original Constitution:

Article I. After the first enumeration, required by the first article of the Constitution, there shall be one representative for every thirty thousand, until the number shall amount to one hundred; after which, the proportion shall be so regulated by Congress, that there shall be not less than one hundred representatives, nor less than one representative for every forty thousand persons, until the number of representatives shall amount to two hundred; after which, the proportion shall be so regulated by Congress, that there shall not be less than two hundred representatives, nor more than one representative for every fifty thousand persons.

Art. II. No law, varying the compensation for the services of the senators and representatives, shall take effect until an election of representatives shall have intervened.

Art. III. Congress shall make no law respecting an establishment of religion, or prohibiting the free exercise thereof, or abridging the freedom of speech, or of the press, or the right of the people peaceably to assemble, and to petition the government for a redress of grievances.

Art. IV. A well regulated militia being necessary to the security of a free state, the right of the people to keep and bear arms shall not be infringed.

Art. V. No soldier shall, in time of peace, be quartered in any house, without the consent of the owner, nor in time of war, but in a manner to be prescribed by law.

Art. VI. The right of the people to be secure in their persons, houses, papers, and effects, against unreasonable searches and seizures, shall not be violated; and no warrants shall issue but upon probable cause, supported by oath or affirmation, and particularly describing the place to be searched, and the persons or things to be seized.

Art. VII. No person shall be held to answer for a capital or otherwise infamous crime, unless on a presentment or indictment of a grand jury, except in cases arising in the land or naval forces, or in the militia when in actual service, in time of war or public danger; nor shall any person be subject, for the same offence, to be twice put in jeopardy of life or limb; nor shall be compelled, in any criminal case, to be a witness against himself; nor be deprived of life, liberty, or property, without due process of law; nor shall private property be taken for public use without just compensation.

Art. VIII. In all criminal prosecutions, the accused shall enjoy the right to a speedy and public trial by an impartial jury of the state and district wherein the crime shall have been committed, which district shall have been previously ascertained by law; and to be informed of the nature and cause of the accusation; to be confronted with the witnesses against him; to have compulsory process for obtaining witnesses in his favour; and to have the assistance of counsel for his defence.

Art. IX. In suits at common law, where the value in controversy shall exceed twenty dollars, the right of trial by jury shall be preserved; and no fact, tried by a jury, shall be otherwise re-examined in any court of the United States, than according to the rules of common law.

Art. X. Excessive bail shall not be required, nor excessive fines imposed, nor cruel and unusual punishments inflicted.

Art. XI. The enumeration in the Constitution of certain rights, shall not be construed to deny or disparage others retained by the people.

Art. XII. The powers not delegated to the United States by the Constitution, nor prohibited by it to the states, are reserved to the states respectively, or to the people.

The recorded vote in the House of Representatives on this historic resolution was ayes 37, noes 14—comfortably above the constitutionally required two-thirds majority. The most significant fact about that vote, the grand finale of the long and arduous congressional struggle to add the Bill of Rights to the Constitution, is that on this momentous occasion the congressional Anti-Federalists and the few others who had regularly voted with them—Aedanus Burke, Elbridge Gerry, James Jackson, Theodoric Bland, John Page, Samuel Livermore, Thomas Tudor Tucker, and others—were recorded as voting no, asserting to the bitter end their disapproval of these amendments.[16] But with that affirmative vote, the work of the First Congress in the making of the Bill of Rights was at long last completed. Now it was up to the state legislatures to complete the process of ratification that would make the new amendments, "to all intents and purposes," a valid part of the Constitution.

On to the State Legislatures

Just as there is no record of the Senate deliberations on the amendments, so there is practically no information on the deliberations of the state legislatures in ratifying the amendments. The only newspaper accounts were brief, factual reports to the effect that ten or eleven or twelve amendments had been approved by one or another state legislature. It may seem strange that a matter that had been so important to the public that it endangered ratification of the Constitution was now, just a few years later, apparently a matter of public indifference, treated with near silence. Bernard Schwartz finds it difficult to explain, in fact "amazing, considering the crucial signifi-

167

cance of the Bill of Rights, that we know practically nothing about what went on in the state legislatures during the ratification process," especially since several states rejected one or two amendments, a definite sign that "there must have been sharp debates in those states on the matter."[17] But the silence would not be "amazing" at all if the press and the general public did not consider the amendments to be of "crucial significance," and that seems to have been clearly the case. The explanation is not difficult; their erstwhile followers had been so successfully detached from the Anti-Federalist leaders that ratification of the amendments had become an anticlimax. The "great mass of the people" had been won over to the Constitution, the public's fears had subsided, and their attention had turned to more pressing matters.

But whether or not that is the full or only explanation, the unquestionable fact is that the debates in the state legislatures over the amendments were not reported in the newspapers. Almost the only matters that were reported were the results of the voting: for instance, that the New Hampshire legislature ratified eleven of the amendments. The fact that some of the amendments were not approved by one state legislature or another indicates that there was controversy and disagreement, especially about the first two of the twelve proposed amendments, and that the state legislators were being discriminating and attentive to the task of ratifying these additions to the Constitution. But although, as Schwartz observes, "even in the states which ratified all twelve proposed amendments, there must have been sharp division and debate,"[18] nevertheless, the disagreements were not the sort to arouse the interest of the public.

When the amendments were submitted to the state legislatures, they were not presented as requiring or deserving any special status or priority over other legislative matters. For example, the governor of New Hampshire, in his message to the two houses of the state legislature at the beginning of their 1790 legislative session, listed the "many acts and resolves of Congress which will require your deliberations": "the proposal of the Federal Government, to take under their care the support of the Light House"; "a law empowering the United States to confine their prisoners in the prisons of this state"; "whether the duties may not be lessened, on account of the impost now drawn by the United States"; and "whether any of the existing laws of the state . . . are repugnant to the laws of the United States, or the constitution of the Federal Government." Only after enumerating these several items of legislative business—the lighthouse, prisons, duties, and so forth—did the governor add: "The amendments proposed by Congress to the constitution of the United States, cannot fail of being considered and determined upon as early as the nature of the business before you will admit."[19]

Virginia Takes a Stand

One state, however, was an exception; there is information about the debates, incomplete but still interesting and informative, that took place in the Virginia legislature. Not from newspapers but from the correspondence of participants and observers, we know how the Virginia legislature came close to derailing the ratification of the Bill of Rights.

The only Anti-Federalists in the United States Senate were the two senators from Virginia, Richard Henry Lee and William Grayson, who had, of course, been chosen by the Anti-Federalist Virginia legislature, dominated by the omnipotent Patrick Henry. When the twelve amendments were finally passed by both houses of Congress, Lee and Grayson sent copies at once to the governor and to the speaker of the House in Virginia, with letters expressing their disappointment and even dismay. To the governor they wrote, "It is with grief that we now send forward propositions inadequate to the purpose of real and substantial Amendments." They assured the speaker "that nothing on our part has been omitted to procure the success of those radical amendments" that had been proposed by the Virginia ratifying convention and approved by the Legislature, but all their efforts to gain passage of those Anti-Federalist proposals had failed in the Federalist-controlled Senate. They went on to warn that unless further amendments were obtained, "the natural operation of the Constitution" would result in "consolidated empire" and "the annihilation of the state governments." The letter concluded with a prediction that "it will not be many years before a constitutional number of Legislatures will be found to demand Convention for the purpose" of securing radical amendments.[20]

Very soon after this, President Washington received a report from Richmond of the reaction of the delegates when this "extraordinary letter from our Senators in Congress" was received and read:

> I was happy in hearing much indignation expressed at it, by many who were strong Antifederalists, and had voted against the constitution in the Convention. . . . Mr. Henry appears to me by no means content—But if the people

continue as much satisfyed, as they at present appear to be, he will be soon alone in his sentiments.[21]

Other reports confirmed that Patrick Henry was losing popular support for his anticonstitutional demands for radical amendments, including especially his strongest desire, an amendment to strip Congress of its power to levy direct taxes. His immediate reaction to the amendments was that "they will tend to injure rather than to serve the Cause of Liberty,"[22] and that a ban on direct taxation would be "worth all the rest" of the amendments.[23]

Edward Carrington wrote to Madison that "Mr. H - - - - was disposed to do some antifederal business, but having felt the pulse of the House on several points and finding that it did not beat with certainty in unison with his own," he left the legislature in the middle of the session. Before his departure Henry proposed a vote of thanks to the two senators for their efforts as described in their letter, "but it not appearing to take well, it was never stirred again." The senators' letter, Carrington informed Madison, "was considered by some of the most violent Anti's as seditious and highly reprehensible," the same reaction that had been reported to President Washington. Carrington described the opposition to the amendments by members of the Virginia senate as out of step with the citizenry. "My information from the various parts of the Country is that the people are at ease on the subject of amendments."

The public may have been at ease with the amendments, but a majority of the Virginia legislators were not. Henry Lee reported that "the antifederal gentlemen in our assembly do not relish the amendments proposed by Congress,"[24] and Hardin Burnley added the observation that "whatever may be the fate of the amendments submitted by Congress it is probable that an application for further amendments will be made by this assembly, for the opposition to the Foederal Constitution is in my opinion reduced to a single point, the power of direct taxation."[25]

The course the Virginia legislators followed on the way to ratifying the amendments was reminiscent of the confused and meandering one the House of Representatives had earlier taken in composing the amendments. In the Virginia House of Delegates, a committee of the whole began by approving the first ten amendments, but not the eleventh and twelfth (that is, what are now the Ninth and Tenth Amendments). But the House then disagreed with the committee's report—that is, disagreed with itself, and approved all twelve of the amendments. When it was their turn, the Senate disagreed with the recommendation of the House approving all the amendments and ended its deliberations by refusing to approve the third, eighth, eleventh, and twelfth amendments (that is, the First, Sixth, Ninth, and Tenth Amendments). When these decisions were returned to the House for their concurrence, the delegates would not accept the rejections and requested a conference committee, which then failed to reconcile the disagreements. And so ratification by Virginia was defeated, or at least stalled.[26]

Many of the partisans of the Constitution were dismayed, but Madison, although angry at first, had a different reaction after reflecting on the situation for a month. He saw that public opinion in Virginia had shifted decidedly against the Anti-Federalists, and that led him to adopt a calculating and surprisingly calm appraisal of the Virginia senate's refusal to ratify. He wrote to President Washington that although

> this event is no doubt to be regretted . . . it will do no injury to the Genl Government. On the contrary it will have the effect with many of turning their distrust towards their own Legislature. The miscarriage of the 3d. art: particularly, will have this effect.[27]

One aspect of the Virginia ratification debacle had been unique. In other states, it was the first two proposed amendments that had run into trouble early in the ratification process: the first had to do with the size of congressional districts, the second with compensation for members of Congress. Six states ended by refusing to ratify one or both of them. But Virginia, while finding no fault with those two amendments, was the only state to object to others of them. More surprising, the opposition to them came from "a friend to the Constitution," one of Madison's and Washington's most important allies in Virginia. It was Edmund Randolph who raised objections to "the powers not delegated" being "reserved" in the twelfth amendment, and in the eleventh amendment to the word *retained* in the provision that "the enumeration in the Constitution, of certain rights, shall not be construed to deny or disparage others retained by the people." "His argument," as one puzzled delegate attempted to describe it to Madison, "if I understood it,"

> was applied in this manner, that as the rights declared in the first ten of the proposed amendments were not all that a free people would require the exercise of; and that as there was no criterion by which it could be determined whether any other particular right was retained or not, it

would be more safe . . . that this reservation against constructive power, should operate rather as a provision
against extending the powers of Congress by their own
authority, than as a protection to rights reducable to no
definitive certainty. But others among whom I am one see
not the force of the distinction.[28]

As we have seen, Madison was able to take this troublesome
development calmly a month after it occurred. But at first, while the
debates were still in progress, he was angered by Randolph's opposition to the amendments, puzzled by his argument, and concerned
about the possible harmful consequences. Madison wrote to President Washington, perhaps with the hope of drawing him into the
matter and having him exert his influence on Randolph:

The difficulty started agst. the amendments is really un-
lucky, and the more to be regretted as it springs from a
friend to the Constitution. It is a still greater cause of regret, if the distinction be, as it appears to me, altogether
fanciful. If a line can be drawn between the powers granted
and the rights retained, it would seem to be the same thing,
whether the latter be secured, by declaring that they shall
or that the former shall not be extended. If no line can be
drawn, a declaration in either form would amount to nothing. If the distinction were just it does not seem to be of
sufficient importance to justify the risk of losing the
amendmts, of furnishing a handle to the disaffected, and
of arming N.C. with a pretext, if she be disposed, to pro-
long her exile from the Union.[29]

Randolph, too, wrote to Washington, apprising him of the difficulties the amendments were encountering, defending his own opposition to the two amendments—one defense, of his opposition to
what would become the Ninth Amendment, not presented with much
clarity; the other, concerning the future Tenth Amendment, remarkably foresighted. He also contended that it would have been possible to ratify the rest of them

if the friends would have joined the enemies of the constitution, in suspending the ratification of the eleventh
amendment; which is exceptionable to me, in giving a
handle to say, that congress have endeavoured to admin-
ister an opiate, by an alteration, which is merely plausible.
The twelfth amendment does not appear to me to have
any real effect, unless it be to excite a dispute between the
United States, and every particular state, as to what is delegated.[30]

Ten days later, December 15, 1789, Randolph wrote again to the president to report that the Virginia Senate had indeed refused to ratify four of the amendments, and that the "friends to the constitution" had thought it best to "let the whole of them rest" and "throw the odium of rejection on the senate." But the reports Madison and others were relying on proved to be accurate, of a decisive shift of public opinion in Virginia in favor of the amendments; exactly two years later, December 15, 1791, after the voters had sufficiently changed the membership of the Virginia Senate, Governor Henry Lee was able to notify President Washington that the General Assembly had adopted "all the amendments proposed by Congress." North Carolina and Rhode Island had by then ratified the Constitution and joined the Union; Vermont also had joined the Union, becoming the fourteenth state; and all three of them ratified the amendments before Virginia did.[31] Ironically, by taking so long, it fell to Virginia, whose legislature had been most vehemently and stubbornly opposed to the amendments, to be the decisive eleventh state to ratify, and thus to become the one to make the amendments "valid to all Intents and Purposes, as Part of this Constitution."[32]

And so, more than two years after Madison's speech to the House of Representatives "introducing the great work"; four years after Jefferson had written that "a bill of rights is what the people are entitled to against every government on earth, general or particular, and what no just government should refuse or take on inference"; and four and a half years after George Mason had said he would "sooner chop off his right hand" than sign the Constitution without a bill of rights, which, he said, could be composed "in a few hours," the issue that had nearly killed the Constitution in its infancy, that had been at the heart of the movement for a second constitutional convention, that had kept two states out of the Union, that had stirred the opposition and made so many of the state ratifying conventions scenes of impassioned controversy, that had been contested heatedly in the press and had been at the center of the election campaigns for Congress finally ended—quietly, unceremoniously, without fanfare, almost unnoticed.

Jefferson Announces Ratification

It fell to Thomas Jefferson, as secretary of state, to deliver the official notice of ratification to the governors of the several states, in a letter remarkable in just one respect: that it would be difficult, perhaps impossible, to find any other message from that inspired pen more devoid of fervor or eloquence.

Sir,   Mar. 1, 1792

I have the honor to send to you herein enclosed, two copies duly authenticated, of an Act concerning certain fisheries of the United States, and for the regulation and government of the fishermen employed therein; also of an Act
to establish the post office and post roads within the United
States; also the ratifications by three fourths of the Legislatures of the Several States, of certain articles in addition
and amendment of the Constitution of the United States,
proposed by Congress to the said Legislatures, and of being with sentiments of the most perfect respect, your
Excellency's &.

Th. Jefferson[33]

The comment of Bernard Schwartz is not surprising: "The Jefferson letter may appear to us a singular way of announcing the ratification of what many now consider the most consequential part of the Constitution itself."[34] Jefferson's letter does indeed seem a strangely undramatic conclusion to a struggle that commenced with so much passion and intensity. How can we account for the rapid cooling down of enthusiasm and interest? Why was there almost no attention paid or excitement expressed when the amendments were ratified? Why were there no public celebrations to greet the great victory, the successful culmination of the struggle to incorporate a popularly demanded bill of rights in the Constitution? Why did the greatest advocate and spokesman of rights seem to give as high a priority to fisheries and post offices as to the addition of "what many consider the most consequential part of the Constitution itself"?

The answer to all these questions would seem to be the same: the legislators who had just taken so much time and expended so much effort to add the amendments to the Constitution never con-sidered them "the most consequential part of the Constitution," and, by this time, neither did the general public. The opponents of the amendments thought they were useless or, even worse, harmful. The only amendments the Anti-Federalists considered consequential were the ones that they themselves had proposed and that the majority had successfully kept out of the Constitution. On the other side, the proponents of the amendments also did not think they were conse-quential, and said so consistently.

As for the general public, it is true that many of them had thought the omission of the amendments from the Constitution was consequential; that omission had in fact caused grave uneasiness among a substantial minority of the people. But Madison's speech to the House introducing the amendments, and their subsequent passage by both houses of Congress two years prior to their ratification, had relieved much if not all of the public's anxieties. By the time they were ratified, the amendments were the solution to a problem that had ceased to exist.

And so when, finally, the ratification of the Bill of Rights was officially announced, there were no great ceremonies, no glowing editorials, no passionate speeches, no grand parades, no fireworks lighting up the sky; there was nothing to indicate that anything had occurred that was more consequential than legislative acts concerning fisheries, fishermen, post offices, and post roads. The Bill of Rights slipped quietly into the Constitution and passed from sight and public consciousness until given a new and very different life by the Supreme Court more than a century later.[35]

Reflections on Part Three

Authors, typically, are not the best judges of their own writings; too often they have a higher opinion of their work than it deserves. But the opposite was the case with the authors of the Bill of Rights. The members of the First Congress, who worked so long, so diligently, so reluctantly to write the amendments, were severely critical of their own handiwork, and some were downright derisive. Those among them who had some few good words to say for the amendments praised them not for their intrinsic worth as an addition to the Constitution but only for some hoped-for beneficial effect they might have on public opinion. Edmund Pendleton thought they "will have a good effect in quieting the minds of many well meaning Citizens."[1] Others were equivocal; William Ellery didn't "think the amendments will do any hurt, and they may do some good, and therefore I don't consider them as of much importance."[2]

The Anti-Federalists, and the few other congressmen who voted with them against the amendments, were unanimous in their denunciations, as we would expect. Richard Henry Lee was scornful: "The english language has been carefully culled to find words feeble in their Nature or doubtful in their meaning!"[3] William Grayson described the amendments as "so mutilated & gutted that in fact they are good for nothing, & I believe as many others do, that they will do more harm than benefit."[4] Samuel Livermore said he knew his constituents "would not value them more than a pinch of snuff, they went to secure rights never in danger."[5] And Thomas Tudor Tucker denounced them as either a joke or a fraud: "You will find our Amendments to the Constitution calculated merely to amuse, or rather to deceive."[6]

In sum, the Anti-Federalist critics were unanimous in decrying the adequacy of the Bill of Rights. Some of the Federalists thought they were inconsequential; others thought they might have beneficial political consequences; but none praised them for intrinsic excellence.

On one point Federalists and Anti-Federalists were agreed: These amendments changed nothing in the Constitution. That was the complaint the Anti-Federalists made repeatedly, and that was why they voted against them. They voted "No" on the amendments primarily because adopting them meant rejecting other amendments, "those solid and substantial amendments" the Anti-Federalists wanted to add to the Constitution.[7] For the same reason—that they changed nothing in the Constitution—the Federalists voted for the amendments. For them, the best recommendation, perhaps the only recommendation, these amendments had was their usefulness in keeping those other amendments out of the Constitution and doing so without altering the original document.

The Transforming Power

But were the members of the First Congress right in their negative assessments? And were they right that these additions left the Constitution unchanged? The amendments had the effect of winning the allegiance of the doubters among the great mass of the people, of luring them away from the Anti-Federalist leaders and converting them to the cause of the Constitution. Could amendments not worth "a pinch of snuff," composed of "words feeble in their Nature," have had that transforming power?

If the amendments could so completely erase the profound uneasiness of a significant portion of the citizenry, does it not follow that there must be in them something that spoke with remarkable persuasiveness to the American mind and heart? Does not the fact that these particular provisions had such an immediate "effect in quieting the minds of many well meaning Citizens" tell us volumes about the significance of these new provisions, and also something about the American people, who were so strongly attracted and powerfully swayed by them? Is it not probable that the American people were won over by these amendments in large part because they saw the Constitution more, now, with the amendments, as *their* Constitution, as fitting their view of what constituted them as a people, the people who are credited by the words of the Preamble as the real Constitution makers?

We the People

The Preamble, as we have seen, begins as it does somewhat by accident, but once those opening words were promulgated and ratified, they took on a significance dear to the hearts of all.[8] "We the People of the United States," it announces with considerable rhetorical power, "do ordain and establish this Constitution for the United States of America." Thirty-nine signatures attest to the fact that a small group of extraordinary leaders had debated and deliberated and then written the document in the Constitutional Convention in Philadelphia. The work of those framers was indispensable, unquestionably, and there can be no pretense that the American people could have, somehow or other, concocted this Constitution without them. But the Framers knew all along that it was not in their power to bring the Constitution into effect, to make that transition from parchment to power, without the wholehearted endorsement of the great mass of the people. The signatures of the Framers could do no more than give witness to the emphatic, explicit, and ineradicable constitutional fact that only "the People of the United States" had the power to ordain and establish this Constitution.

But what else did the original Constitution tell us about "the People of the United States" other than that they were the true founders? The complete answer to that question is very short, and indisputable: it tells us absolutely nothing at all about them. After the first words of the Preamble, the original Constitution never again mentions "the People of the United States."[9] In sharp contrast to this silence, the Bill of Rights speaks of "the people" again and again. Perhaps therein lies a clue to the amazing power these amendments had in truly establishing the Constitution, in winning for it not just the acceptance but the devotion of the whole community. The people were included now, as an integral part of the Constitution, in a way they had not been before.

The People Article

The original Constitution is made up primarily of descriptions of the institutions it establishes and the powers vested in those institutions.

Article I is the Legislative Article, Article II the Executive Article, and Article III the Judicial Article. Each article defines and describes a branch of the government by enumerating the powers vested in it. But the unamended Constitution had no article dealing with the people and the powers vested in them, as individuals and as a people. The first ten amendments added that new article; it might justly be described as the People Article.

The Bill of Rights, considered as the People Article, is similar in structure to the first three articles of the Constitution. Just as those articles enumerate the respective powers of the three branches of government, so this new article enumerates the people's rights, each right analogous to a power delegated to the legislature, or the executive, or the judiciary.[10] One important difference, however, must be noted; the people's powers, their rights, are not delegated or granted. The first ten amendments do not speak of granting the rights of the people to the people; the amendments instead do no more than recognize and declare explicitly the existence of those rights, which were understood to exist before they were enumerated in the Constitution. In order to declare that the new government was denied the power to trifle with them, the existence of the rights had to be made formally explicit. But in doing so the government was not granting the rights, it was acknowledging them.

It is also important to understand that the Bill of Rights was not intended to be universal, but was constructed with a particular people in mind. It is true that the basic premise underlying the doctrine of natural rights is that rights are universal, that we are all equal in our rights, that we have rights simply because we are human beings. Spokesmen of the natural rights teaching, from John Locke to Abraham Lincoln, have always argued that although human beings may be very unequal in other respects, we are all equal in our rights.[11] As a consequence, there is an important difference, in this respect, between the Declaration of Independence and the Constitution, our two great founding documents. The Declaration speaks with the voice of "one people" addressing all "mankind" with its universal message of the equality of "all men" in their rights to "Life, Liberty and the pursuit of Happiness." But the Constitution, including the Bill of Rights, is addressed only to the American people. Whatever the relationship may be of the provisions of the Bill of Rights to natural rights, they are demonstrably applicable to a specific people, the American people, and cannot be understood as meant to be universal, however wise we may think them to be, and however beneficial we think it might be if other peoples were to adopt them.

Consider, for example, the first clause of the First Amendment, the Establishment Clause. It is uncommon, even among modern democratic nations, to insist that there shall be no established church. Among most of the less modern and more traditional peoples it is a decidedly unacceptable principle. Nations with one form or another of established church include such disparate populaces as those of England, Israel, and all the Islamic nations (with the partial exception of Turkey).

Furthermore, in many, perhaps in most countries, the rights of freedom of speech, of the press, and of assembly are set forth in their constitutions, but are so severely hedged and qualified as to nullify the protections in those extraordinary circumstances when they are most needed. The rights of the accused in criminal cases are also regarded very differently in most other countries. Legal protections enumerated in the Bill of Rights are not universally accepted, including trial by jury, speedy and public trials, the right to counsel, and more broadly, the emphasis given throughout that the powers of government officials are understood to be limited in very specific ways by the requirements of due process of law. In short, the Bill of Rights was quite specifically designed—tailored, one might say—to fit not all mankind but rather one specific people, the "People of the United States."

A Portrait of the People

If we regard the Bill of Rights as a verbal portrait of "the People of the United States," what do we see? Starting with the opening words of the First Amendment, we see that this is a people who takes religion very seriously, seriously enough to insist that all Americans be free to choose how they will worship, if they choose to worship at all; who cannot be required to follow governmental or any other sort of dictate in matters of religion, or be denied the right to follow ancient religious practice, if that is their choice; who will not seek to impose their religious beliefs or practices on others, or allow others to impose their beliefs on them. This is a people who will insist that their voices be heard, in speech and print; who will not hesitate to broadcast their own opinions, however unpopular, or to hear them from others, no matter how unwelcome they may be; who expect to have much to say about the governing of their nation; and who will gather together, if and when they so choose, to let the government know, peaceably but unmistakably, when they have grievances.

In addition, the opening words of the First Amendment, "Congress shall make no law," tell us that this is a people who, though fully committed to the principle of the rule of the majority, understands full well that the majority is not authorized to do whatever it may want; that there are certain things that the majority, as represented in Congress, is forbidden to legislate, by the authority of "the whole community," as expressed in the Constitution by "the People of the United States," which prevails over the majority whenever the majority may seek to violate the constitutional rights of the people.

The Second Amendment tells us that this is a sturdy, courageous, and self-sufficient people who insist that they shall not be denied the right to participate in their state's militia as disciplined, "well regulated" citizen-soldiers in the defense of their homes and families, not only for the fulfillment of their private concern for safety, but for "the security of a free State," and will not rely on others who are not of their community for their defense against foreign enemies.

The Third Amendment tells us that this is a people composed of many owners of private homes who, however hospitable they may be, have decided views about the limits of hospitality; who put a high value on the privacy of their private property, and therefore will not welcome uninvited house guests, especially not soldiers whom the executive authority may seek to impose on them, without their consent, in time of peace.

The Fourth Amendment tells us, with increased emphasis and specificity, about the extent of the domain of the people that is to be protected from incursion by law-enforcement officials or the judiciary. "Their persons, houses, papers, and effects" are *theirs*, and private, and officials must show "probable cause," properly sworn to, before even attempting to look at them, let alone seize them. In short, with respect to the many things that are none of the government's business, this is a people not to be trifled with.

The Fifth, Sixth, Seventh, and Eighth Amendments tell us that this is a law-respecting people who insist on living under laws only of their own choosing, laws they expect to protect them from the abuses of arbitrary executive and judicial powers, laws to be enforced fairly and within clear, preestablished limits; and who also insist on participating in judging and being judged by their peers; that is, they are a law-abiding people who acknowledge no superiors in matters of law, only equals.

The Ninth Amendment acknowledges that the people have

more rights than can ever be enumerated, because, both as individuals and as a community, they are more complex than can be depicted in a page or two of constitutional text. These rights are unenumerated because they are countless. In the early congressional debates only two were mentioned—the right to wear a hat or not and the right to go to bed and to rise when one chooses.[12] We can add many others that are certainly rights of considerable importance but that are not mentioned in the Constitution: the right to marry or to remain single; the right to have children, a dozen or more, or none at all; the right to own a house, or to be a renter, or to be a transient; the right to have a dog, or some other pet, or none; the right to own and drive an automobile, or to rely instead on public transportation, or to walk. The list, one can see, can be endless. The people have innumerable rights, and one must not think that because certain rights are enumerated that doubt is cast on other rights not enumerated; that is, as the Ninth Amendment tells us, enumerating certain rights "shall not be construed to deny or disparage others retained by the people." It must be added, however, that regulation of these unenumerated rights also does not deny or disparage them; that is, the burdens imposed by requiring persons to obtain marriage licenses, birth certificates, deeds to property, dog licenses, auto registrations and drivers' licenses do not deny or disparage unenumerated rights, even when, as sometimes happens, such licenses are denied for cause.

The conclusion of the People Article, the Tenth Amendment, is unique among the amendments because it speaks directly not of the rights of the people but of the powers of the people: "The powers not delegated to the United States" by the Constitution are "reserved . . . to the people."[13] This amendment asserts the full scope of the people as the originators of the Constitution, as the true source of all the powers of the government. The powers of the government were originally, naturally, the powers of the people, and have been delegated by them to the government through the instrument of this Constitution. That is what Madison meant when, in the Constitutional Convention, he spoke of the people as "the fountain of all power."[14] But not all the natural powers of the people have been delegated; many have been "reserved" to the people. And which powers have been delegated to the government and which have been reserved to the people cannot be known with crystal clarity because the word "expressly" was deliberately kept out of the text of the amendment. But one fact does emerge with full clarity from the last four words of the Bill of Rights: the body of constitution-making citizens it portrays is a citizenry with powers, a powerful people.

Are We That People?

The description of the people of the Constitution derived by reading the Bill of Rights as the People Article raises this question: What progress have we, the American people at the end of the twentieth century, made in becoming like that people of the Constitution? Madison persuaded himself, we must recall, at that critical turning point in his correspondence with Jefferson, that a bill of rights would be effective in developing in the people those traits of thought and action that could suppress or restrain an oppressive majority, should one arise to threaten the rights of the people:

> The political truths declared in that solemn manner ac-
> quire by degrees the character of fundamental maxims of
> free Government, and as they become incorporated with
> the national sentiment, counteract the impulses of interest
> and passion.[15]

Have the political truths declared in the Constitution and the Bill of Rights persisted as our "fundamental maxims of free government"? Have we absorbed them into the core of our national character? And most important, to what extent have those solemn truths been effective in counteracting "the impulses of interest and passion" in our national life? Those are necessary questions to ponder if we care about the future of American constitutionalism.

The people portrayed in the Bill of Rights are religious, tolerant, public spirited, self-sufficient, jealous of their rights and respectful of the rights of others, and responsibly conscious that they are "the fountain of all power" and therefore must use that power with prudent restraint. That is not a portrait many Americans of today would claim for ourselves. Despite this disparity between the wonderful people the Bill of Rights sets before us as a standard to which we ought to aspire and the reality of today's American people, I see little cause for pessimism. Even though no one can sensibly maintain that Madison's hope for a people steadily improved by the influence of the political truths of the Bill of Rights has been completely fulfilled, I would maintain that the Constitution has done and continues to do its formative work. It may be true that the Constitution suffers much abuse and distortion from judges, legal scholars, and self-serving litigants, but fortunately the Constitution is a sturdy structure, not at all fragile, and it retains very considerable power to shape us as a people. The American people never quite measure up to the expectations established for them by the Constitution, but it keeps pulling them upward, or at least seems always to keep them from sinking into the depths of tyranny or oppression. And to that extent, Madison has been justified.

Closing the Parenthesis

In the seminal essay that led me to write this book, the late Herbert Storing wrote that "The Bill of Rights provides a fitting close to the parenthesis around the Constitution that the Preamble opens."[16] He did not, unfortunately, explain the meaning of his "parenthesis" metaphor. My understanding of it is that by proclaiming in the Preamble the ordaining and establishing role of "the People of the United States," and then never again mentioning them anywhere in the text that follows, the unamended Constitution opened a theme of great consequence—the central role of the people themselves in the founding of their constitutional republic—and then left that theme woefully unfinished. The addition of the Bill of Rights provided that "fitting close" previously lacking, by telling us so much about the people for whom, and by whom, this Constitution was established, and making it abundantly clear not only what their rights are but also that they are the original source of all the constitutional powers.

As we have seen, Madison and his congressional colleagues did not alter anything in the original text when they added the Bill of Rights. They also did not introduce any new elements that were in tension or opposition to the principles of the original Constitution. But by adding an enumeration of the rights and powers of the people who made the Constitution, and thereby portraying a constitution-making people that would be worthy of the republic they founded, a citizenry that would be fit to sustain it for their posterity, they closed the parenthesis left open by the Framers, won the allegiance of the great mass of the people, and completed thereby, at long last, the making of the Constitution.

Notes

CONSTITUTION MAKING

1. Albert P. Blaustein, "The 162 National Constitutions—Latest Revision Dates," January 1, 1991 (unpublished). The late Professor Blaustein, editor of *Constitutions of the Countries of the World* (18 vols.), kept track of the dates of constitutional revisions in all countries.

2. "Les représentants du peuple Français, constitués en assemblée nationale, considérant que l'ignorance, l'oubli ou lé mépris des droits de l'homme sont les seules causes des malheurs publics et de la corruption des gouvernements." Decreed by the National Assembly during the sessions of August 20–26 and October 1, 1789, and accepted by the king on October 5.

3. Jean Foyer, "The Drafting of the French Constitution of 1958," and Francois Luchaire, "Commentary," in *Constitution Makers on Constitution Making: The Experience of Eight Nations*, ed. Robert A. Goldwin and Art Kaufman (Washington, D.C.: AEI Press, 1988), pp. 7–68.

4. Barry L. Strayer, "The Canadian Constitution and Diversity," and Robert C. Vipond, "Commentary," in *Forging Unity Out of Diversity: The Approaches of Eight Nations*, ed. Robert A. Goldwin, Art Kaufman, and William A. Schambra (Washington, D.C.: AEI Press, 1989), pp. 157–205.

5. Alexis de Tocqueville, "Author's Preface to the Twelfth Edition" (1848), *Democracy in America* (New York: Alfred A. Knopf, 1948), pp. cvi–cvii. Despite Tocqueville's advice and efforts, the Second Republic was short-lived, from 1848 to 1851.

6. Michael Shaara, *The Killer Angels* (New York: Ballantine Books, 1974), p. xiii.

7. Jack N. Rakove, *James Madison and the Creation of the American Republic* (Glenview, Ill.: Scott Foresman/Little, Brown Higher Education, 1990), pp. ix, x.

8. *Burke's Politics: Selected Writings and Speeches of Edmund Burke on Reform, Revolution, and War*, ed. Ross J. S. Hoffman and Paul Levack (New York: Alfred A. Knopf, 1949), pp. 379–80.

9. Madison to Jefferson, October 17, 1788, in *The Roots of the Bill of Rights*, ed. Bernard Schwartz (New York: Chelsea House Publishers, 1971), vol. III, p. 614. Emphasis added.

10. Plutarch, *The Lives of the Noble Grecians and Romans* (New York: The Modern Library, n.d.), pp. 49–74, 97–117.

11. Jack N. Rakove, "The Road to Philadelphia, 1781–1787," in *The Framing and Ratification of the Constitution*, ed. Leonard W. Levy and Dennis J. Mahoney (New York: Macmillan Publishing Co., 1987), pp. 98–111.

CHAPTER 1: PHILADELPHIA

1. Resolution of Congress, February 21, 1787: "Resolved that in the opinion of Congress it is expedient that on the second Monday in May next a Convention of delegates who have been appointed by the several states be held at Philadelphia." *Documents Illustrative of the Formation of the Union of the American States*, ed. Charles C. Tansill (Washington, D.C.: Government Printing Office, 1927), p. 46.

2. In the course of discussion, in the Constitutional Convention, June 16, 1787, James Wilson of Pennsylvania described the power of the convention as "authorized to conclude nothing," but "at liberty to propose any thing." *The Records of the Federal Convention of 1787*, ed. Max Farrand, Revised Edition in 4 vols. (New Haven, Conn.: Yale University Press, 1937), vol. I, p. 253.

3. James Madison, in debate in the House of Representatives, April 6, 1796: "As the instrument came from them [the delegates of the Constitutional Convention], it was nothing more than the draught of a plan, nothing but a dead letter, until life and validity were breathed into it, by the voice of the people, speaking through the several state conventions." Quoted in Jack N. Rakove, *Original Meanings: Politics and Ideas in the Making of the Constitution* (New York: Alfred A. Knopf, 1996), p. 362.

4. Articles of Confederation, Article XIII, in Tansill, *Documents*, p. 35.

5. On March 24, 1788, in a statewide referendum, voters in Rhode Island rejected ratification of the Constitution by a vote of 2,711 to 239. Two years later, when all the other states had ratified and the Constitution was established, the Rhode Island convention finally ratified, grudgingly and narrowly, 34 to 32. John P. Kaminski, "Rhode Island," in *Ratifying the Constitution*, ed. Michael Allen Gillespie and Michael Lienesch (Lawrence, Kans.: University Press of Kansas, 1989), pp. 379, 385.

6. Report of Proceedings in Congress, Feb. 21, 1787, in Tansill, *Documents*, p. 46.

7. In *Federalist* No. 40, Madison asserted that the instructions to the convention contained an extensive end—to frame a new government, adequate to the exigencies of government and preservation of the Union. But those same instructions gave the delegates limited means to achieve that end—revising and altering the Articles of Confederation. He argued that when the means and the end conflict, "the less important should give way to the more important part; the means should be sacrificed to the end, rather than the end to the means." Alexander Hamilton, James Madison, John Jay, *The Federalist Papers*, ed. Clinton Rossiter (New York: New American Library, 1961), p. 248.

8. Edmund C. Burnett, "Our Union of States in the Making," lecture, Washington, D.C.: Carnegie Institution of Washington, 1935.

9. Farrand, *Records*, vol. II, pp. 555–56.

10. Ibid., p. 665.

11. In many printings of the Constitution it is unclear whether the final sentence of the Constitution, starting with the words "Done in Convention by the Unanimous Consent of the States present," is part of Article VII, or whether it should be understood to stand alone. I take the latter position, that the sentence quoted, about ratification by nine states, is the whole of Article VII, bolstered by the authority of Philip B. Kurland and Ralph Lerner, eds., *The Founders' Constitution* (Chicago: University of Chicago Press, 1987), vol. IV, p. 647.

12. Farrand, *Records*, vol. II, p. 561.

13. Ibid., p. 562.

14. Ibid.

15. Ibid., p. 475.

16. Ibid., p. 476.

17. Ibid.

18. George Graham, "Pennsylvania," in Gillespie and Lienesch, *Ratifying the Constitution*, p. 63.

19. Farrand, *Records*, vol. II, p. 632.

20. Ibid., pp. 645–46.

21. Ibid., p. 479.

22. Ibid., p. 563.

23. Ibid., pp. 587–88.

24. Ibid., p. 588.

25. On the question of the importance of this provision in Mason's mind, see note 13 in chapter 3.

26. Farrand, *Records*, vol. II, p. 631.

27. Ibid., p. 632.

28. Ibid., p. 633.

29. Ibid., p. 645.

30. All these remarks were made on September 17, the final day of the convention, with the exception of Mason's (which he uttered on August 31). Ibid., pp. 645–46.

31. Ibid., p. 632.

32. Ibid., p. 645.

CHAPTER 2: NEW YORK

1. *Journals of the Continental Congress 1774–1789*, ed. Roscoe R. Hill, from the original records in the Library of Congress (Washington, D.C.: United States Government Printing Office, 1936), vol. XXXIII, p. 549.

2. *Letters of the Members of the Continental Congress*, ed. Edmund C. Burnett (Washington, D.C.: Carnegie Institution of Washington, 1936), vol. VIII, p. 660.

3. Ibid., William Grayson to William Short, April 16, 1787, pp. 580–81.

4. Ibid., "The North Carolina Delegates to the North Carolina General Assembly," December 15, 1787, p. 689.

5. Ibid., p. 635. In a circular letter to the state governors, dated August 10, 1787, the secretary of Congress wrote: "Since the first Monday in November last

the United States have not been represented more than three days by 10 states, thirty days by nine states, and forty days by 7 and 8 states."

6. Edmund C. Burnett, *The Continental Congress* (New York: W. W. Norton & Co., Inc., 1964), p. 693.

7. Ibid., p. 695; Richard Henry Lee to John Adams, September 5, 1787.

8. Ten members of the Continental Congress, nearly one-third of the entire body, had been delegates to the convention: John Langdon and Nicholas Gilman, New Hampshire; Nathaniel Gorham and Rufus King, Massachusetts; William Samuel Johnson, Connecticut; Madison, Virginia; William Blount, North Carolina; Pierce Butler, South Carolina; and William Few and William Leigh Pierce, Georgia. Clinton Rossiter, *1787: The Grand Convention* (New York: W. W. Norton & Co., Inc., 1987), p. 275.

9. Burnett, *Letters,* vol. VIII, p. 651; James Madison to George Washington, New York, September 30, 1787.

10. Ibid., p. 658. Richard Henry Lee to the governor of Virginia (Edmund Randolph). Lee emphasized this point in letters to others he hoped would join with him in opposing ratification of the unamended Constitution. To George Mason (October 1, 1787; ibid., pp. 652–53), he wrote, "They found it most eligible at last to transmit it merely without approving or disapproving provided nothing but the transmission should appear on the journal. This compromise was settled and they took the opportunity of inserting the word unanimously, which applies only to simple transmission, hoping to have it mistaken for an unanimous approbation of the thing. It states Congress having received the Constitution unanimously transmit it etc. It is certain that no approbation was given . . . ." And to Samuel Adams (October 5, 1787; ibid., p. 654), he wrote, "You will have been informed by other hands why these amendments were not considered and so not appear on the Journal, and the reasons that influenced a bare *transmission* of the Convention plan, without a syllable of approbation or disapprobation on the part of Congress."

11. Ibid., p. 660; Edward Carrington to Thomas Jefferson, New York, October 23, 1787.

12. Ibid., p. 662; James Madison to Thomas Jefferson, New York, October 24, 1787. In his previous letter to Washington on September 30, Madison had acknowledged that instead of mere transmittal, "a more direct approbation would have been of advantage in New York and some other states," but he concluded by emphasizing his expectation that unanimity would prove more useful because "the circumstances of unanimity must be favorable everywhere."

13. John P. Kaminski, "A Revolution in Favor of Government: The Ratification of the United States Constitution," lecture brochure (Collegeville, Minn.: Saint John's University, 1987), p. 9; Washington to Madison, October 10, 1787.

CHAPTER 3: THE STATES

1. George J. Graham, Jr., "Pennsylvania: Representation and the Meaning of Republicanism," in *Ratifying the Constitution*, ed. Michael Allen Gillespie and Michael Lienesch (Lawrence, Kans.: University Press of Kansas, 1989), p. 58.

2. Michael Allen Gillespie, "Massachusetts: Creating Consensus," in ibid., pp. 142–44.

3. Ibid., p. 147.

4. Edward P. Smith, "The Movement towards a Second Constitutional Convention in 1788," in *Essays in the Constitutional History of the United States in the Formative Period, 1775–1789*, ed. J. Franklin Jameson (Boston and New York: Houghton, Mifflin, and Company, 1889), p. 72.

5. Ibid.

6. Jackson Turner Main, *The Antifederalists: Critics of the Constitution, 1781–1788* (New York: W. W. Norton and Co., 1974), p. 204.

7. John P. Kaminski, "A Revolution in Favor of Government: The Ratification of the United States Constitution," lecture brochure (Collegeville, Minn.: Saint John's University, 1987), p. 10.

8. Ibid., pp. 10–11. Hancock had many detractors. Madison was certainly not one of his admirers. In a letter to Jefferson evaluating several possible vice presidential candidates, Madison wrote (October 17, 1788) that "Hancock is weak ambitious a courtier of popularity given to low intrigue." This sentence in Madison's letter was written in secret code and decoded interlinearly by Jefferson.

9. Edward Smith, and other historians, suggest that Hancock stayed away from the convention until it became apparent which side would prevail, and then jumped on the bandwagon. Only when "he had begun to fear that the Constitution might be carried in opposition to his opinion" did Hancock decide to appear at the convention in favor of ratification. Smith, "Movement towards a Second Convention," p. 76.

Michael Allen Gillespie disputes this account. "This explanation is dubious, because even with Hancock's considerable support, ratification was not assured." A more probable explanation, according to Gillespie, is that Hancock "waited until the most opportune moment to present his proposal for a modified ratification." "Massachusetts," in Gillespie and Lienesch, *Ratifying the Constitution*, p. 152.

10. "The support of Samuel Adams and John Hancock was crucial to the ratification of the Constitution in Massachusetts. . . . In contrast to the conventional wisdom, the success of the Constitution at this crucial juncture was thus due, not to the youth and vigor of the Federalists, but to the wisdom of two old patriots. Their success was largely the result of their belief in a politics of consensus, which suggested to them an alternative between simple ratification and outright rejection. The conciliatory proposition that they presented, however, was not a compromise between two competing views but a concrete proposal that rested on a comprehensive conception of the appropriate character of a good regime." Ibid., p. 161.

11. "To sympathize with southern feelings, which were nowhere more acute than in Virginia, we must realize that as of 1786, the West was everywhere perceived as an extension of the South. Western settlement was still almost exclusively on lands southwest of the Ohio. Settlers in Kentucky or in Tennessee were often literally the kin or former neighbors of important southern families, and a great deal more than family ties and family fortunes seemed at stake in their continued membership in the American union. For years, Virginians had identi-

fied the economic future of their commonwealth with improvements that would make the Chesapeake the entrepot for European imports to the West. More recently, as population had moved increasingly into the old Southwest, it had become increasingly apparent that admission to the Union of new southwestern states could fundamentally affect the federal balance, guaranteeing southern dominance within the federation or assuring the emergence of a national majority whose agricultural character and interest would accord with Virginia's republican ideals. All of this seemed threatened by the Jay-Gardoqui treaty." Lance Banning, "Virginia," in ibid., p. 265.

12. Just prior to the convening of the Constitutional Convention, Madison wrote to Jefferson (March 10, 1787), mostly in their secret code, that "The *Spanish project sleeps*. . . . A late accidental conversation with *Guardoqui proved to me* that *the negociation is arrested*. . . . [A]lthough it appears that the intended *sacrifice of* the *Mississippi will not be made, the consequences of the intention* and the *attempt are likely to be very serious*. . . . Mr. *Henry's disgust exceeded all measure* and I am not singular in ascribing his refusal to *attend the [Constitutional] Convention* to the *policy of keeping himself free to combat or espouse the result of it according* to the result *of the Mississippi business*. . . ." *Letters of the Members of the Continental Congress,* ed. Edmund C. Burnett, (Washington, D.C.: Carnegie Institution of Washington, 1936), vol. VIII, p. 561. (Underlined words were written in code by Madison and decoded interlinearly by Jefferson.)

13. Oliver Ellsworth, a delegate to the Constitutional Convention from Connecticut, was skeptical that the absence of a bill of rights in the Constitution was Mason's chief reason for withholding his signature. He contended that Mason had refused to sign the Constitution only because his motion for a two-thirds majority on navigation acts had failed to pass and that the rest of his objections were window-dressing. Frank Donovan, *Mr. Madison's Constitution: The Story Behind the Constitutional Convention* (New York: Dodd, Mead & Co., 1965), p. 100.

14. Banning, "Virginia," in Gillespie and Lienesch, *Ratifying the Constitution,* p. 263 ff.

15. Ibid., p. 263.

16. Smith, "Movement towards a Second Convention," p. 61; Forrest McDonald, *E Pluribus Unum: The Formation of the American Republic, 1776–1795* (Indianapolis: Liberty Press, 1979), p. 340.

17. Smith, "Movement towards a Second Convention," p. 87.

18. Ibid., pp. 89–90. Forrest McDonald suggests less lofty reasons for Randolph's switch: "Exactly who converted Randolph to Federalism—or how or when—no one knows. That Washington, Madison, and John Marshall tried to convert him is known. So also are some facts that suggest the means of conversion: that Randolph's objections were doctrinaire, and thus subject to persuasive reasoning; that he was financially embarrassed in 1788 and emerged in 1790 on solid footing and as the holder of more than $10,000 in public securities; that he was politically ambitious and emerged in 1789 as the first attorney general of the United States." McDonald, *E Pluribus Unum,* pp. 339–40.

19. Smith, "Movement towards a Second Convention," p. 90.

20. Ibid., p. 93.

21. Ibid., p. 95.

22. Ibid., p. 96.

23. Ibid., p. 97.

24. Washington to Hamilton, August 28, 1788, in Bernard Schwartz, ed., *The Roots of the Bill of Rights* (New York: Chelsea House Publishers, 1980), vol. IV, p. 927.

REFLECTIONS, PART ONE

1. There is a widespread misconception that the Swiss constitution is the world's oldest. The Swiss confederation celebrates its birthday as the first of August 1291, but the document establishing it was not a constitution, but rather a treaty of mutual defense among several small sovereign cantons. The first Swiss constitution was adopted in 1848. A new Swiss federal constitution, adopted in 1874, is still in force today, although it has been amended more than one hundred times. Otto K. Kaufmann, "Swiss Federalism," in Robert A. Goldwin, Art Kaufman, and William A. Schambra, eds., *Forging Unity Out of Diversity: The Approaches of Eight Nations* (Washington, D. C.: AEI Press, 1989), pp. 206–8.

CHAPTER 4: WHAT USE CAN A BILL OF RIGHTS SERVE?

1. Madison to George Eve, January 2, 1789, in *The Papers of James Madison,* ed. Robert A. Rutland, et al. (Charlottesville: University Press of Virginia, 1977), vol. XI, pp. 404–5. A subsequent campaign letter, entitled "To a Resident of Spotsylvania County," January 27, 1789, making the same arguments, was printed in the Fredericksburg, Virginia, *Herald,* January 29, 1789, with a heading, "Extract of a letter from the Hon. James Madison, jun. to his friend in this county." Ibid., pp. 428–29. Madison won the statewide election handily, but he did not carry Spotsylvania County, the home county of James Monroe, his opponent in the election.

2. Madison to Jefferson, October 24, 1787, in Bernard Schwartz, ed., *The Roots of the Bill of Rights* (New York: Chelsea House Publishers, 1980), vol. III, pp. 593–605.

3. Ibid., p. 601.

4. Ibid., p. 598.

5. Francis Canavan, "A New Fourteenth Amendment," in *The Human Life Review,* Winter 1986, vol. XII, no. 1, p. 38. The concluding section of the Fourteenth Amendment (section 5) stipulates that "The Congress shall have power to enforce, by appropriate legislation, the provisions of this article."

6. Schwartz, *The Roots,* vol. III, p. 616.

7. Ibid., p. 621; Jefferson to Madison, March 15, 1789.

8. Ibid., p. 615; Madison to Jefferson, October 17, 1788.

9. Ibid., p. 621; Jefferson to Madison, March 15, 1789.

10. Ibid., p. 606; Jefferson to Madison, December 20, 1787.

11. Ibid., p. 607.

12. Ibid., p. 609; Jefferson to William Stephens Smith, February 2, 1788.

Jefferson conveyed the same message in letters to Alexander Donald on February 7, 1788, and to C. W. F. Dumas, February 12, 1788.

13. Jefferson to Edward Carrington, May 27, 1788: "My first wish was that 9 states would adopt it in order to ensure what was good in it, & that the others might, by holding off, produce the necessary amendments. But the plan of Massachusetts is far preferable, and will I hope be followed by those who are yet to decide." Stephen L. Schechter and Richard B. Bernstein, eds., *Contexts of the Bill of Rights* (Albany: New York State Commission on the Bicentennial of the United States Constitution, 1990), p. 29.

In a subsequent letter, to Francis Hopkinson, March 13, 1789, Jefferson added this comment: "But I was corrected in this wish the moment I saw the much better plan of Massachusetts and which had never occurred to me." Schwartz, *The Roots*, vol. III, p. 619.

14. Ibid., p. 615; Madison to Jefferson, October 17, 1788.

15. Ibid.

16. Lance Banning, for example, calls this assertion of Madison's "as disingenuous . . . as he ever was about a previous political position." *The Sacred Fire of Liberty: James Madison and the Founding of the Federal Republic* (Ithaca, N.Y.: Cornell University Press, 1995), p. 281. Banning adds (p. 283) that "Except for the remark that he had always been in favor of a declaration, Madison's reply to Jefferson was candid."

Herbert Storing, however, sees no lack of candor in the remark: "The significant fact is not that Madison came to favor a bill of rights—he said truthfully that he had always favored it under the right circumstances. What is significant is the time he chose to move for a bill of rights, the kinds of rights protected, and the form the Bill of Rights took." "The Constitution and the Bill of Rights," in *How Does the Constitution Secure Rights?*, ed. Robert A. Goldwin and William A. Schambra (Washington, D.C.: AEI Press, 1985), p. 29. This essay was originally published in *Essays on the Constitution of the United States*, ed. M. Judd Harmon (Port Washington, N.Y.: Kennikat Press, 1978), and has since been reprinted in *Toward a More Perfect Union: Writings of Herbert J. Storing*, ed. Joseph Bessette (Washington, D.C.: AEI Press, 1995).

17. Schwartz, *The Roots*, vol. III, p. 615.

18. Ibid., p. 616.

19. Ibid.

20. Ibid.

21. Ibid., pp. 598–99. Madison to Jefferson, October 24, 1787.

22. Ibid., p. 599.

23. Ibid.

24. Ibid.

25. Ibid., pp. 599–600.

26. Ibid., p. 600.

27. According to Max Farrand, the eminent editor of *The Records of the Federal Convention*, Madison was "unquestionably the leading spirit" in the achievement of the convention; "Madison," of all the delegates to the convention, "stands pre-eminent"; "Madison's ideas were the predominating factor in the framing of the constitution." But then, along with this unstinting praise of Madison,

Farrand adds: "He seems to have lacked imagination, but this very lack made his work of peculiar value at the moment. His remedies for the unsatisfactory state of affairs under the Confederation, were not founded on theoretical speculations, they were practical." *The Framing of the Constitution of the United States* (New Haven, Conn.: Yale University Press, 1913), pp. 196, 198. Farrand's inability to appreciate the power of Madison's combining mind, his talent for deriving practical "remedies" from "theoretical speculations," seems inexplicable in the light of the kind of reasoning Madison displayed in his contributions to *The Federalist* and in his correspondence with Jefferson, especially in "this immoderate digression."

28. Schwartz, *The Roots*, vol. III, p. 617.

29. Article I, sec. 9, clause 2.

30. Article I, sec. 8, clause 8. It is noteworthy that this is the only place in the original Constitution where the word "right" occurs. Robert A. Goldwin, "How the Constitution Promotes Progress," in *Why Blacks, Women, and Jews Are Not Mentioned in the Constitution* (Washington, D.C.: AEI Press, 1990), pp. 37–41.

31. Schwartz, *The Roots*, vol. III, p. 618.

32. Ibid., p. 616.

33. For example, the Singapore Constitution proclaims in Article 14, Clause 1, Part A, that "every citizen has the right of freedom of speech and expression," but then, in effect, nullifies this right by adding that "Parliament may by law impose on these rights such restrictions as it deems necessary or expedient in the interest of the security of Singapore."

34. Article 352 of the Indian Constitution enabled the president of India, at the request of Prime Minister Indira Gandhi, to declare a state of emergency in June 1975, which lasted until December 1977. During more than two years, emergency restrictions were imposed on the press. Both Indian and foreign journalists were subjected to fines and imprisonment for publishing anything objectionable or embarrassing to the government or likely to bring "hatred or contempt or excite disaffection toward the government and thereby cause or tend to cause public disorder."

35. Schwartz, *The Roots*, vol. III, p. 616.

36. Ibid.

37. Ibid.

38. Rossiter, *Federalist* No. 51, p. 324.

CHAPTER 5: TO INTRODUCE THE GREAT WORK

1. Robert A. Rutland, "How the Constitution Protects Our Rights: A Look at the Seminal Years," in *How Does the Constitution Secure Rights?*, ed. Robert A. Goldwin and William A. Schambra (Washington, D.C.: AEI Press, 1985), p. 3.

2. Madison to Jefferson, October 17, 1788, in Bernard Schwartz, ed., *The Roots of the Bill of Rights* (New York: Chelsea House Publishers, 1980), vol. III, p. 615.

3. The Continental Congress designated March 4, 1789, for the convening of the First Congress, but the two houses of Congress did not have a quorum present until April 6. Schwartz, *The Roots*, vol. V, p. 1,012.

4. Ibid., p. 1,015.

5. "Although the term *committee* commonly implies a relatively small number of persons appointed to give a task more detailed attention than is possible in a body the size of the assembly, . . . an assembly can also designate all of its members present to act as a committee, which is called a *committee of the whole*. In large assemblies, the use of a committee of the whole is a convenient method of considering a question when it is desired to allow each member to speak an unlimited number of times in debate." "In a committee of the whole, the results of votes taken are not final decisions of the assembly, but have the status of recommendations which the assembly is given the opportunity to consider further and which it votes on finally under its regular rules." However, "even though the committee consists of the entire body of members in attendance at the assembly's meeting, it is technically not 'the assembly.'" General Henry M. Robert, *Robert's Rules of Order* (Glenview, Ill.: Scott, Foresman and Co., 1970), pp. 406–7, 443, 444.

6. Schwartz, *The Roots*, vol. V, p. 1,016.

7. Ibid., p. 1,018.

8. Ibid., p. 1,020.

9. Ibid., p. 1,021.

10. Ibid., p. 1,022.

11. Ibid. Except as noted, all the quotations in this section are taken from pp. 1,024–26.

12. Ralph A. Rossum, "*The Federalist*'s Understanding of the Constitution as a Bill of Rights," in *Saving the Revolution*, ed. Charles R. Kessler (New York: The Free Press, 1987), pp. 219–33.

13. Shortly before the First Congress began its sessions, Madison wrote to Jefferson, predicting that "with regard to the Constitution . . . the disaffected party" would be a very small minority. He then continued, "Notwithstanding this character of the Body, I hope and expect that some conciliatory sacrifices will be made, in order to extinguish opposition to the system, or at least break the force of it, by detaching the deluded opponents from their designing leaders." Madison to Jefferson, March 29, 1789. *The Papers of James Madison*, ed. Charles F. Hobson, Robert A. Rutland, William M. E. Rachal, and Jeanne K. Sisson (Charlottesville, Va.: University Press of Virginia, 1979), vol. XII, p. 38.

14. Madison's proposal dealing with excessive bail (now the Eighth Amendment) passed through five stages of deliberation without having one word altered: "Excessive bail shall not be required, nor excessive fines imposed, nor cruel and unusual punishments inflicted."

An example of Madison's proposals that received some slight modification is, "No soldier shall in time of peace be quartered in any house without the consent of the owner, nor at any time, but in a manner to be prescribed by law." The final form (now the Third Amendment) was, "No soldier shall, in time of peace be quartered in any house, without the consent of the owner, nor in time of war, but in a manner to be prescribed by law."

What is now the Ninth Amendment was proposed by Madison in these words: "The exceptions here or elsewhere in the constitution, made in favor of particular rights, shall not be construed as to diminish the just importance of other rights, retained by the people, or as to enlarge the powers delegated by the constitution; but either as actual limitations of such powers, or as inserted merely for greater caution." It was completely reworded as follows: "The enumeration in the Constitution of certain rights, shall not be construed to deny or disparage others retained by the people."

15. Schwartz, *The Roots*, vol. V, pp. 1,026–28.

16. Herbert J. Storing, "The Constitution and the Bill of Rights," in *How Does the Constitution Secure Rights?* ed. Robert A. Goldwin and William A. Schambra (Washington, D.C.: AEI Press, 1985), p. 22.

17. Except as noted, all citations in this section are taken from Schwartz, *The Roots*, vol. V, pp. 1,026–28.

18. The fact that Madison could not find an appropriate place to insert the Tenth Amendment suggests that it is, more than the other amendments, truly an addition of something that was absent in the original Constitution.

19. In almost all printings, this heading is included as if a valid part of the Constitution, but it was not voted on and ratified by the states.

20. For discussion of the importance of negative and imperative provisions in a bill of rights, see Robert A. Goldwin, *Why Blacks, Women, and Jews Are Not Mentioned in the Constitution* (Washington, D.C.: AEI Press, 1990), pp. 4, 70–71, 89–90.

21. Schwartz, *The Roots*, vol. V, p. 1,026.

22. Storing, in *How Does the Constitution*, p. 33.

23. *Popular Sources of Political Authority: Documents of the Massachusetts Constitution of 1780*, ed. Oscar and Mary Handlin (Cambridge, Mass.: Belknap Press of Harvard University, 1966), pp. 442–47.

24. "To promote their happiness and to secure the good order and preservation of their government, the people of this Commonwealth have a right to invest their legislature with power to authorize and require, and the legislature shall, from time to time, authorize and require, the several towns, parishes, precincts, and other bodies-politic, or religious societies, to make suitable provision, at their own expense, for the institution of the public worship of God, and for the support and maintenance of public protestant teachers of piety, religion, and morality, in all cases where such provision shall not be made voluntarily."

"And every denomination of christians, demeaning themselves peaceably, and as good subjects of the Commonwealth, shall be equally under the protection of the law: And no subordination of any one sect or denomination to another shall ever be established by law." Ibid., pp. 442–43.

25. All the citations in this section are taken from Schwartz, *The Roots*, vol. V, pp. 1,026–33.

26. Ibid., p. 1,029.

27. Ibid., p. 1,027.

28. Ibid., p. 1,028.

Reflections, Part Two

1. Rutland, "Our Rights," in Goldwin, *How Does the Constitution Secure Rights*, pp. 1–4.

2. Schwartz, *The Roots*, vol. III, p. 616. Madison to Jefferson, October 17, 1788.

3. Ibid., p. 600. Madison to Jefferson, October 24, 1787.

4. Alexander Hamilton, James Madison, John Jay, *The Federalist Papers*, ed. Clinton Rossiter (New York: New American Library, 1961), p. 323.

5. Ibid., pp. 323–24.

6. Ibid., pp. 324–25.

7. Schwartz, *The Roots*, vol. III, p. 617. Madison to Jefferson, October 17, 1788.

8. Rossiter, *Federalist* No. 84, p. 515.

Chapter 6: Rats and Anti-Rats

1. Bernard Schwartz, ed., *The Roots of the Bill of Rights* (New York: Chelsea House Publishers, 1980), vol. V, p. 1,034.

2. *The Papers of James Madison*, ed. Charles F. Hobson, Robert A. Rutland, William M. E. Rachal, and Jeanne K. Sisson (Charlottesville, Va.: University Press of Virginia, 1979), vol. XII, p. 219.

3. See Madison's letters to Samuel Johnston and Edmund Pendleton, June 21, 1789; and letters to Madison from Joseph Jones, June 24, Edward Stevens, June 25, and Edmund Randolph, June 30; in ibid., pp. 249–50, 251–53, 258–60, 261, 273–74.

4. Tench Coxe to Madison, June 18, 1789. Coxe went on in this letter to inform Madison that he had submitted "short papers" for publication in support of the proposed amendments. His "Remarks on the . . . Amendments to the Federal Constitution" appeared in the Philadelphia *Federal Gazette*, June 18 and June 30. He also spoke of getting them reprinted in papers in New York state. By June 24 Madison was able to inform Coxe that his printed remarks had already appeared "in the Gazettes here" in New York and that he was "indebted to the co-operation of your pen." Ibid., pp. 239–41 and 257.

5. Edward Stevens to Madison, June 25, 1789. Ibid., p. 261.

6. Schwartz, *The Roots*, vol. V, p. 1,050.

7. For the account of the proceedings throughout August 13, see ibid., pp. 1062–75.

8. Great significance was ascribed to *We the people of the United States* in several state ratifying conventions, especially in Virginia, as well as in this congressional debate. In the Constitutional Convention, the first draft of the Preamble, prepared by the Committee of Detail, began by listing the states from north to south: "We the people of the states of New Hampshire, Massachusetts [and so forth, until Georgia]." The opening of the Preamble remained in that form until the Committee of Style changed it to *We the people of the United States*. Nothing in the record of the proceedings of the convention explains the change, but the reasons for deleting the list of the states seem obvious. No one could be sure that all the states would ratify the Constitution, and it would be imprudent and insulting to state legislators to take them for granted, to assume that the ratification deliberations were simply a formality, as if the states had no choice but to vote for ratification. Furthermore, such a list of states would quickly have become an embarrassment as new states were admitted to the Union.

9. For the account of the debate throughout August 14, see Schwartz, *The Roots*, vol. V, pp. 1,076–87.

10. Herbert J. Storing, "The Constitution and the Bill of Rights," in *How Does the Constitution Secure Rights?* ed. Robert A. Goldwin and William A. Schambra (Washington, D.C.: AEI Press, 1985), pp. 30–33.

11. Later in the deliberations, the question was raised whether amendments, in the committee of the whole, required a two-thirds majority for passage, or whether a simple majority sufficed. The chairman ruled that a simple majority was enough in committee, but two-thirds would be required in the voting in the House itself, as required by Article V. The narrow majorities for some of the proposed articles, as in the case of the pre-Preamble, foretold difficulties in the next stage in the proceedings.

12. "No law varying the compensation for the services of the Senators and Representatives shall take effect, until an election of Representatives shall have intervened." Only six states ratified this amendment by the end of 1791; one more state ratified it in 1873, and another in 1978. But then in the 1980s a campaign was mounted to win the ratification of the necessary thirty additional states. Between April 1983 and May 1992, thirty-one states ratified it and, despite the lack of "contemporary consensus," it became the 27th Amendment. The amendment does not prohibit congressmen from voting themselves a pay raise, but it does require incumbents who voted for the increase to face the electorate before they can begin to collect it. If an incumbent loses his bid for re-election, the victorious challenger is entitled to collect the new, higher salary.

13. For the account of the debate throughout August 15, see Schwartz, *The Roots*, vol. V, pp. 1,087–1107.

14. Gillespie, "Massachusetts," in *Ratifying the Constitution*, ed. Michael Allen Gillespie and Michael Lienesch (Lawrence, Kans.: University Press of Kansas, 1989), pp. 148–49.

15. Gerry's view seemed to be that the Constitution had to be either federal or national. Madison had a more complex understanding of the Constitution. He treated this question at length in *Federalist* No. 39, concluding that the Constitution "is, in strictness, neither a national nor a federal Constitution, but a composition of both. In its foundation it is federal, not national; in the sources from which the ordinary powers of the government are drawn, it is partly federal and partly national; in the operation of these powers, it is national, not federal; in the extent of them, again, it is federal, not national; and, finally in the authoritative mode of introducing amendments, it is neither wholly federal nor wholly national." Alexander Hamilton, James Madison, John Jay, *The Federalist Papers*, ed. Clinton Rossiter (New York: New American Library, 1961), p. 246.

16. See John Locke, *Two Treatises of Government* (Cambridge: Cambridge University Press, 1960), Book II, chapter 13, sec. 149, pp. 384–85: "Though in a Constituted Commonwealth . . . there can be but one Supream Power, which is the Legislative, . . . yet the Legislative being only a Fiduciary Power to act for certain ends, there remains still in the People a Supream Power to remove or alter the Legislative, when they find the Legislative act contrary to the trust reposed in them. . . . And thus the Community may be said in this respect to be always the Supream Power, but not as considered under any Form of Government, because this Power of the People can never take place till the Government be dissolved."

The Lockean paradox of two "supreme" powers is explained in my chapter

"John Locke," in *History of Political Philosophy*, ed. Leo Strauss and Joseph Cropsey (Chicago: University of Chicago Press, Third Edition, 1987), p. 501.

17. Sillabub, according to the Oxford English Dictionary, is a drink or dish made of milk, curdled by the admixture of wine, cider, or other acid, and then sweetened or flavored; figuratively, it means "something unsubstantial and frothy, especially floridly vapid discourse or writing."

18. "Seamen have a custom, when they meet a whale, to fling him out an empty tub by way of amusement, to divert him from laying violent hands upon the ship." Jonathan Swift, *Tale of a Tub*, as quoted in Kenneth R. Bowling, *"A Tub to the Whale": The Founding Fathers and Adoption of the Federal Bill of Rights* (Virginia Commission on the Bicentennial of the United States Constitution, 1988), p. 1.

19. Cox v. Louisiana, 379 U.S. 559 (1965).

20. Texas v. Johnson, 491 U.S. 397 (1989).

21. Barnes v. Glen Theater, 501 U.S. 560 (1991).

22. Jefferson to Madison, Aug. 28, 1789. *Papers of James Madison*, vol. XII, p. 363. Emphasis in the original.

23. See note 11 above.

CHAPTER 7: SOLID AMENDMENTS DEFEATED

1. For the account of the debate throughout August 17, see Bernard Schwartz, ed., *The Roots of the Bill of Rights* (New York: Chelsea House Publishers, 1980), vol. V, pp. 1,107–20.

2. For fuller discussion of this view of the subject matter of the Second Amendment, see Robert A. Goldwin, "Gun Control Is Constitutional," *The Wall Street Journal*, December 12, 1991, and Garry Wills, "To Keep and Bear Arms," *The New York Review*, September 21, 1995. For a review of six books with opposing views on the Second Amendment and gun control, see Jacob Sullum, "Shooting Gallery," in *Reason*, vol. XXVII, no. 7, December 1995, pp. 50–55.

3. For the account of the debate throughout August 18, see Schwartz, *The Roots*, vol. V, pp. 1,114–20.

4. One would think that the deliberate decision by the members of the First Congress to omit the word "expressly" would forever settle the matter for the Justices of the Supreme Court. In McCulloch v. Maryland, 4 Wheat. 316 (1819), Chief Justice Marshall wrote that "the 10th amendment . . . omits the word 'expressly,' and declares only that the powers 'not delegated to the United States, nor prohibited to the states, are reserved to the states or to the people'; thus leaving the question, whether the particular power which may become the subject of contest has been delegated to the one government, or prohibited to the other, to depend on a fair construction of the whole instrument."

Nevertheless, fifty years later, in Lane County v. Oregon, 7 Wall. 71 (1869), Chief Justice Chase inserted the omitted word in his reading of the Tenth Amendment: "in many articles of the Constitution the necessary existence of the States, and, within their proper spheres, the independent authority of the States, is distinctly recognized. To them nearly the whole charge of interior regulation is committed or left; to them and to the people all powers not expressly delegated to the National Government are reserved." And fifty years after that, Justice Day, in Hammer v. Dagenhart, 247 U.S. 251 (1918), continued the effort to rewrite the Amendment: "In interpreting the Constitution it must never be forgotten that the nation is made up of states, to which are intrusted the powers of local government. And to them and to the people the powers not expressly delegated to the national government are reserved."

5. Congressional control over elections of representatives and senators continues to be a matter of great significance in federal-state relations. It was the issue in Voting Rights Coalition v. California, 60 F. 3d 1411 (1993), a case before the Ninth U. S. Circuit Court of Appeals, in which the state of California challenged the constitutionality of the National Voter Registration Act of 1993, popularly known as the "motor voter" act. The governor complained that the act would cost California an additional $18 million beyond the federal funding for the registration law and that state autonomy was at stake, "since once Congress can commandeer state agencies . . . Congress can shift with ease the cost of any federal measure to the states." But the Court held that the Constitution gives Congress authority over the states on election matters and that "Congress may conscript state agencies to carry out voter registration," and, furthermore, "the exercise of that power by Congress is by its terms intended to be borne by the states without compensation." On January 22, 1996, the Supreme Court refused to hear California's appeal, thus allowing the Circuit Court's decision to stand.

6. D. Stuart to George Washington, September 12, 1789: "The success of amendments will leave but a few scattering opponents. . . . Mr. Henry is the only one of the party, I have heard of, who disapproves of it—He still thinks too that the single amendment proposed in our [Virginia] Convention, respecting direct taxes, worth all the rest." *Documentary History of the Constitution,* vol. V, p. 205.

7. *The Records of the Federal Convention of 1787,* ed. Max Farrand (New Haven, Conn.: Yale University Press, 1937), vol. II, p. 350.

8. Hylton v. United States, 3 Dallas 171.

9. Edward L. Barrett, Jr., "Direct and Indirect Taxes," *Encyclopedia of the American Constitution,* ed. Leonard W. Levy, Kenneth L. Karst, and Dennis J. Mahoney (New York: Macmillan Publishing Company, 1986), vol. II, pp. 564–65.

10. Pollock v. Farmers Loan & Trust Co., 157 U.S. 429, and 158 U.S. 601 (1895).

11. "Pollock v. Farmers' Loan & Trust Co.," in *Encyclopedia of the American Constitution,* ed. Leonard W. Levy, Kenneth L. Karst, and Dennis Mahoney (New York: Macmillan Publishing Co., 1986), vol. III, pp. 1,423–24. Adoption of the Sixteenth Amendment put an end to significant direct-tax disputes. For a concise listing of all the taxes that the Supreme Court has ruled are *not* direct taxes—including on carriages kept for pleasure, on receipts of insurance companies, on the circulating notes of State banks, on the use of foreign-built yachts, on the privilege of selling property on exchanges and Boards of Trade, etc.—see *The Constitution of the United States of America (Annotated)* (Washington, D.C.: United States Government Printing Office, 1938), pp. 285–87.

12. Speeches in reply to William Grayson and Patrick Henry, June 12, 1788. *Papers of James Madison,* vol. XI, pp. 121–33.

13. See *Foreign Policy and the Constitution,* ed. Robert A. Goldwin and Robert A. Licht (Washington, D.C.: AEI Press, 1990), especially the essays by Nathan

Tarcov, "Principles, Prudence, and the Constitutional Division of Foreign Policy"; Edmund S. Muskie, "The Reins of Liberty—Congress, the President, and American Security"; and Dick Cheney, "Congressional Overreaching in Foreign Policy."

14. Compare this with the language of the Articles of Confederation (Article VI): "No state shall lay any imposts or duties, which may interfere with any stipulations in treaties, entered into by the united states in congress assembled."

15. Cecelia M. Kenyon, *The Antifederalists* (Indianapolis: The Bobbs-Merrill Company, Inc., 1966), p. lxvii.

16. Morton Borden, *Jews, Turks, and Infidels* (Chapel Hill, N.C.: University of North Carolina Press, 1984), pp. 11–13.

17. The Constitution does not prescribe the wording of the oath that is required, in Article VI, for all executive officers, legislators, and judges, but the Constitution does give the text, in Article II, of the oath the president is to take: "I do solemnly swear (or affirm) that I will faithfully execute the office of President of the United States, and will to the best of my ability, preserve, protect and defend the Constitution of the United States." At his inauguration, George Washington added the words, "So help me God," and presidents have ever since done the same.

18. Amendment XVI: "The Congress shall have power to lay and collect taxes on incomes, from whatever source derived, without apportionment among the several States, and without regard to any census or enumeration."

19. Amendment XVII: "The Senate of the United States shall be composed of two Senators from each State, elected by the people thereof."

CHAPTER 8: KILL THE OPPOSITION

1. Madison to Edmund Pendleton, September 14, 1789. *Papers of James Madison*, ed. Charles F. Hobson, Robert A. Rutland, William M. E. Rachal, and Jeanne K. Sisson (Charlottesville, Va.: University Press of Virginia, 1979), vol. XII, p. 402.

2. Helen E. Veit, Kenneth R. Bowling, Charlene Bangs Bickford, eds., *Creating the Bill of Rights: The Documentary Record from the First Federal Congress* (Baltimore: Johns Hopkins University Press, 1991), p. 198. The Congressional Register, August 19, 1789.

3. Ibid., p. 120.

4. Ibid., p. 117.

5. Earlier consideration of this question is discussed above and in note 2, chapter 7.

6. For a persuasive explanation of why the Federalists opposed "a frequent recurrence to fundamental principles" in the Constitution, see Herbert J. Storing, "The Constitution and the Bill of Rights," in *How Does the Constitution Secure Rights?* ed. Robert A. Goldwin and William A. Schambra (Washington, D.C.: AEI Press, 1985), pp. 30–32.

7. Only eleven states were represented in the first session of the First Congress, as North Carolina and Rhode Island had not yet ratified the Constitution.

8. Veit, Bowling, and Bickford, *Creating the Bill of Rights*, p. 287. Madison to Alexander White, August 24, 1789. Emphasis in original.

9. Ibid., p. 280. William Smith (of Maryland) to Otho H. Williams, August 17, 1789: "The Antis have opposed their being brot. forward in every Stage & I am inclined to believe the proposed amendments will fail, for although they are approved by the federalists & a majority will no dou[b]t vote for the whole of them, I woud. question if two thirds will concur. A small party are opposed to all amendments. And others . . . do not think they go far enough. . . ."

Ibid., p. 288. Robert Morris (senator from Pennsylvania) to Richard Peters, August 24, 1789: "The Waste of precious time is what has vexed me the most, for as to the Nonsense they call Amendments I never expect that any part of it will go through the various Trials which it must pass before it can become a part of the Constitution."

10. *The Papers of James Madison*, vol. XI, pp. 301–3 and 353–56. Peters to Madison, July 20 and August 24, 1789, enclosing rhymed fables he had written.

11. Ibid., p. 283. Peters to Madison, July 5, 1789.

12. Veit, Bowling, and Bickford, *Creating the Bill of Rights*, p. 288. Robert Morris, senator from Pennsylvania, addressed Peters as "you, who know everything." Morris to Peters, August 24, 1789.

13. See James H. Hutson, "The Drafting of the Bill of Rights: Madison's 'Nauseous Project' Reexamined," *Benchmark*, vol. III, November–December 1987, pp. 309–20.

14. Veit, Bowling, and Bickford, *Creating the Bill of Rights*, p. 285. William Smith to Otho H. Williams, August 22, 1789: "Very high words passed in the house on this occasion, & what nearly amounted to direct challenges, the weather was excessive hot, & the blood warm. On the change in the Air the heat of the Debate subsided, & all are now in good humor."

According to Elbridge Gerry, at one point some members were ready to resort to dueling pistols to settle their disagreements. John P. Kaminski, "The Making of the Bill of Rights: 1787–1792," in Stephen L. Schechter and Richard B. Bernstein, eds., *Contexts of the Bill of Rights* (Albany, N.Y.: New York State Commission on the Bicentennial of the United States Constitution, 1990), p. 47.

15. See, for example, Jack N. Rakove, *James Madison and the Creation of the American Republic* (Glenview, Ill.: Scott, Foresman/Little, Brown Higher Education, 1990), pp. 81–84.

16. *The Papers of James Madison*, vol. XII, p. 348. Madison to Edmund Pendleton, August 21, 1789; Madison to Edmund Randolph, August 21, 1789.

17. Veit, Bowling, and Bickford, *Creating the Bill of Rights*, p. 281, fn. 1. The editors offer their explanation of the phrase, "the nauseous project": "Madison is referring to Peters' poem of July 20, which compared the process of amending the Constitution to cooks spoiling a fine soup." But the word *nauseous* does not occur in that poem.

18. The legislatures of Virginia and New York had already submitted applications to Congress, on May 5 and 6, 1789; eight more states would have to submit applications to activate the provision for the calling of "a Convention for proposing amendments," as provided for in Article V of the Constitution.

19. *Papers of James Madison*, vol. XII, pp. 353–56. Peters to Madison, August 24, 1789.

20. Ibid., p. 38. Madison to Jefferson, March 29, 1789.

CHAPTER 9: FISHERIES AND POST ROADS

1. Bernard Schwartz, *The Roots of the Bill of Rights* (New York: Chelsea House Publishers, 1980), vol. V, pp. 1,124–37.

2. For some unexplained reason, the addition of the phrase *or to the people* got lost twice. It was initially approved by the committee of the whole on August 18 but then was missing from the text when the provision came before the House itself. Sherman then moved its addition on August 21, which was approved without debate, and then was apparently lost again; that is, when the text of the amendments adopted by the House was transmitted to the Senate, the phrase *or to the people* was, once again, not included in Article the Seventeenth. The Senate, however, voted to add it (for the third time) to what became the Tenth Amendment.

3. Helen E. Veit, Kenneth R. Bowling, and Charlene Bangs Bickford, ed., *Creating the Bill of Rights: The Documentary Record from the First Federal Congress* (Baltimore: Johns Hopkins University Press, 1991), pp. 37–41.

4. See note 2 above for an account of the missing phrase, *or to the people.*

5. Veit, Bowling, and Bickford, *Creating the Bill of Rights*, p. 297. Fisher Ames reported that after the Senate amended the amendments "many in our house, Mr. Maddison, in particular, thinks that they have lost much of their sedative Virtue." Roger Sherman, on the other hand, judged the amendments as changed by the Senate "considerably abridged & I think altered for the Better."

6. Ibid., p. 289.

7. Ibid., p. 288.

8. Veit, Bowling, and Bickford, *Creating the Bill of Rights*, p. 46. This record of the editing of the amendments is in the hand of Senator Oliver Ellsworth of Connecticut.

9. Schwartz, *The Roots*, vol. V, pp. 1,148–51.

10. Veit, Bowling, and Bickford, *Creating the Bill of Rights*, p. 188.

11. Schwartz, *The Roots*, vol. V, p. 1,150. Senator Ellsworth's record of these changes (Veit, Bowling, and Bickford, *Creating the Bill of Rights*, p. 47) is in the following cryptic form. It records the deletions of the two House amendments, the two important additions to what is now the Tenth Amendment, and finally, at the end, the strikingly matter-of-fact statement of the passage of the House amendments as amended by the Senate:

> To erase the 14th. article & the words —*article the fourteenth.*
> To erase the word—*Fifteenth*—& insert *Eleventh.*
> To erase the 16th. article & the words *"Article the Sixteenth."*
> To erase the word *Seventeenth,*—& insert *Twelfth*—&
> To insert in the seventeenth article after the word *delegated*— *to the United States.* &
> To insert at the end of the Same article—*or to the people;*
> It passed in the affirmative, two thirds of the Senators present concurring.

12. Michael J. Malbin, *Religion and Politics: The Intentions of the Authors of the First Amendment* (Washington, D.C.: AEI Press, 1978), p. 9.

13. *Documents of American History*, 6th Edition, ed. Henry Steele Commager (New York: Appleton-Century-Crofts, Inc., 1958), p. 131.

14. Malbin, *Religion and Politics*, pp. 14–17.

15. Schwartz, *The Roots*, vol. V, pp. 1,164–65, and Veit, Bowling, and Bickford, *Creating the Bill of Rights*, p. 50.

16. Veit, Bowling, and Bickford, *Creating the Bill of Rights*, p. 53.

17. Schwartz, *The Roots*, vol. V, p. 1,171.

18. Ibid.

19. Ibid., pp. 1,182–83. This message of the governor of New Hampshire, given "at the Council Chamber in Portsmouth, the 23d day of Dec. 1789," was published in the *Maryland Gazette*, January 22, 1790.

20. Ibid., pp. 1,186–88. Richard Henry Lee and William Grayson to the governor of Virginia, September 28, 1789, and to the speaker of the House of Representatives in Virginia, September 28, 1789.

21. Ibid., p. 1,189. D. Stuart to President Washington, December 13, 1789.

22. Veit, Bowling, and Bickford, *Creating the Bill of Rights*, p. 289. Patrick Henry to Richard Henry Lee, 28 August 1789.

23. "The success of amendments will leave but a few scattering opponents . . . . Mr. Henry is the only one of the party, I have heard of, who disapproves of it—he still thinks too that the single amendment proposed in our Convention, respecting direct taxes, worth all the rest." David Stuart to George Washington, September 12, 1789, in *Documentary History of the Constitution*, vol. V, p. 205.

"Mr. H[enry]., (As Colo. Leven Powell tells me,) is pleased with some of the proposed amendments; but still asks for the great desideratum, the destruction of direct taxation." Edmund Randolph to James Madison, August 18, 1789, in Veit, Bowling, and Bickford, *Creating the Bill of Rights*, p. 281.

24. Schwartz, *The Roots*, vol. V, p. 1,186. Henry Lee to Alexander Hamilton, Nov. 16, 1789.

25. Ibid., p. 1,188. Burnley to Madison, November 28, 1789.

26. Ibid., p. 1,192. Edward Carrington to Madison, Dec. 20, 1789.

27. Ibid., p. 1,193. Madison to Washington, Jan. 4, 1790. The "3d. art." was, of course, what is now the First Amendment. One month earlier, Madison had been much more concerned about the possible consequences of the failure to ratify; see his letter to Washington, December 5, 1789, below.

28. Ibid., p. 1,188. Burnley to Madison, November 28, 1789.

29. Ibid., p. 1,190. Madison to President Washington, December 5, 1789.

30. Ibid., p. 1,191. Randolph to President Washington, December 6, 1789.

31. North Carolina ratified the Constitution on November 21, 1789, and all of the amendments, December 22, 1789. Rhode Island ratified the Constitution, May 29, 1790, and all of the amendments, except the second, June 7, 1790. Vermont ratified the Constitution on January 10, 1790; was admitted to the Union as the first new state as of March 4, 1791; and ratified the amendments November 3, 1791.

32. Because there were now fourteen states in the Union, eleven states had to

ratify to meet the constitutional requirement of three-fourths. Three of the original states—Massachusetts, Connecticut, and Georgia—either did not ratify or failed to notify the president that they had ratified the amendments. In 1939, on the occasion of the Sesquicentennial of the Bill of Rights, those three states celebrated by ratifying the amendments.

33. Schwartz, *The Roots*, vol. V, p. 1,203. Schwartz gives as the source of this letter *Harper's*, June 1963, where it appeared under the heading, "First Things First."

34. Ibid., p. 1,171.

35. Walter Berns, *Taking the Constitution Seriously* (New York: Simon and Schuster, 1987), pp. 126–27. "What is . . . beyond dispute, although very little attention has been paid to it, is that during what is still the greater part of our history (1789–1925), the Bill of Rights played almost no role in the securing of rights.... The religious liberty enjoyed by Americans owed nothing, absolutely nothing, to judicial enforcement of the First Amendment, and the same is true respecting the freedom of speech and press; not once during these first 136 years did the Supreme Court invalidate an act of Congress on First Amendment grounds . . . ."

REFLECTIONS, PART THREE

1. Veit, Bowling, and Bickford, *Creating the Bill of Rights*, p. 291. Edmund Pendleton to James Madison, September 2, 1789.

2. Ibid., p. 291. William Ellery to Benjamin Huntington, September 8, 1789.

3. Ibid., p. 299. Richard Henry Lee to Patrick Henry, September 27, 1789.

4. Ibid., p. 300. William Grayson to Patrick Henry, September 29, 1789.

5. Ibid., p. 210.

6. Ibid., p. 300. Thomas Tudor Tucker to St. George Tucker, October 2, 1789.

7. Although he was not one of the congressional authors of the Bill of Rights, George Mason provided a prime example of the persistence of the Anti-Federalist objection to what the First Congress had done, and especially to what it had not done, concerning amendments. In a letter to Samuel Griffin, September 8, 1789, he made it clear that the Bill of Rights was insufficient for winning his allegiance "to the new Government" because of the amendments that had been left out: "I have received much Satisfaction from the Amendments to the Federal Constitution . . . . With two or three further Amendments such as confining the federal Judiciary to Admiralty & Maritime Jurisdiction, . . . fixing the Mode of Elections . . . securing the Regulation of them to the respective States—Requiring more than a bare Majority to make Navigation & Commercial Laws, and appointing a constitutional [sic] amenable Council to the President, & lodging with them, most of the Executive Powers now rested in the Senate—I cou'd cheerfully put my Hand & Heart to the new Government." Ibid., p. 292.

8. See chapter 6, note 8.

9. In Article I, Section 2, the phrase occurs, "the people of the several states," but thereafter the words "the people" will not be found in the text of the original Constitution.

10. John Locke, often called "America's philosopher" because of the influ-

ence of his teachings there in the eighteenth century, linked rights and powers, showing how political powers derive from the natural rights of individuals. Consider the opening words of his famous definition of political power: "*Political Power* then I take to be *a Right* of making Laws." *Two Treatises of Government*, ed. Peter Laslett (Cambridge: Cambridge University Press, 1960), Book II, chap. 1, sec. 3 (emphasis in the original). Also, "Man being born . . . with a Title to perfect Freedom, and an uncontrouled enjoyment of all the Rights and Priviledges of the Law of Nature, equally with any other Man, . . . hath by Nature a Power . . . to preserve his Property, that is, his Life, Liberty, and Estate, against the injuries and Attempts of other Men." Ibid., sec. 87.

11. Ibid., Book II, chapter 6, sec. 54. "Though I have said . . . that all men by nature are equal, I cannot be supposed to understand all sorts of equality: age or virtue may give men a just precedency: excellency of parts and merit may place others above the common level: birth may subject some, and alliance or benefits others, to pay an observance to those to whom nature, gratitude or other respects may have made it due; and yet all this consists with the equality I there spoke of, as proper to the business in hand, being that equal right that every man hath, to his natural freedom, without being subjected to the will or authority of any other man."

Lincoln gave a similar explanation of equality in his Reply to Douglas in the First Debate at Ottawa, Illinois, August 21, 1858, in *Abraham Lincoln: His Speeches and Writings*, ed. Roy P. Basler (Cleveland: The World Publishing Company, 1946), p.445: "There is no reason in the world why the negro is not entitled to all the natural rights enumerated in the Declaration of Independence—the right to life, liberty, and the pursuit of happiness. I hold that he is as much entitled to these as the white man. I agree with Judge Douglas he is not my equal in many respects—certainly not in color, perhaps not in moral or intellectual endowment. But in the right to eat the bread, without the leave of anybody else, which his own hand earns, he is my equal, and the equal of Judge Douglas, and the equal of every living man."

12. Schwartz, *The Roots*, vol. V, p. 1,090.

13. For the history of this twice-forgotten and thrice-adopted phrase, "or to the people," see chapter 9, note 2.

14. *The Records of the Federal Convention of 1787*, ed. Max Farrand, revised edition in 4 vols. (New Haven, Conn.: Yale University Press, 1937), vol. II, p. 476.

15. Schwartz, *The Roots*, vol. III, p. 617. Madison to Jefferson, October 17, 1788.

16. Herbert J. Storing, "The Constitution and the Bill of Rights," in Robert A. Goldwin and William A. Schambra, eds., *How Does the Constitution Secure Rights?* (Washington, D.C.: AEI Press, 1985), p. 35.

Index

Adams, Samuel, 39, 41, 52–53, 189n10
Amendments. *See also* Constitution; Bill of Rights in the committee of the whole, 197n11; demand for, 5, 11, 61–62, 72–74, 89; Hancock, John and, 40; Henry, Patrick and, 43; Jefferson, Thomas and, 61–62, 68–71; Madison, James and, 9, 57–59, 62–64, 65, 67–74, 75–95; Massachusetts formula, 40–41, 44, 46, 51, 61, 192n13; political issues, 80–82, 201n9; resistance to, 7, 24; selection of, 89–91
Amendments, Anti-Federalist: Bill of Rights and, 57; constitutional structure and, 53, 100, 120–24; issues and their defeat, 127–39, 144, 151, 154–55, 161; opposition to, 11, 76, 90–91; ratification of the Constitution and, 50
Amendments, specific. *See also* Bill of Rights; Rights and freedoms; Eighth, 181–82, 194n14; Fifth, 129, 130, 161, 181–82; First, 86, 124–25, 160, 161, 180, 181; Fourteenth, 59–60, 124–25, 139; Fourth, 181; Ninth, 182, 194n14; Second, 127–30, 161, 181; Seventeenth, 139, 200n19; Seventh, 129, 130, 181–82; Sixteenth, 139, 199n11, 200n18; Sixth, 181–82; Tenth, 130, 155, 161, 182, 195n18, 198n4, 202n2; Third, 129, 181, 194n14; Twenty–seventh, 197n12
Ames, Fisher, 106, 125
Anti-Federalists. *See also* Amendments; Bill of Rights, 167, 174, 176–77; in the First Congress, 53, 120–21, 144; governmental powers and, 90; Madison, James and, 146, 152; in New York, 45; opposition to Constitution, 81; as party name, 113; ratification and, 43, 45, 46, 50; in

Virginia, 43, 46, 169–73
Armies, standing, 68–69, 127–30, 143, 161
Articles of Confederation: characteristics of, 12, 15; Constitutional Convention and, 16–17; ratification of Constitution and, 11, 20, 22; revising of, 186n1
Assembly. *See* Rights and freedoms

Bahamas, 1
Bangladesh, 1
Banning, Lance, 192n16
Berns, Walter, 204n35
Bill of Rights. *See also* Amendments; Constitution (U.S.); Madison, James; Rights and freedoms arguments against, 92–93; Congress and, 181; Congressional debate on, 105–139, 144–45, 154–64; Constitution and, 5–6, 8, 73–74, 92–94, 100, 101, 177; goal and effects of, 91–95, 177–84, 204n35; guarantees of, 86–88; heading for, 84–85, 87–89; negative and imperative character of, 85; opposition to, 100–102, 130–39, 169–73; "the people" and, 178–84; political issues, 73, 81–82, 88–89, 90–91, 94–95, 96, 99–100, 110, 112, 122, 138–39, 140–53; procedural history, 105–39, 147–49, 164; ratification of, 11, 85, 167–75; selection of, 89–91; text approved by House of Representatives, 156–59; text approved by House and Senate, 165–67; unratified amendments, 111, 171; wording and organization of, 82–89, 100, 108–12, 130, 136–38, 141–42, 145, 159–64, 171–72, 176
Blair, John, 27
Bland, Theodoric, 76–77, 167
Blount, William, 26–27

207

Russia, 1, 74
Rutland, Robert, 96, 101, 102

St. Clair, Arthur, 30–31
Sao Tome, 1
Schwartz, Bernard, 107, 167–68, 174
Scott, Thomas, 143
Seychelles, 1
Shays's Rebellion, 38
Sherman, Roger, 106, 108, 109, 111, 141–42, 155
Singapore, 193n33
Slavery, 18, 60, 134
Smith, Melancton, 46, 53, 126
Soviet Union. *See* Russia
Spain, 1, 12, 42
Speech. *See* Rights and freedoms
State governments: *See also* Government, Anti–Federalist amendments, 131–32; bills of rights, 85, 88, 91, 92–93, 97, 139; Congressional resolution, 29; Constitution and, 17–18; military issues, 135; ratification of Bill of Rights, 167–75; ratification of Constitution, 19–20, 22, 36–48; religious issues, 137; trade issues, 136
Storing, Herbert, 83, 184, 192n16
Sumter, Thomas, 120
Sweden, 1
Switzerland, 191n1

Taxation, *see* Direct Taxation
Tobago, 1
Tocqueville, Alexis de, 4–5

Trade issues, 136
Trinidad, 1
Tucker, Thomas Tudor: amendments to Constitution, 110, 115, 123–24; Anti–Federalist amendments, 130–39, 155; Bill of Rights, 167, 177
Turkey, 1

Vermont, 173, 203n30
Vining, John, 79, 106, 109–10, 118–19
Virginia: *See also* Madison, James, Constitutional Convention, 16, 27; election of Madison, James, 152–53; Mississippi navigation and, 42, 189n11; ratification of the Bill of Rights, 169–73; ratification of the Constitution, 37, 41–44, 46, 47, 61–62, 89

War Powers Resolution of 1973, 135
Washington, George: Continental Congress and, 34; ratification of the Bill of Rights and, 169–70, 172–73; ratification of the Constitution and, 43, 47, 52–53; signing the Constitution, 27
Western settlements, 189n11
Wilson, James, 21, 23, 52–53, 186n2

Yemen, 1
Yugoslavia, 74

Zambia, 1

211

About the Author

ROBERT A. GOLDWIN is a resident scholar of constitutional studies at the American Enterprise Institute. He has served in the White House as special consultant to the president and, concurrently, as adviser to the secretary of defense. He has taught political science at the University of Chicago and at Kenyon College and was dean of St. John's College in Annapolis. He is the editor of more than a score of books on American politics, senior editor of the AEI series of volumes on the Constitution, and author of numerous articles, many of which appear in *Why Blacks, Women, and Jews Are Not Mentioned in the Constitution* (AEI Press, 1990).

William M. Landes
Clifton R. Musser Professor of
  Economics
University of Chicago Law School

Sam Peltzman
Sears Roebuck Professor of Economics
  and Financial Services
University of Chicago
  Graduate School of Business

Nelson W. Polsby
Professor of Political Science
University of California at Berkeley

George L. Priest
John M. Olin Professor of Law and
  Economics
Yale Law School

Murray L. Weidenbaum
Mallinckrodt Distinguished
  University Professor
Washington University

Research Staff

Leon Aron
Resident Scholar

Claude E. Barfield
Resident Scholar; Director, Science
  and Technology Policy Studies

Cynthia A. Beltz
Research Fellow

Walter Berns
Resident Scholar

Douglas J. Besharov
Resident Scholar

Robert H. Bork
John M. Olin Scholar in Legal Studies

Karlyn Bowman
Resident Fellow

Kenneth Brown
Visiting Fellow

John E. Calfee
Resident Scholar

Lynne V. Cheney
W. H. Brady, Jr., Distinguished Fellow

Stephen R. Conafay
Executive Fellow

Chuck Downs
Assistant Director, Asian Studies

Dinesh D'Souza
John M. Olin Research Fellow

Nicholas N. Eberstadt
Visiting Scholar

Mark Falcoff
Resident Scholar

John D. Fonte
Visiting Scholar

Gerald R. Ford
Distinguished Fellow

Murray F. Foss
Visiting Scholar

Diana Furchtgott-Roth
Assistant to the President and Resident
  Fellow

Suzanne Garment
Resident Scholar

Jeffrey Gedmin
Research Fellow

James K. Glassman
DeWitt Wallace–Reader's Digest
  Fellow

Robert A. Goldwin
Resident Scholar

Robert W. Hahn
Resident Scholar

Robert B. Helms
Resident Scholar; Director, Health
  Policy Studies

Glenn Hubbard
Visiting Scholar

Douglas Irwin
Henry Wendt Scholar in Political
  Economy

James D. Johnston
Resident Fellow

Jeane J. Kirkpatrick
Senior Fellow; Director, Foreign and
  Defense Policy Studies

Marvin H. Kosters
Resident Scholar; Director,
  Economic Policy Studies

Irving Kristol
John M. Olin Distinguished Fellow

Dana Lane
Director of Publications

Michael A. Ledeen
Resident Scholar

James Lilley
Resident Fellow; Director, Asian
  Studies Program

John H. Makin
Resident Scholar; Director, Fiscal
  Policy Studies

Allan H. Meltzer
Visiting Scholar

Joshua Muravchik
Resident Scholar

Charles Murray
Bradley Fellow

Michael Novak
George F. Jewett Scholar in Religion,
  Philosophy, and Public Policy;
  Director, Social and
  Political Studies

Norman J. Ornstein
Resident Scholar

Richard N. Perle
Resident Fellow

William Schneider
Resident Scholar

William Shew
Visiting Scholar

J. Gregory Sidak
F. K. Weyerhaeuser Fellow

Herbert Stein
Senior Fellow

Irwin M. Stelzer
Resident Scholar; Director, Regulatory
  Policy Studies

Daniel Troy
Associate Scholar

W. Allen Wallis
Resident Scholar

Ben J. Wattenberg
Senior Fellow

Carolyn L. Weaver
Resident Scholar; Director, Social
  Security and Pension Studies

Karl Zinsmeister
Resident Fellow; Editor, *The American
  Enterprise*

A NOTE ON THE BOOK

This book was edited by
Cheryl Weissman of the publications staff
of the American Enterprise Institute.
The index was prepared by Julia Petrakis.
The text was set in Palatino, a typeface
designed by the twentieth-century Swiss designer
Hermann Zapf. Jennifer Lesiak set the type,
and Edwards Brothers, Incorporated,
of Lillington, North Carolina,
printed and bound the book,
using permanent acid-free paper.

The AEI Press is the publisher for the American Enterprise Institute for Public Policy Research, 1150 Seventeenth Street, N.W., Washington, D.C. 20036; *Christopher DeMuth*, publisher; *Dana Lane*, director; *Ann Petty*, editor, *Leigh Tripoli*, editor; *Cheryl Weissman*, editor; *Jennifer Lesiak*, editorial assistant.